HAUNTS AND HOBBIES
OF
AN INDIAN OFFICIAL

HAUNTS AND HOBBIES OF AN INDIAN OFFICIAL

BY MARK THORNHILL

GYAN

Published by

Gyan Publishing House
5, Ansari Road
Daryaganj, New Delhi-110002
Phone: 011-47034999, 9811692060
E-mail: books@gyanbooks.com

Distribution Network
gyanbooks.com
India, USA, Canada, UK, Australia

ISBN: 978-93-6433-694-9 (PB)
First Published, 1899

2nd Impression 2024

Printed at: Gyan Press, Delhi.

HAUNTS AND HOBBIES OF AN INDIAN OFFICIAL
Author: MARK THORNHILL

HAUNTS AND HOBBIES OF AN INDIAN OFFICIAL

HAUNTS AND HOBBIES
OF
AN INDIAN OFFICIAL

By MARK THORNHILL

AUTHOR OF
"ADVENTURES OF A MAGISTRATE IN THE INDIAN MUTINY"

LONDON
JOHN MURRAY, ALBEMARLE STREET
1899

PREFACE

DURING the latter period of my residence in India I kept a diary. The diary was chiefly devoted to observations on the birds, insects, and animals whose acquaintance I made in my garden, or which I beheld on the bed of the river beyond. But it also contained memoranda on the weather and the changes of the seasons, notes of interviews with native visitors, and of any interesting information I happened to acquire. When I finally left India I brought the diary with me, together with a variety of Persian manuscripts and other Eastern books and papers. For many years it remained unnoticed, half forgotten; then one day the fancy took me to open and peruse it.

I found it interesting, sufficiently so to warrant the hope that if expanded and arranged in the form of a narrative it might prove a volume of entertaining reading. After much delay and many interruptions I have carried this idea into execution.

The insects and animals described in the earlier parts of the narrative are mostly those which in India are very common, very insignificant, and on that account but little regarded. Nevertheless I found them interesting to observe, and I trust that they may be interesting to read about ; and although my observations are quite unscientific, they may perhaps add a little to the store of popular information, and by exciting an interest in the humble creatures with which they deal they may tend to develop kindly feelings towards them.

The animals that I have spoken of towards the end of my narrative are of a grander kind, such as the tiger, the bear, the deer, and the rhinoceros, the shooting of which forms the subject of most sporting works. Such works are popular from the adventures they record, but I think my narrative will show how much interest, even excitement, may be derived from observing these animals without injuring or destroying them.

I have added to my account of the domesticated elephants, as they now are, a description of the far grander position they held in the days of the emperors; then in trappings of silk and cloth of gold they added to the splendour of the court, and formed one of the most formidable and important accompaniments of the armies.

In regard to the elephants and some other of the larger wild animals, I have noted the fact of their disappearance, within comparatively recent times, from many extensive regions where they were formerly abundant, a disappearance for which in many cases there is apparently no sufficient cause.

Although I have devoted much of my narrative to the animals, I have treated also of other matters. Indian society in the hills and at the large stations has been frequently described, and as such descriptions are popular I have thought that a picture of the quiet life of a European official in the plains might also be worthy of record. In order to render my picture accurate I have described, and at some length, many ordinary matters which, in works on India, are usually either left unnoticed or but incidentally alluded to. I have, for example, not only described the appearance of my house, but also the arrangement of the rooms; I have said much on the weather and the climate and the changes of the seasons; I have besides given a brief account of my office, and also, as in a way connected with it, of the jail and its inmates; and I have added to my account some weird stories, all true and within my own experience.

In various parts of my narrative I have introduced notices of native habits, institutions, and superstitions, all of which may, I hope, be interesting, and many of them new, to most readers; some few will be so even to those acquainted with India.

I have concluded my narrative with an account of a tour I made during one cold season through the valley of the Doon, but I have introduced into the account recollections of an earlier period, when the valley was under my charge, and a description of the little Sikh monastic establishment, with its tranquil surroundings and bitter internal dissensions; the Government tea plantations, as they then existed; the curious marriage customs prevailing in the adjacent mountains; and lastly, the discovery of the deserted palace, round which a forest had grown up, and the "beauty" that was found reposing within it

CONTENTS

CHAPTER VI.

CHAPTER VII.

CHAPTER VIII.

CHAPTER IX.

CHAPTER X.

CHAPTER XVI.

CHAPTER XVII.

CHAPTER XVIII.

CHAPTER XIX.

CHAPTER XX.

HAUNTS AND HOBBIES OF AN INDIAN OFFICIAL

CHAPTER I.

ANTS

SOME few years after the Mutiny, I was appointed to a station up the country. The station stood on the bank of the Ganges. In the early days of our rule it had been to some extent a seat of government. It was the headquarters of several of the chief civil offices, and a strong military force was maintained at it, but as time passed the importance of the station had declined. One by one the great offices had been removed elsewhere, and the number of the troops had been reduced. Just previous to the Mutiny they consisted only of a portion of a native regiment. The station, however, was still a tolerably large one; but the many unoccupied houses and uncared-for gardens gave to it a rather deserted and melancholy appearance.

I arrived at the station about the middle of the month of May, the very hottest period of the year. Some few days were occupied in selecting a house and settling myself in it; and then one afternoon, when the sun had set, I took a stroll round the garden. The garden extended to the river, and descended to near the water's edge in a succession of terraces. The garden had originally been a pretty one, and well stocked with flowers, but for many years it had been sadly neglected. In England a neglected garden becomes a wilderness; in India, where all cultivation depends on irrigation, it assumes much the aspect of a desert. This garden had done so. There were a few magnificent trees, several more of smaller size, some flowering shrubs, and here and there a rose-bush; but generally the surface displayed only one monotonous expanse of bare brown earth. In places, however, there were clumps of pampas grass, forming quite little jungles, and among them were crops of the hardiest of weeds. The appearance of the lower terraces was rather more cheerful, for they were still partly cultivated, though only with native vegetables of the commonest kinds.

It was uncertain how long I should remain at the station. I did not, therefore, think it worth while to put the garden in order; I amused myself instead by studying its living inhabitants—the insects and other small animals, for all these it contained in great abundance. I directed my attention at first to the ants. My acquaintance with them thus commenced: I was strolling through the garden, as before, soon after sunset, when I noticed on the rough surface of the ground a broad, smooth track; it was much the sort of mark that the trunk of a tree or a beam of timber would leave, if dragged along.

I had with me two attendants. I pointed to the track, and inquired if any of the trees of the garden had been lately felled and drawn away. The men smiled, and informed me that the track was not that of a tree, but was the foraging path of an ants' nest.

I was at first incredulous. It seemed to me impossible that such light, diminutive insects as ants could have made so broad and smooth a track as this over the rough, hard earth; but I was presently convinced. We followed the track; it extended from the point where I had noticed it for some sixty or seventy yards; then it abruptly terminated in the centre of what had once been a flower-bed. At the point where the track terminated the ground was slightly raised, something in the form of a wide but very shallow inverted saucer.

In this low mound I noticed that there were four small holes. These holes, my attendants informed me, were the entrances to the passages that led down to the nest. A few ants only were about. The rest, my attendants said, had retired below for the night; but in the morning, about sunrise, they would be out again and in full activity.

In India during the hot weather we all rise at earliest dawn. By six o'clock the sun is high in the heavens, and his rays unpleasantly penetrating. It was about this time the next morning that I returned from my ride. I went at once to the ants' nest. It was situated, I may mention, on the uppermost of the terraces—the one nearest to the house. The track now presented a very different appearance to that of the previous evening, for, broad and long as it was, it was nevertheless completely covered with ants going out and returning. The track, I now found, led from the nest to one of those clumps of pampas grass I have above alluded to. Here it widened out and ended, and the ants dispersed themselves among the grass and weeds to gather their seeds.

Having collected their seeds, the ants returned to the nest, each ant, as I imagined, carrying a single seed. It was a scene of peaceful industry most interesting to behold, so interesting that, notwithstanding the heat, I sent for a chair and sat down to observe it. I am sorry to say that I had not looked long before I became aware that the ants were neither so peaceful nor so industrious as I had at first supposed. Although the seeds were abundant, not one ant in six took the trouble to gather any. Many of the ants, indeed, never proceeded to the clumps at all. Instead, they lay in wait in different places along the track, and robbed of their seeds the industrious of their comrades who had been there and were returning laden.

If the industrious ant was much the smallest, he usually accepted the situation. He dropped his seed, turned, and with wonderful patience went back to the grass clumps to gather another. If the ants were at all of equal size, the affair generally ended by both conveying on the seed together. Sometimes, though rarely, the small ant would hold on to his seed so resolutely that the larger, robber ant had to drag him along with it to the nest.

I had supposed at first that, as the ants were foraging among the grass clumps, it was the seed of the grass that they were gathering. To make sure, however, on this point, I sent for my magnifying-glass, and with it I examined the seeds. I found, rather to my surprise, that the seeds were not the seeds of the grass, but those of the akâwâ, a small, juicy wild plant that grew among the grass clumps, and also elsewhere near them.

I remained for a long time watching the ants; in fact, I remained till the rays of the sun got too hot for endurance. Then I retired to the house. The servants told me that in another hour or so the ants would retire also. They would enter their nest, and there remain till the day declined. They would then reappear, forage as before, and a little before sunset return again for the night.

I was curious to ascertain if this statement was correct. I waited till a full hour had elapsed, and then, shaded by a thickly wadded umbrella, I went back to the nest. Not an ant was visible. The track was as bare and deserted as I had seen it on the previous evening. And not only had the ants retired, but the entrances to the nest were also closed; and I noticed that over each a little mound of pellets had been erected. The pellets were minute fragments of brick or small pieces of hard earth, the like of which were everywhere strewed about the garden.

The mounds were so neatly constructed that I imagined at first that they were the work of some of the children of the servants who lived on the premises; but I was assured by my attendants that they were erected by the ants themselves. It was the custom, they said, of these ants always thus to close and cover over the entrances to their nests whenever they retired within them. They added that if I would come out when the ants retired again at sunset, I could witness them doing so.

This account of my attendants so interested me that I looked forward to the afternoon with some little impatience. In fear lest I might be too late, I left the house while the sun was yet well above the horizon. I found the track still covered with ants, but all were returning. Their numbers were so great that it was a considerable time before the whole had entered the nest. A small party, however, some twenty or thirty, remained without; and these now, to my extreme satisfaction, set about the work of closing the entrances. Their mode of procedure was as follows:—

They first separated themselves into four groups of about equal numbers. Each group appeared to undertake the duty of closing one of the four entrances. The ants next dispersed, and collected pellets from the fragments of brick and hard earth lying around. With these pellets they then commenced to cover over the entrance holes. It was a work requiring some care, for, small as were the entrance holes, a good many of the pellets were even still smaller. But all the while I looked on I did not observe a single pellet fall in.

The ants worked rapidly. Before many minutes had passed, all the four entrances were closed. In the covering over one entrance a small aperture was left. The other three entrances were closed completely, and over these three the ants now proceeded to erect the mounds. When the mounds were completed, all the ants but one retired into the nest, through the aperture left, as above mentioned, in the covering over the fourth entrance. One ant remained, and now, all unaided, he set about erecting a mound over this last entrance. I noticed that as he placed the pellets he was very careful to preserve the aperture. As the mound rose around it, the aperture assumed something the appearance of a roughly constructed, most diminutive well.

I watched this ant's proceedings with great interest, wondering much how when the mound was completed, and he retired himself into the nest, he would manage to close the aperture behind him. My curiosity on this point was not destined to be gratified. Before the mound was completed, I was called away to the house by the arrival of a visitor. I have a vague recollection that on another occasion I did see the mound completed, and this last ant retire; but how the aperture was closed I do not remember, nor, I am sorry to say, do my notes record.

I had hitherto visited the ants; before very long the ants returned the compliment, and visited me. It was in the late afternoon, the sun was just sinking, the outer doors had been opened, and I was sitting in the verandah waiting to take my evening drive. I happened to look down, and saw that the floor was covered with a multitude of small moving, dusky spots. On nearer inspection I perceived that these spots were ants, and ants of one of the diminutive red varieties. I had seen none previously. From whence had these come?

On searching about I discovered that these ants were

issuing from a crack in the cemented floor, and they were not only issuing from the crack, but they were returning to it again and descending. With the aid of my magnifying-glass, I further ascertained that each ant as he came out of the crack carried in his jaws a minute pellet of mortar. The ants ran along the floor, deposited their pellets upon it, and then raced back to the crack, and disappeared within it. The reason of their presence was now explained. They had come not merely to visit, but to reside. They were engaged in excavating chambers and galleries, in which to establish a colony. In this work of excavation they must have been engaged for some hours, for the floor of the verandah, to the distance of many feet from the crack, was covered with the little pellets of mortar which they had brought up from beneath and deposited.

The sight suggested some speculations. From whence did these ants come? for I had seen none exactly like them in the garden. Then why, with so much space of earth all around, should they have selected this solid masonry floor in which to excavate their residence? And, lastly, how did such soft, diminutive little creatures manage to tunnel through it? To none of these problems am I able to afford any solution.

These small red ants having arrived, they remained for the rest of the season; and I was glad that they did, for the watching their proceedings was a source of constant interest. They were followed by other ants; but these later arrivals, though much varying in size, belonged all to the black varieties. They also, for some reason or other, almost entirely confined themselves to another verandah—the one which faced to the north; and, with few exceptions, they were only day visitors. They came in the morning, and departed again as the sun declined. Those that remained permanently were ants of the most diminutive species. They also, like the small red ants, excavated residences for themselves in the solid masonry flooring.

The larger ants, the day visitors, were to be numbered by thousands. Whenever I entered the verandah I found the entire surface of the floor and walls thickly speckled with them. Their activity, too, was wonderful. They appeared to pass their time in ceaseless wanderings, hardly ever, that I could observe, resting even for an instant. The object of their wanderings was not apparent. I suppose it was in search of food, though what food they could find in the verandah was a puzzle, for the room that served as a larder was on the other side of the house.

Except in the larder, ants are one of the few Indian insects that are not an annoyance. They are so clean; they confine themselves so entirely to the walls and floors, and mostly to those of the verandahs; but in the larder, or wherever else there is anything eatable, then there they are a pest. However carefully food may be hidden away or protected, the ants are sure before long to discover and devour it. The only receptacle that will protect food from the ants is a safe with wire gauze sides, and supported on long legs, the legs resting in wide stone saucers kept filled with water; and this requires constant attention, for the dust, with which the air in the hot season is always thickly laden, soon forms a film on the water, and over this film, thin as it is, the ants are able to pass.

But now a question arises: By what means do the ants discover the food? Is it by sight or by scent? Or in the course of their incessant wanderings do they come on it by accident? This question has been much debated, but never, that I am aware, been quite satisfactorily determined. Having so many ants about, I resolved to try some experiments to throw, if I could, some light on the subject. My experiments were very numerous; one or two of them I will relate.

The first experiment was performed in this north verandah. It was suggested by a long, thick nail that projected from the wall, driven in by some former occupant of the house. The nail was about six feet above the floor, and projected some three inches from the face of the wall. From the end of this nail I suspended a piece of stiff paper by means of some fine twine. I passed the twine through the four corners, so that the paper hung flat like a small platform. Then on the upper surface of the paper I placed a little heap of powdered sugar. I did this one day on returning from my early morning ride.

For three days the sugar remained untouched; not an ant came near it. Then I varied the experiment. It was in the morning: the floor, as usual, was covered with ants; I carefully lifted one with a card and placed him on the paper. He ran at once to the sugar and commenced to eat it. Towards sunset, when the heat had diminished, I went again to the verandah. I found a score or more of ants on the paper, and all eagerly devouring the sugar. In the course of the next day it was entirely consumed.

Now during the three days that the sugar had remained untouched the ants had been swarming on the wall; many hundreds must have passed by the nail. They were evidently, therefore, not attracted to the sugar either by sight or smell. How, then, did they eventually discover it? I think it may be assumed that they were directed to it by the ant that I placed on the paper. Probably, when he had eaten as much sugar as he desired, he ascended the twine, passed along the nail to the wall, and then by some means or other informed the other ants of the existence of the sugar and where it was situated.

The experiment, however, was not conclusive. In another day or two the sugar might have been found accidentally by some ant walking on to the nail; also the sugar may have been scentless; and, further, the ants, wandering always with their faces to the wall, may not have perceived it. In order to determine these points, I repeated the experiment in a different form.

I filled two empty jam-pots with earth nearly to their brims. On the earth in each pot I placed a small heap of powdered sugar. Near the house, a few feet in front of the verandah which faced to the east, there was an ants' nest. The ants were of the same species as those of the nest on the terrace, only considerably smaller. In the evening, after these ants had retired to their nest and closed the entrances, I placed the two pots one on each side of their foraging track, and both at equal distances from it.

The next morning, on returning from my ride, I went at once to inspect them. I found the pot on the right of the track completely covered with ants, all busily engaged in devouring the sugar. They must have been thus engaged for some time, for the sugar was nearly all consumed. But the sugar in the pot to the left was untouched, nor was there a single ant on the pot itself or anywhere near it. Now, the ants could not have discovered the sugar on the right-hand pot by sight, for it was not visible from the ground; nor can we suppose that they were attracted to it by scent, for if so, the scent would have equally attracted them to the sugar in the other pot. We may fairly assume that, of the hundreds of ants that passed along the track, about as many would have gone to the one pot as to the other.

We may therefore conclude, I think, that the sugar in the pot to the right was discovered by accident. Some ant, or ants, must have noticed the pot, and out of curiosity approached it, then climbed the sides, found the sugar, eaten as much as they cared to, descended again, and informed the other ants on the track. A further experiment supported this conclusion. I placed as much jam as would fill a teaspoon on a half-sheet of notepaper. I laid the paper by the side of the foraging track of the ants on the terrace, and distant from the track about nine inches. The track at the time was crowded with ants going out from the nest and returning.

For some minutes none of them noticed the paper. Then a single ant left the track and advanced towards it. In the meanwhile the heat of the sun's rays had caused the edges of the paper to curl slightly upwards—the curl was only very slight, but it was sufficient to prevent the ant from perceiving the jam—the ant came up to the paper, paused for a second or so, looked at it, and departed. A second and a third ant did the same: each in succession left the track, advanced to the paper, paused, looked at it, and passed on.

Next there came an ant of very unusual stature; his great height, perhaps, enabled him to see over the curled edge, for, on reaching the paper, he at once proceeded to climb on it. He then bit off a piece of the jam and descended; and in his descent he met with an accident. He tripped over the curled edge, stumbled, and fell; and in his fall he dropped his piece of jam. Nor was this all. In picking up the jam some of it got smeared over his body and legs. He now moved with difficulty; soon he could hardly move at all. The ground was covered with dust. All sticky as he now was, much of the dust adhered to him. The nest was about a yard distant. It was many minutes before he succeeded in reaching it; and then it was without his piece of jam, for that he had been compelled to abandon in the course of his journey.

And now occurred something very interesting. The large ant had not long entered the nest, when a multitude of ants of ordinary size came trooping out of it. They went direct and at full speed to the paper; they climbed on it without a moment's delay, and commenced at once to devour the jam. They were so many, and they atc so eagerly, that in a very few minutes the jam had all disappeared. I think that we may confidently assume that these ants had been informed of the jam and been directed to it by the large ant after he had entered the nest. By what means he had done so it would be endless to conjecture. I think we may also assume that the first ants, those that went to the paper but did not ascend it, were attracted to it by sight merely, for if they had become aware from scent of the jam that lay on its surface, then assuredly they would have climbed the paper, as the other ants did, and devoured it.

I made, as I have said, many other experiments. It would be tedious to describe them. I found that in most cases the ants discovered the food I placed merely by accident. One or more of them came upon it in the course of their ceaseless wanderings, and then communicated their discovery.

In several cases, however, they certainly became aware of the presence of the food by sight, and in some few instances they must have been attracted to the food either by scent or else by some sense which we do not possess, for though the food was placed where they could not have seen it, they went to it at once and in a multitude.

CHAPTER II.

MY HOUSE AND GARDEN

MY house is a bungalow; that is, it consists of a single story and has a thatched roof. The outer walls being low, and the roof large and lofty, the house when seen from a distance has a good deal the appearance of a gigantic haystack. The term "bungalow," I may mention, is the English corruption of the Hindostanee word "Bungâlâ," which signifies "of" or "relating to" Bengal. The term is applied to these thatched houses because it was from the province of Bengal that they were originally introduced.

The house is a tolerably large one; nevertheless it contains only six rooms. But then these are very spacious. They all communicate with each other by doorways, for in Indian houses there are no passages, and all open on verandahs. There is a verandah on each side of the house, and at their ends are small apartments. These form the bathing and dressing rooms, one, however, being devoted to the combined purpose of pantry and larder. The house, I may add, is placed on a masonry terrace some three feet high. The upper surface of this terrace, which is coated with fine cement, forms the floors. The terrace does not extend beyond the walls of the house, and so is not much noticeable from without.

As the house has no passages, so neither has it any special windows. The outer doors, those that open on the verandahs, are fitted with panes of glass, and though always spoken of as doors, they form also the windows. Immediately before these window-doors are other doors. They are of wood, painted dark green, and, in place of panels, contain arrangements of flat bars much resembling venetian blinds. These arrangements are termed "jilmils." I may often hereafter have occasion to mention them.

I will conclude this account of the house with a few words regarding its grounds, or, as in India they are termed, its "compound."

The compound is some five acres in extent, and of this about half the area is occupied by the garden; the rest is open space dotted with trees. Along the eastern end of the compound runs the river; the opposite end is bounded by one of the station roads. Here, with their back to the road, are the stables, and close by them are the entrance gates. In about the centre of the compound stands the house. The huts of the servants and a variety of sheds and outhouses stretch along one of the sides; and beyond them, but well apart, is the kitchen, usually here in India described as the "cook-room." The boundaries on either side are the compounds of my neighbours.

And now, having described my house, I will endeavour to depict the life I lead within it at this season of the year. I rise at earliest dawn. It is hardly well light when I commence my ride, but the day comes quickly on. The prospect it discloses is but dreary. The sky is a grey-white; a dull brown band stretches all along the eastern horizon: it is the dust with which the air is laden. Presently the brown becomes tinged with red. The red grows brighter, then it turns to yellow, and I know that the sun has risen; but it is not till the sun has mounted well above the band of dust that he becomes plainly visible, and then he appears not as a glowing ball, but as a mere pale white disc.

It is not yet six o'clock when I return home, but the sun's rays are already powerful. Still, shaded by an umbrella, I stroll for half an hour about the garden. I look at the river; I pay a visit to my friends the ants and note their proceedings; perhaps I make acquaintance with some new insects. The heat has now become oppressive; I retire to the house. The outer doors are closed, and also the green "jilmil" doors beyond them, and I commence the long indoor day. To describe it in detail would be tedious. I read or I answer letters; I receive native visitors, for these early hours are when, during the hot season, they mostly call; I bathe; I dress; I depart for my office; about five I return and dine.

Dinner finished, I sit and read, the punkah swinging monotonously above me. An hour passes; the light has grown softer; it assumes a mellow hue, and I know that the long day is at length drawing to a close. The doors are now thrown open. I go outside. Though the sun is setting, the heat is still extreme, but after the long confinement in the house the open air, hot though it is, feels pleasant. I now take my evening drive; it is dusk before I return. The time that follows is the pleasantest in the day. I have my tea—a meal in this hot weather very enjoyable. Then I read, or, if there is a moon, I sit outside. The Indian moonlight is always beautiful; even though obscured by the haze of dust, it still preserves its soft, dreamy radiance. I often sit till near midnight tranquilly enjoying it.

In this manner, but little varied, the hot weather days pass by, very monotonous, often wearisome, yet leaving a memory of calm tranquillity not unpleasing.

It remains to say a few words on the weather. The heat is extreme. It is something that only those who have experienced it can fully realize. Nevertheless, owing to its perfect dryness, it is not unhealthy, nor, so long as the wind blows from the west, is it within the house at all oppressive. A bamboo frame is very lightly thatched with the fibrous roots of a certain grass. The frame, which when thus thatched is termed the tattie, is then placed in one of the outer doorways, and kept continually wetted. The burning wind evaporates the moisture, and in doing so its own temperature is lowered. It passes into the house refreshingly cool. It also diffuses a faint but agreeable aroma. For the grass roots have the peculiarity of possessing a natural scent. This grass is of a very coarse description; it is termed by the natives "khus," a name by Europeans altered into "kuskus." The roots are, or were, imported into this country, and used by perfumers. I saw some once years ago in a shop in

Bond Street. It was there known under the name of "vitivert."

The heat and the extreme dryness produce some curious effects. Sealing-wax if left about becomes soft, and bends and twists into all sorts of odd shapes; a sheet of paper placed on a table rolls up; and one's hair becomes electric like that of a cat: when brushed it crackles and emits sparks. More singular still, the country assumes something of the aspect which we associate with the winter of the far North. There is the same dim lurid sky, and the clouds of dust as they sweep by recall recollections of the driving snow. The appearance of the natives, the few who at this season venture abroad, increases the resemblance. To protect themselves from the terrible heat, they envelop their heads in enormous turbans, and wrap round their persons great cloaks wadded thick with cotton.

But it is not only in appearance that this season resembles winter: it produces also very similar effects on certain forms of animal life. The frogs, the toads, even some of the fishes, as the heat increases burrow into the mud while it is still moist, and there lie torpid till the rains recall them to life.

The landscape, as I have said, has a dim wintry aspect. Nevertheless the light is intense. Of its intensity I shall hereafter give examples. At present one will suffice. During the day all the outer doors of the house are closely shut, both the window-doors and also the green wooden ones beyond them. The sunshine is further excluded by reed screens hung along the outer side of the verandah. And yet, all this notwithstanding, the light that comes through the raised bars of a single jilmil panel suffices amply to illuminate the largest of the rooms.

I have spoken above of the intensity of the sunlight at this season of the year. Of its intensity I will give two further illustrations.

The first I witnessed at another station, and some years ago. The house I occupied, like this, had small rooms, mere closets, at the ends of the verandahs. I happened one day, during the hot weather, to enter one of them. I noticed with surprise that the white wall opposite the outer door appeared bright blue, and also that feathery streaks of green seemed moving over the blue surface. Next, to my greater surprise, the figure of a man, only upside down, passed by, as if reflected in a looking-glass.

The phenomenon was now explained. There was a hole in the upper part of the door, and the intense sunlight passing through this hole pictured on the wall, like as in a camera obscura, the objects in the garden. The blue colour was the reflection of the sky, the green feathery streaks were the waving branches of the trees, and the figure of the man was one of the servants who happened to be passing by. But, the hole not being fitted with a lens, all the objects appeared inverted. Having discovered the fact of these reflections on the wall, I used afterwards often to enter the room and amuse myself by observing them.

Subsequently I was residing elsewhere, and in a much larger house. A friend had been staying with us. On his departure I accompanied him to the outer door. His buggy was drawn up before it, the syce standing at the horse's head. I remained outside in the porch for a few minutes till my friend had mounted his buggy and driven off. Then I re-entered the house.

In contrast to the glare without, the house within appeared to me almost dark. I could see only just sufficiently to make my way to the room where I had been previously sitting. The jilmils of this room were all closed. It appeared to me so absolutely dark that I stood for a short time at the door, lest I might fall over some obstacle. As I thus stood, I appeared to see before me, as clearly as if I was actually beholding them, only all black, the outlines of the horse, the buggy, and the syce, just as I had looked at them from the porch. Now at least three or four minutes had passed since I had re-entered the house. How intense must have been the sunlight that the picture it had impressed on the retina of my eyes should have continued for all that time!

The intensity of the sunlight may be judged of also by its effect on the roses. At early morning the leaves of the flowers are a deep red; by noon they have faded to a pink; by evening they are almost white. Whether they renew their colouring during the night I do not remember. I rather think by the next day they have entirely faded. I should mention that the roses I speak of are the common native roses, the ones from which the rosewater and otto of roses are made.

Neither the heat nor the glare, however, has the least effect in diminishing the activity of the ants. Those that frequent the verandahs run all day about the walls and the floors, apparently quite indifferent to the burning sunshine, while my friends in the nests pursue their morning and afternoon duties with just the same regularity and energy as before.

Of their energy I have recently had an example. A day or two ago, on visiting the lower nest, I found that the ants had laid out a new foraging path, or rather, to speak quite correctly, they had extended the one already existing. This path used to terminate at the edge of the pampas grass. I found that it now went partly through this grass, then made a sharp bend round to the right, and continued on to a small patch of akâwâ plants that stood about six or seven yards away. I presumed from this that the seeds of the akâwâs which grew among the pampas grass had become exhausted, and that the ants had pushed on to these other plants to obtain a further supply. On examination I found my supposition was correct. The akâwâ plants among the pampas grass had been so thoroughly exhausted that among the whole number I could not find one plant that now possessed a single seed.

The new plants seemed, however, to be yielding an abundant supply of seeds, and the ants were most actively engaged in gathering them and carrying them home to their nest. As I watched the little creatures I was struck, as I often was subsequently, with the extreme rapidity with which their foraging tracks become marked. This track could not have been frequented for more than three, or at the most four, hours, for there had been no trace of it when I had visited the nest the previous morning. It traversed also very rough ground, and it was several inches wide, and yet for its entire length and breadth it was already quite distinctly marked. The dust was everywhere brushed away, and the rough surface of the ground had been trodden into some approach to smoothness.

The track showed the diligence of the ants, but it displayed also their stupidity. The new patch of akâwâ plants was very much nearer the nest than the old one among the pampas grass, but, instead of making a direct track to the new patch, the ants continued to go all the way round by the old one, thus adding at least a third to the length of every journey. I noticed afterwards on various occasions many similar instances of apparent stupidity on the part of the ants, occasions where they underwent a vast amount of labour, and even exposed themselves to some danger which a very little sense would have enabled them to avoid. Some of these instances in due course I shall relate.

After watching the ants for some time on the track I went back to the nest and amused myself, as I often did, in testing the facility of the ants in discovering different kinds of food. I put down, some little way from the nest, a handful of a yellow lentil termed "dâl," and in a different direction I placed also a small heap of flour. The "dâl" some of the ants found accidentally, but took no notice of; the flour they made for at once, and in a multitude. By what sense they became aware of its presence was a puzzle, for it was too far off for them to see, and to our perceptions it had no odour. However, they found it, and at once, and forthwith began to carry it into the nest. It was a work of great labour, for the flour was too dry to adhere well together, and so nearly half what they collected fell off on the way.

The proceedings of one ant interested me greatly. He was of unusually large size, and with energy proportionate. On first emerging from the nest he went full pace to the heap, made one rush to the summit, and at once began to collect together with feet and jaws as much flour as he could reach. This he pressed into a ball against his chest, and with it he tore back to the nest, darted into the entrance, and presently reappeared. I recognized him by his great stature and the white patches of flour on his body and limbs. He went off again at once to the heap, collected another ball of flour, and returned. And this performance he continued to repeat without a moment's pause or intermission all the while that I remained watching him. So much of his collections of flour fell off on the way that his various returns to the nest were marked by little threads of white.

By the evening all the flour had been carried into the nest. The "dâl" remained where I had placed it till the afternoon of the third day. The ants paid it no attention, and it appeared to have no attraction for any other insect, nor even for the birds. On the third afternoon the ants suddenly changed their minds and conveyed the whole into their nest. Owing to the size of the grain, and its distance from the nest, nearly a yard, the conveying it must have been a work of considerable labour, and, as it subsequently appeared, of labour entirely thrown away.

It was shortly after this last proceeding of the ants that I made the acquaintance of those deadly enemies to the smaller members of their species, the ant-lions.

Close by the house—indeed, only just on the other side of the carriage drive—there is an extremely bare and dusty patch of ground, perhaps the very barest and dustiest in the whole garden. One morning, on returning from my drive, I happened to pass by this patch. As I did so I noticed that the surface was thickly dotted over with little circular, funnel-shaped pits. These little pits were so many and so close together that there was hardly a square foot of the ground that did not contain two or three. I recognized them as the pits of the ant-lion.

While I was standing looking, a dozen or so very small ants appeared on the patch. They were wandering seemingly aimlessly about, as is the habit of these small ants. One of the ants in the course of his wanderings happened to pass close by one of the many pits. It apparently excited his curiosity. He stopped, looked, and then advanced cautiously to the extreme edge of the pit, and bent his head as if gazing down it. As he did so the loose sandy soil gave way, and the ant commenced to slide down the side of the little abyss. In the course of his descent he managed, however, to turn, and then made frantic efforts to reascend. His struggles loosened more of the sand ; a whole quantity began to roll down.

Immediately on this in the narrow bottom of the pit

a pair of great horns appeared, and commenced to throw up the sand in a perfect shower. The sand as it fell descended on the poor ant, and as fast as he climbed up it threw him back again. I was on the point of going to his assistance, when by an extreme effort he managed to reach the edge, to clamber over it, and escape. The sudden appearance of the great horns from the bottom of the pit had in it something weird and mysterious. I was curious to behold the creature to which they belonged, for somehow I had never as yet, either at home or in India, seen an ant-lion. The servants informed me that the easiest way of procuring an ant-lion would be to angle for one with a horse-hair; for if dug out it required much trouble and time to discover it among the sand. This angling for ant-lions, I was also told, was a common amusement with the native children. The process is this: A horse-hair is held in the hand by one end; with the other end of the hair the sand at the bottom of the pit is gently stirred. The movement arouses the ant-lion; he supposes that an ant has fallen in, seizes the hair with his jaws, and clinging to it, is drawn up.

The process in description appeared simple enough, but we found that in practice it required some little dexterity to be successful. A horse-hair was got from the stables; the servants all tried, I also tried, but it was a very long time before an ant-lion was captured. His appearance was a disappointment. Seen out of his pit, he was a most ordinary-looking insect, with no sort of mystery whatever about him, nor indeed anything at all remarkable except his large, flat head and great jaws.

Having gratified my curiosity as to the appearance of the ant-lions, I was next desirous to observe by what process they constructed their pits, especially how they contrived to make the sides so perfectly circular, even, and funnel-shaped. I commenced my observations a day or two after. An ant-lion was speedily procured, for the servants had now acquired the knack of managing the horse-hair. I had the ant-lion carefully placed on the flat surface of a large lump of earth, and, to guard against the danger of his running away, the lump of earth was deposited at the bottom of a very wide, shallow earthen pan.

These arrangements completed, we stood by to watch the little captive's proceedings. We waited, but nothing occurred. The ant-lion lay perfectly still and motionless on the spot where we had placed him; then it occurred to me that perhaps the position did not suit him, so I had him conveyed away to a piece of ground very much resembling that from which we had originally taken him. The change produced the desired result. The ant-lion was no sooner placed on the ground than he began to wander about it; and I noticed that he moved both backwards and forwards with equal facility. He made frequent pauses, apparently testing the quality of the soil with the sharp-pointed end of his body. At length, I suppose, he found a spot sufficiently soft to suit him, for he stopped, dug the pointed end of his body into the ground, and commenced to move round in a circle as on a pivot. As he moved he shovelled up the dusty soil with his great head and jaws, throwing it in quite a shower beyond the circle. He worked so energetically, that in less than a minute he had not only outlined his pit, but had lowered the entire area quite perceptibly below the surface of the ground around.

I was watching his proceedings with the greatest interest, when they were suddenly put a stop to by a most unfortunate occurrence. A troop of small ants from some neighbouring nest made their appearance. At the sight of the ant-lion they seemed seized with fury; they rushed towards him, threw themselves on him, and buried their jaws in his body. Their bite seemed poisonous; the ant-lion at once became motionless, either dead or paralyzed.

I subsequently several times repeated the experiment, but the result was never altogether satisfactory. Most frequently the ant-lions, when placed on the ground, simply burrowed beneath the surface, and there remained. On some few occasions the experiments were put a stop to before they had well commenced. A troop of small ants suddenly appeared on the scene, and before we succeeded in driving them off the ant-lion was killed or entirely disabled. So far as I remember, it was only on two, or at the most three, occasions that the ant-lions when drawn out of their old pit proceeded to construct another. Their method then was precisely the same as that I have above described.

They moved about probing the ground for a soft spot. That found, they dug in the pointed end of their bodies, moved round on them in a circle, throwing up the sandy soil with their heads and jaws. They continued this till they had lowered the surface to the depth of a little more than the eighth of an inch. This much accomplished, they discontinued their labours. They buried themselves in the centre of the circle, and however long I might wait, they did not again appear.

My experiments had shown me how the ant-lions commenced their pits and the means by which they rendered the surface outline so exactly circular; but I remained still in ignorance as to how the pits were finished, and especially how the sides, down to the very bottom, were made so smooth, so straight, and so perfectly funnel-shaped.

On other points also regarding the ant-lions my curiosity to the last continued ungratified, and especially on this, namely, how, living solely on ants as they did, they managed to exist on the very small number of ants they appeared to capture.

I used to pass by the piece of ground where the ant-lion pits were nearly every morning, and I used generally to stop some little while to observe them. I never saw any very large number of ants on the ground, and of these I do not think one in twenty ever fell into the pits. Either more fell in at other times of the day, or else the ant-lions were able to subsist on an extraordinarily small amount of food.

Another thing also struck me as curious. The ant-lions subsist upon ants, and yet when out of their pits they never made any attempt to capture them. The condition of things was, indeed, then reversed: the ants were the assailants, the ant-lion the victim.

The ant-lion is not at all a large insect. None that I

saw very much exceeded in dimension an ordinary house fly. Still, small as the ant-lions were, to the diminutive ants they must have seemed giants. Nevertheless the ants appeared to regard the ant-lions with no sort of apprehension. On seeing one they immediately attacked it, and without the least delay or hesitation. To be sure, they generally attacked in overwhelming numbers, but it was not their numbers that gave them confidence. The ants attacked with equal boldness when they were few, and, so far as I saw, always successfully.

On the other hand, the ant-lions showed just as little fear of the ants. They did not flee when the ants approached, nor did they seek refuge by burying themselves in the sandy earth; they remained just as they were till the ants came close, and then they gave them the warmest reception. Their weapons were their great jaws, and at each nip of these an ant was left headless. If the attack of the ants had only been confined to the front, with our assistance the ant-lion would have escaped; but some few of the ants always at the same time approached from behind, and it was their attack that proved fatal. They were so small, and they came on so quickly, that neither I nor the servants perceived them till they were already on the ant-lion's body; and then it was too late. The ant-lion's jaws could not reach them, nor could we pull them off. To prevent any misapprehension, I think it as well to state that these combats between the ants and the ant-lions were always accidental, and they occurred, notwithstanding all the efforts of myself and the servants to prevent them.

I used at first to suppose that the attacks of the ants were the result of instinctive animosity. I thought that in the ant-lion the ants recognized their natural enemy, their implacable foe; and certainly the extreme ferocity of their attack did suggest such an explanation. I afterwards came to the conclusion that the ants attacked the ant-lion merely as they did caterpillars and other small insects—for the sake of prey; for these small ants, though they devour anything, are especially carnivorous. Their attacks, too, on the ant-lions were not more furious, I found, than their attacks on grubs and caterpillars. Besides, as the ant-lion devours the ants only when concealed in his pit, the ants could hardly have identified him with the insects they saw lying on the ground. I may add that it was only the very small varieties of ants that ever attacked the ant-lions; the larger ants, if they happened to approach, passed by with entire indifference. But these large ants are very little, if at all, carnivorous.

I have spoken of the rapidity with which the ant-lion outlines and excavates the upper portion of his pit. More remarkable still is the rapidity with which, when on suitable soil, he buries himself beneath it. I have watched an ant-lion as he lay on the ground. My attention has been distracted for a few seconds. When I looked again the ant-lion was no longer on the surface. In this short interval he had concealed himself beneath it.

CHAPTER III.

THE RIVER

I HAVE spoken of how the present extreme heat gives to the landscape and atmosphere something of the aspect of winter—the same lurid sky, the same appearance of driving snow. To-day there was still the wintry aspect, but it was of winter of a more agreeable phase. The wind had fallen, much of the dust had subsided, the sky was faintly blue, and the sun shone cheerfully, no longer wan and pale. The air was also tolerably clear, but more intensely hot and dry than ever. The air was so hot, so absolutely dry, that when I left the house to proceed to the office it seemed almost as if I had entered a bath of heated sand. Nevertheless there was something in the appearance of both landscape and atmosphere that recalled recollections of a hard frost and a bright winter day. The air had the same glistening look, the same crisp, bracing feel, and it also to some extent conveyed the same exhilarating sensation — a sensation, however, which did not very long continue.

In the course of the afternoon and evening I had experience of other effects of the combined heat and dryness. Some few months previously, in the course of the last cold season, I had received from England a box of stationery. The box, among other things, contained a few packets of sealing-wax; the packets were most neatly done up, all the sticks of the sealing-wax being separated from each other, except at the ends, by slips of thin paper.

In the afternoon, when I had returned from the office, for some reason or other I wanted some sealing-wax. I went to the box and took out one of the packets. I found it distorted out of all shape; the sticks of sealing-wax had not exactly melted, but they had softened sufficiently to twine and twist, and to unite at the ends where they were not separated by the paper. At the same time, and what struck me as most curious, was that, though the sealing-wax had thus twisted and joined, it still to the touch seemed as hard and firm as ever; and when I attempted to separate one of the sticks it broke off with a perfectly clean and sharp fracture, thus in a way illustrating the modern theory of the movement of glaciers.

While engaged with the sealing-wax I had left lying on the writing-table a sheet of notepaper. I found it now coiled up by the heat into a complete cylinder.

My evening experience was, however, perhaps the most curious. I was brushing my hair before the looking-glass by the light of a candle. As I brushed my hair crackled loudly, and it gave out sparks that even in the candle-light were faintly visible. In order to ascertain their full brilliancy, I had the candle removed; and then as I brushed my hair in the dark the sparks that issued were so many and so bright, that

D

I could distinguish, not only the outline of the looking-glass, but also, though certainly faintly, the reflection of my head and face on the surface of the glass.

The intense heat continued for some days, and then, as is usually the case, it was succeeded by a dust storm. It happened to be a native holiday, and the office was closed. It was about two o'clock in the afternoon. I was sitting reading near the tattie in the drawing-room; the punkah was swinging above me. According to custom, I had that morning risen early. The heat, the cool breeze from the tattie, the monotonous swing of the punkah, and my early rising, all combined to make me drowsy. Without knowing it, I think I must have fallen into slumber. I was suddenly aroused by the sound of a great commotion in the verandah outside. The servants were rushing about slamming to the doors and shouting to each other. I called out, but in the confusion I could get no answer; and then I noticed that the room was becoming dark. I rose and went out to ascertain what had happened.

As soon as I passed into the verandah the cause of the disturbance and of the darkness was revealed. A great dust storm was approaching. The servants were hurrying about closing all the doors and jilmils and letting down the reed blinds before the storm should be on us.

The appearance of the storm as it approached was very grand. It was coming on from the west, a great cloud of dust, black and solid-looking almost as a wall. This great wall of dust stretched along the entire horizon, and reached upwards to the very firmament.

All around us there was perfect stillness: not a leaf moved; there was not a breath of air. But the cloud of dust was rapidly advancing, and as it advanced it shut out all behind it. In a minute or two it had reached the houses on the other side of the road; it seemed to swallow them up. As I looked it crossed the road, and hid the compound wall; then came a rush of wind; a few drops of rain fell. I had only just time to get back into the house before the cloud of dust enveloped us. It hid the sun: it dimmed the light; inside the house there was utter darkness.

The darkness was so intense, that till the candles were lighted I had to grope my way, and even the candles when lighted only faintly illumined the room. They seemed to shine as through a dense haze, for, though every door was closely shut, the dust had found its way in, and filled the air.

This intense darkness continued for at least an hour, then there came a faint twilight, and gradually day reappeared. It was near sunset, however, before the storm had entirely passed away, and it was not till well into the night that the dust in the atmosphere had altogether subsided.

The time while the storm lasted was a time of much discomfort. Dinner had to be postponed, and even then was cooked and served with great difficulty. A thick layer of dust spread over the floors and carpets, and covered the beds, the chairs, and every other article of furniture, besides filling my hair and every fold in my clothes.

These discomforts, however, afterwards had their

compensations. The storm cleared the air, and left behind it a most agreeable coolness. This coolness was increased by a second storm, which came on a day or two after. It was quite an insignificant storm compared to the storm I have described; but then it was accompanied by a fall of rain, and though the amount of rain which fell was but slight, yet it so lowered the temperature that I was able to sit all the evening without using the punkah: also the next morning I was able to stay out much longer in the garden after returning from my ride. I took advantage of the circumstance to make a rather protracted visit to the ants in the lower nest.

I found them engaged in what I may describe as a complete house-cleaning. They were bringing out of the nest all the rubbish that apparently had for a very long time been accumulating within it. The articles brought out were of the most varied description. I noticed pellets of earth, husks of seeds, stalks of grass, small pieces of stick, and also what looked very like the fragments of bodies of insects, besides much else that I have forgotten.

But what most excited my surprise was that among the rubbish thus brought out was all that "dâl," or yellow lentil, that only the other day the ants had carried into the nest with so much labour and trouble. Perhaps they had found it too hard to eat, or perhaps they had found the taste disagreeable. But then why had they not satisfied themselves on both these points before conveying it in?

The pleasant effect of the storm was apparent in the

afternoon. It was so comparatively cool, and the air so free from dust, that before taking my evening drive I sat for a long time—an hour or more—on a low masonry terrace on the edge of the bank that overlooks the river. The end of the garden, as I have said, descends to the river in a succession of terraces, but not for its entire breadth. Along one side a narrow strip of the garden runs level to the edge of the river bank, which is there precipitous. I may add that the bank of the river on this its western side is generally precipitous, but it is broken at intervals by sloping gaps, worn away by the rains of centuries. It is one of these gaps that at the end of my garden has been converted into the terraces.

The bank is here about forty feet high, perhaps a little more; but, small as the elevation is, it is sufficient in this level country to afford a tolerably extensive view. As I sit I see across the river, which is from bank to bank fully three miles wide. I see down the river for a still greater distance, and I also obtain some slight prospect of the fields and groves of the country on the other side.

The view is pleasant from its being so open, but I cannot describe it as exactly pretty. At this season of the year the volume of the river is much reduced, and what water there is flows almost entirely along the opposite bank. Foreshortened by the distance, it appears from here only as a thin blue line; the rest of the bed is one wilderness of bare earth and sand. Through this dreary expanse wind several narrow streams. Some are really streams, and do actually flow, though with a movement hardly perceptible; the rest are mere long-stagnant pools—water left in the deeper hollows of the bed when, after the last rainy season, the river subsided.

The largest of the real streams runs immediately below me; it flows along the base of the bank on which the terrace is situated. This stream is sufficiently broad and deep, indeed, to merit the appellation of a river, and its current, though slow, is still quite easily apparent. On the other side of this stream there are a number of melon gardens; they extend along the margin of the stream for a quarter of a mile or more, and form quite a little oasis, and one most pleasant to contemplate. Hardly anything can be prettier than the contrast of the bright yellow of the melons and the deep, rich, cool green of their great broad leaves.

The chief interest of the river-bed lies, however, in its animals. Although it is but a mere strip of sand and stream, yet, as regards the living creatures that inhabit it, it appears like another region, so many are the birds, reptiles, and other forms of life upon it which are never seen in the vast tracts of country that lie on either side.

This afternoon, as I sit on the terrace, the creatures most in evidence are a party of some five or six great alligators. They lie basking on a sand bank not far distant; they lie with their bodies flat on the sand, much resembling so many logs of timber, as large, as rough, and quite as motionless. Three of them have their mouths wide open; the lower jaws stand out horizontally; the upper jaws point upwards, almost perpendicularly, to the sky. Long, narrow, sharp at the ends, they suggest the idea of three enormous pairs of open scissors.

These huge creatures will lie on the sand banks for hours thus motionless. When sailing on the river I have often watched them. Suddenly one is moved by some impulse. Perhaps the approach of the boat has alarmed it. It starts into life; it makes a rush to the river, throws itself over the edge of the bank, and falls into the stream with a thud and a splash that resound over the water far and wide.

Considering what awkward, short-legged creatures alligators are, it is surprising to observe the speed with which they can run, but of course only for a very limited distance. It is said that they can overtake a man, and there are many stories of their having done so. Some native has ventured too near an alligator and provoked or disturbed him; a chase has ensued, and the man been overtaken and devoured. On the other hand, I have often been assured that a man, if pursued by an alligator, can always escape by suddenly turning, for the alligator can only turn after making a considerable circuit; and by the time the circuit is completed the man is too far off to be overtaken. It is necessary, however, that the man when turning should keep his head, for otherwise, instead of passing the alligator, he may probably run into his jaws.

But I have not much faith in these stories. It is possible that men may sometimes have been seized and devoured by alligators on the land, but I never myself knew of an instance. The alligators, however, do certainly occasionally seize and carry off human beings in the water, especially women and children at the bathing-places. Many alligators when shot and opened have been found with ornaments of children and females inside them.

I remember when I was magistrate of Muttra being told of a rather remarkable instance that had occurred there some few years previously. An alligator had established himself in the river not far from the chief bathing-places. He was an enormous brute of the short-nosed variety. He was believed to have carried off several of the bathers, chiefly women. He established quite a terror. At length he was captured and dragged ashore, killed, and then cut open. I was told that an immense number of women's ornaments and fragments of dresses were found within him.

But sometimes when bathers disappear the alligators are unjustly accused, as the following story will show. The incidents occurred also at Muttra, but before my time. They were thus related to me, and I entertain no doubt of their general correctness :—

Several women had disappeared suddenly when bathing. Each gave a shriek and vanished under the surface. It was supposed at first that they had been seized and dragged below by the alligators, but presently suspicions were excited. It came to be noticed that all the women who disappeared were well-to-do, and at the time of their disappearance they were wearing valuable ornaments. Before long the suspicions became certainties. The body of one of the women was found floating in the river. It bore no mark of injury from any alligator, but her ornaments were gone, and there were rents and gashes in the flesh where they had been torn or cut off.

Inquiries were then instituted, and it was discovered that the women had been the victims of a gang of a species of Thugs. Some of the gang were expert swimmers. They remained near the bathing-places, ostensibly amusing themselves in the water. When a woman with rich ornaments came down to bathe, their confederates signalled them; one of them swam to the bathing-place, swimming the latter part of the distance under water. The woman was seized by the feet, dragged to where the stream was deep, her ornaments there cut and dragged off, and the body allowed to float down with the current.

With regard to the human beings really devoured by alligators, the number is surprisingly small, that is considering how the alligators abound in the rivers and the thousands and thousands of natives—men, women, and children—that each day resort to the rivers and are at all hours bathing in their waters.

Of all the rivers in India the Ganges has the reputation of being the one in which the alligators the most swarm. It is also the river to which the Hindoos most resort for religious bathing. The Mahomedans make these two circumstances a subject of joke against the Hindoos. They say that the sins washed off by the bathing take bodily form in the persons of these huge reptiles, their vast number indicating the wickedness of the bathers.

The alligators live in the rivers, but it is said that they are also occasionally found in some of the great reservoirs, or, as they are termed by the English, the tanks. It is not easy to understand how they find their way to them, for though an alligator can live on the land, he could not travel far over it without attracting observation, and once observed, his destruction would be speedy.

On this matter I remember once hearing a curious story. There is a tank held very sacred by the Hindoos among the hills in a very wild part of India, somewhere, I think, near the frontiers of Bengal. In this tank there lives always a single alligator, never more. When this alligator dies, in the course of a few days another takes its place, but where this last alligator comes from, how it finds its way to the tank, or how it becomes aware that the tank is tenantless, are mysteries that have never been explained. In the neighbourhood of this tank there is, or used to be, a small military station. The story was told me by an English officer, who held a command there; he was himself quite persuaded of its truth.

I will conclude this discourse on the alligators by mentioning that there are in India two distinct varieties of these creatures; they are termed respectively the "gurriâl" and the "mugger." The two varieties differ only, at least to an ordinary observer, in the shape of their heads. The "gurriâl" has a comparatively small, long head and enormously lengthened pointed jaws, resembling, as I have already remarked, the blades of a pair of gigantic, long, thin scissors. The head of the "mugger" is squarish and clumsy-looking to a degree. It calls to mind a good deal the head of a hippopotamus.

The "gurriâl" is the variety which is much the most commonly seen. I presume that it is also the most numerous. Certainly the "mugger" is but seldom to be observed lying on the sand banks.

Both varieties are sufficiently ugly—hideous, I might even say—but of the two the palm for ugliness must be given to the "mugger," for its great clumsy head lacks the picturesqueness which the long, sharp-pointed jaws give to the head of the "gurriâl." But, hideous as both varieties of alligators are, their appearance does not excite the same feeling of loathing and repulsion as does that of a rat and some other animals who are certainly more symmetrically formed.

Although about here, on the Ganges, the long-nosed alligator is termed the "gurriâl," and the short-nosed alligator the "mugger," this nomenclature does not universally prevail. In other parts of Upper India the names are oppositely bestowed: the long-nosed variety is termed the "mugger," and the short-nosed variety is designated as the "gurriâl."

I had been sitting on the terrace for some time contemplating the alligators, the melon beds, and the great expanse of sand beyond them. Then by chance I happened to cast my eyes down the sluggish stream immediately below me.

The opposite bank was very broken and uneven. As I looked it seemed to me that fifty yards or so away there was something moving along the bottom of the bank, close by the water's edge. I looked attentively, and was sure. It was a long, large animal, slowly making its way up the stream in my direction. It came nearer, and I perceived it was an otter, what the natives term the "jul-mânus," or water-man.

I now became very interested. The otter continued to advance; it was most pretty to watch his movements. He crept along with the utmost caution, evidently quite unaware that I was observing him. Every few paces he paused, raised his head, and looked around, as if to make sure that no danger threatened. He presently came on till he was nearly opposite where I was seated. I was wondering where he would go, and what was his object, when something appeared to alarm him. He stopped, raised his head, gave a sharp glance behind, and then made a plunge into the stream, and was out of sight below the surface in an instant.

I sat regretting his departure, when, to my delight, in a minute or two he reappeared, and now on my side of the stream, and immediately below me. He had also altered his course, and was proceeding downwards. On account of the bank, I could not now so well observe him, but I caught occasional glimpses of him, proceeding always in the same slow, cautious manner as before. At length he reached a place where the bank projected. He went round the projection, and I saw him no more. I waited a few minutes, but he did not return, and then I left to take my evening drive.

The next morning I came across some old acquaintances in the shape of a species of ant, termed by the natives the "burtunga." I had known these ants very well at former stations, but had not as yet met them here. This is one of the largest of the Indian ants, and it appears even larger than it is from its standing so very high on its legs. Most ants seem to crawl with their bodies close to the ground, but this ant runs, and with its body well elevated above the surface. It differs from most other ants also in this: it makes its nest in the ground, but passes nearly all its existence on a certain species of tree.

I came on these ants this morning quite by accident. I was sauntering down one of the paths of the garden, when I saw a very large ant come out of a hole in the path; I recognized him as a "burtunga." On seeing me he paused, appeared alarmed, turned, and fled hurriedly back. Once within his hole, he seemed re-assured; he remained standing just within the entrance calmly regarding me. I concluded from this that the hole was the passage to his nest; and this it proved to be.

Curious to see what his next proceedings would be, I withdrew to a little distance, and there remained and watched. In a minute or so the ant came out; he seemed to look around; he could not, I imagine, see me where I stood. I suppose also that, thinking all safe, he gave some signal, for presently a whole multitude of other ants came swarming out. I noticed that each ant carried in his mouth a small pellet of earth. The ants ran with their pellets to a short distance, dropped them, and returned to the hole, I presume, to bring out more. There was such a continued stream of ants coming out, and all bearing pellets of earth, that I concluded that the galleries of a nest were being excavated or enlarged. Whatever the work was on which the ants were engaged, they were evidently anxious to complete it quickly. They rushed in and out, dropped their pellets, and returned for more at quite racing speed.

After looking on for some little while, I came forward. My appearance evidently caused alarm. So soon as the ants perceived me, the whole multitude at once dropped their pellets, fled back to the hole, and buried themselves in its furthest recesses. One or two, however, must have remained near the entrance to watch, for as soon as I retired again, then, in a minute or so, the whole body of ants reappeared and resumed their labours. I repeated the experiment once or twice, and always with the same result: when I appeared, the ants fled; as soon as I had retired, they came out, carrying their pellets as before.

In this fear of man these burtunga ants are peculiar. I never noticed the same fear exhibited by ants of any other species. Nay, more, so far as my observation goes, other species of ants not only exhibit no fear of man, but do not even manifest any apparent consciousness of man's presence. What is still more curious is that these burtunga ants exhibit this fear of man only when they are on the ground. When swarming about the trees, I never saw them display the least apprehension when I approached them, or even show at all by their movements that they were aware I had done so.

The tree that the burtunga ants most frequent is of a species something resembling the "peepul," which is allied in a way to our poplar. The tree has a smooth, light-coloured bark and rather scanty foliage. The movements of the ants on the trunk and branches are, therefore, very plainly observable. It is very interesting to watch them; they swarm over the tree in thousands, for what purpose I could never clearly determine. They did not appear to feed, or to carry away seeds to the nest, or to repose, or, in short, to do anything save to roam incessantly about, and always at full speed. The rapidity of their movements used always to excite my wonder. They ran up the trunk apparently with as much facility as they ran down it, and they raced along the under and the upper sides of the branches with just the same ease and rapidity. One might almost fancy that the force of gravity did not affect them.

The burtunga ants are not only themselves of great size, but they have especially large and powerful jaws. They are capable consequently of inflicting, for an ant, a very severe bite. Their power in this respect is utilized in native surgery. They are used, as thread is with us, to stitch together the sides of wounds, especially sword cuts. The mode of procedure has been thus described to me: A number of these ants are caught and held in readiness; the edges of the wound are then pressed together, and the ants placed on them, each at short intervals. The ants immediately bite, digging their jaws into the flesh on either side of the wound. The necks of the ants are next snipped off with a pair of scissors; the bodies fall to the ground, leaving the edges of the wound firmly held together by the line of heads and jaws.

The English surgeon of the station, to whom I

once described the procedure, declared it to be impossible, and gave many reasons why it must necessarily be so. Nevertheless, though I have never witnessed it, yet I cannot but believe it, for I have heard the fact of its performance so often stated, and that by persons of entire credibility, and who had no possible object for deceiving me. Lately, too, I have somewhere read that ants are similarly used to fasten wounds in parts of South America.

I have mentioned that the second dust storm, that I have described above, was accompanied by a slight fall of rain. The fall was a mere shower, and such showers are nothing unusual. They commonly occur at this season, and also occasionally at other times. I remember, however, two that were rather remarkable. One occurred at this station shortly after my arrival in the country; I was then residing here with my brother. It was towards the end of the cold season. We were taking our morning walk along a road that leads to the city by the bank of the river.

There was not a cloud in the sky, nor any appearance of vapour, when suddenly it commenced to rain. The rain did not last long, and was not exactly heavy, but the drops of rain, I remember, were unusually large; and, what was the most singular, they appeared to fall from vacancy, for, during all the few minutes that the shower continued, the sky remained as unclouded and as clear as before.

The other shower occurred at Delhi, and during the hot weather. It came almost as suddenly as the shower I have just described, and it did not last much longer; but so filled was the air with dust that the rain descended less in the form of water than of liquid mud. I was out walking at the time, and when I had returned home, and my clothes were dried, there was to be seen on every spot where a drop of rain had fallen a little round patch of earth.

CHAPTER IV.

VISITORS

I HOLD here a high official position; I receive in consequence many native visitors. Some call to ask favours, some merely to pay their respects. In the matter of these visits there is a good deal of etiquette. The day previous a message is sent desiring permission to call, and that given, an hour is appointed. Some further preliminaries have, however, still to be arranged. I have to ascertain if the visitor is of sufficient social standing to entitle him to a chair, and if so, whether his position also permits him to bring with him an attendant, that is into the room. Then, further, I must make myself aware as to what distance I should advance to receive my visitor when he arrives, whether to the door of the house, the door of the room, or merely a few steps over the carpet.

It is, however, only in the case of natives of the very highest rank that these last questions arise, and of such about here there are few or none. As regards the visitors I at present receive, the only points I ever have to determine are as to the granting the chair and the admission of the attendant.

Neither of these points arose this morning, for the

visitor was my landlord; and his family being old residents in the city, his social position had been long ago settled. He receives a chair, and being a young man, he never cares to bring an attendant.

He had several times called on me already; but I mention his visit to-day because he told me a story which, as an illustration of the early days of our rule, much interested me. I have introduced the mention of the visit at this stage of my narrative, but I must confess that I do not exactly remember when it really took place, whether before or after the occasion of the dust storm.

In speaking of my visitor, I ought in strictness to describe him, not as my landlord, but as one of my landlords, for the house belongs equally to him and his elder brother. The two brothers are bankers and traders in the city. My visitor, however, though the younger brother, chiefly manages the business; he does so on account of the long and frequent absences of his elder brother.

The elder brother has a passion, I cannot exactly say for travelling, but for making journeys. He goes frequently to Simla, to various places in the Punjaub, and occasionally in the opposite direction as far as Benares, and even Calcutta. As the journeys have no very special object, they are regarded by his fellow-townsmen with some astonishment, and are generally attributed to the influence of a ghost, one of the variety known as the "Burram Râkshus."

The story goes that the grandfather of my landlord once purchased a house; afterwards he discovered in it a vault containing a great treasure. This treasure he kept, whereas he ought to have made it over to the late owner or his heirs. In consequence of his not doing so, the spirit of the late owner has ever since haunted him and his descendants; and at various times it has also done them much evil: it has caused them pecuniary losses, sickness, deaths, and other misfortunes. Of late years the ghost has attached itself in especial to the elder brother. It appears to him at night and terrifies him, and fills his mind during the day-time with all kinds of worries and apprehensions. It is to escape from the influence of the ghost that he makes these frequent journeys.

Possibly the story of the treasure may have some slight foundation in fact, but it was not by such means that the family obtained their fortune. How they did really acquire it, in the course of his visit to-day, the younger brother informed me.

"My grandfather," he said, "was head gomâshtah (agent) in the Commercial Residency here. It was in the old days when the Company (the East India Company) traded. Mr. Dillon (so I will call him) was the Resident. He was a very kind gentleman, and very friendly to my grandfather. Every now and then orders came from London to buy cotton. Mr. Dillon as Resident was, of course, informed of the orders before they were published. My grandfather, as was the custom, used to go to Mr. Dillon every day to pay his respects. Some day or other Mr. Dillon would ask, 'What is the price of cotton?' My grandfather would inform him. Mr. Dillon would be silent for a minute or two; then he would say, 'I think it would be a good time to purchase.' My grandfather understood, and when the visit was over he went into the bazaar and bought all the cotton in the markets far and near. Presently the orders of the Company to buy were published. The price of cotton went up, and my grandfather sold at a great profit. And thus in the course of a few years, without any injury to the Company and without any fraud or oppression to other persons, my grandfather, simply by the favour and kindness of Mr. Dillon, accumulated a fortune of very many lacs of rupees."

It might be supposed that Mr. Dillon also benefited himself. Not in the least. He drew an immense salary, lived in great style, and left but comparatively little money behind him. What he did was out of pure good-nature, and was, in native opinion, only a very amiable and quite legitimate method of benefiting a subordinate.

The feelings of the English of that day were on many matters much more in harmony with those of the natives than they are at present, especially as regarded their servants and subordinates. It was not considered consistent with the dignity of any high official that those who had served him for long and faithfully should afterwards be compelled to enter the service of another master. On leaving the country every high official either pensioned his servants or otherwise provided for them.

Sometimes the methods adopted were rather amusing, as in the following instance. When in another district many years previously I often heard the story related.

Mr. Smith—that name will do as well as another—was the magistrate of the district in the early days of our rule. When he was about to retire from the service and return home, he proceeded to provide for his servants. Some he pensioned; some he gave money to; for the rest he had arranged Government appointments. Then Mr. Smith called before him these servants, and asked what situation each would prefer. One said he would be a thannahdar—that is, head of a police district—another said he would be a jemmahdar—that is, a chief officer of police—and so on. One servant chose one appointment; another servant chose another. And whatever appointment they selected, that appointment they received. At length all were provided for except the cook, and he as yet had not spoken.

So Mr. Smith called him forward, and addressing him, said, "Bawâchee Sahib" ("My Lord Cook"), "and what would you like to be?" The cook answered, "I would like to be nazir" (sheriff). "But," said Mr. Smith, "you cannot read or write. How then will you be able to do the work of sheriff?" Said the cook, "By the blessing of Providence and the good fortune of your honour, I shall do the work sufficiently well."

Mr. Smith tried to dissuade him, and so also did his fellow-servants, but without effect. The cook remained obdurate to all the arguments addressed to him; he merely replied, "I will be sheriff, or I will be nothing." So in the end Mr. Smith gave way, and the cook was made sheriff. Soon after Mr. Smith retired from the service, and Mr. Jenkins came as magistrate in his place. Mr. Jenkins heard the story of the cook, and was much amused at it. The first day Mr. Jenkins held office, the cook as nazir had to present some report. It was his duty to read it, but he excused himself. "Unfortunately he had left his spectacles at home." Mr. Jenkins smiled and said, "Well, bring them to-morrow."

The next day the spectacles were all right. But the nazir explained that he had a pain in his eyes that prevented his using them. Mr. Jenkins smiled again, and hoped that by the following morning the pain would have departed. But though the next day the pain had left, the nazir was still unable to read on account of a hoarseness that had come on in the night.

On this Mr. Jenkins laughed, and said to the cook, "I know all about it. I cannot keep you as nazir, but I will give you another appointment just as good where reading and writing are not required"; and so he did.

The cook held this appointment, whatever it was, I believe, till his death. He had his son educated, and in due time got him into the Government service. In my day this son was the kotwal (mayor) of the city, and a very efficient officer he was considered to be.

I am fond of conversing with the natives who call on me. I often in this way obtain much curious information about the early days of our rule and the times that preceded it. Also occasionally the stories related are in themselves very interesting. Especially so was one quite recently told me. The narrator was a Mahomedan, a man advanced in years, and who held a Government appointment of some importance. He had called to pay his respects, being in a way one of my subordinates. In the course of conversation he happened to mention that his family came originally from Persia, and had only been settled in India for three generations; and then he proceeded to tell me the reason of their coming.

His grandfather, he said, whom I will term Ismael Khan, had been a noble of rank at the court of Nadir Shah, the king of Persia who in the last century invaded India, captured Delhi, and carried away the world-famous peacock-throne and countless other treasures. He was besides one of the most bloodthirsty tyrants that even Asiatic history records.

One day, my visitor went on to relate, Nadir Shah was holding audience. Nadir Shah, arrayed in all his splendour, was seated on his throne. On his right hand and on his left his nobles stood before him. They stood in an attitude of reverence, their hands folded, their eyes cast down. But his grandfather, Ismael Khan, in a moment of forgetfulness, raised his eyes. As ill-fortune would have it, at that moment Nadir Shah happened to be looking towards where Ismael Khan was standing. Their eyes met. "So you stare at me?" Nadir Shah exclaimed, and his voice was angry. Nadir Shah said no more, but that was sufficient.

As soon as the audience was over Ismael Khan returned in haste to his house; he summoned his steward, and bade him have saddled all the fleetest horses in the stables, and to collect the most trustworthy of his followers, and to tell them each man to get his arms and some provisions, and to make ready at once for a long journey. Ismael Khan then entered his zenana and collected all his jewels, and hid them about his person, and desired his favourite wife and one of her attendants to do the same. He also tied about him in a long purse as many gold pieces as he could safely carry, and gave as many more in charge to his steward.

By the time these preparations were completed evening was approaching. Ismael Khan waited till darkness had fallen, then he mounted his horse, and, accompanied by his favourite wife and her attendant, his steward and five-and-twenty horsemen, he rode silently out of the city and directed his course towards Hindostan.

I pass over the narrative of the journey, though, as told me, it was very interesting. It was a journey of terrible hardship, of cold, hunger, danger, and privation. And, above all, there hung over them the never-ceasing dread of pursuit and capture; and capture would be death. At length, after many weeks, the party reached the river Indus. Once across it, they were safe, for the Indus formed the boundary of Nadir Shah's dominions.

But the crossing the river was not easy: there was trouble and much delay in procuring boats, and then the embarking on them was a slow process; and in the midst of it a troop of horsemen appeared, descending the range of hills behind them to the west. One may imagine then the hurry, the terror, and all the while the horsemen drawing nearer and nearer. At length the men, the two women, and the horses were got on board, and the boats shoved off, and none too early, for before half the stream was crossed the troop of horsemen had reached the river bank. They shouted to the fugitives to return; they threatened; they entreated; they endeavoured to persuade. And this they continued till the boats had touched the opposite shore; then the troopers turned their horses and rode slowly away.

Ismael Khan, now in safety, proceeded on to Oude, and presented himself before the then Nawab, the celebrated Munsoor Ally Khan, better known by his title of Sufder Jung (breaker of the ranks in battle). Sufder Jung was himself a Persian. He took an interest in Ismael Khan as a fellow-countryman, and bestowed on him some appointment. "To this appointment," my visitor continued, "his son, my father, in due course succeeded. But, alas! though the salary was good, my father did not save. When he died he left but little, and so, as it was necessary for me to obtain employment, I entered the Government service, and by diligence, the blessing of Providence, and the kindness of my superiors, I have attained to my present position."

Since the day that followed the dust storm I have generally sat on the terrace that overlooks the river for some little while before taking my evening drive. The cooling effect of the storm has, however, long ago passed away. Indeed, the heat for some days has, if possible, been even more intense than before. The river shows its effects. Many of the pools have dried up, and the water in all the streams has perceptibly diminished. The stream immediately below the terrace has become all but stagnant, and in the places where the water is shallow its breadth has diminished by fully a third. The brown patches where the sand was moist have disappeared, and the river-bed displays one uniform dry white surface, most dazzling to the eye.

The shrinking of the streams and the drying up of the sand have almost put an end to the display of animal life, at least as it used to appear from this terrace. The alligators have migrated to deeper waters, the otter no more puts in an appearance, and even the birds have moved eastward and taken up positions in the neighbourhood of the main stream—not, however, quite all: some three or four still remain. They stand motionless, each well apart from the others, on a sand bank nearly in front. These are "buggolahs," a species of "waders," always to be found on the margins of the rivers and drying ponds. The buggolah is not a pretty bird, nor its ways interesting, yet, seen here on the river-bed, it has a sort of odd attractiveness. With its dingy plumage and melancholy aspect, it seems the embodiment of the dreariness of the great, sandy waste. Its quietude, its utter inoffensiveness, excite, too, for it a sort of sympathy. One can almost fancy it as oppressed by some great sorrow.

Its powers of immobility are really extraordinary. They almost equal those of the alligator. The buggolah will stand by the riverside for hours, its head sunk between its shoulders, its long beak resting on its breast. It stands thus motionless as if carved out of wood. Then, like the alligator, a sudden impulse possesses it: it starts to life, mounts with a spring into the air, and is transformed. The under-plumage of the wings and body is a brilliant white. The flight of the buggolah is not long nor particularly graceful, but while it lasts the bird, with its pure white plumage, is really a pretty object. But soon it alights, and becomes again a dull grey wooden statue.

In justice to the buggolah, I must, however, admit that very few, if any, of our resident river birds are gaily coloured; but we occasionally have from the east some very gorgeous visitors. A short time since a party of six flamingoes made their appearance one morning on the sands. They remained for two days, moving about with extreme stateliness. Their scarlet crests and wing feathers quite illumined the river-bed.

This afternoon as I sit on the terrace the only colour that relieves the monotonous expanse of sand is that afforded by the melon beds, and this is diminishing. The leaves have lost something of their first cool freshness, and a good deal of the fruit has been gathered; still enough remains to make a pretty display. It is only the yellow melons that catch the eye here from the terrace; the green varieties too much resemble the leaves in tint to be distinguishable.

Gay and bright as the yellow melons appear among the green leaves at this distance, their colouring when seen near is far inferior in beauty to that of some of the green varieties, and of these for variety and loveliness of tints and harmony of blending the palm must be certainly assigned to the water-melon. It is, perhaps, when these melons are cut that their colouring is seen in its greatest perfection, for to the deep green without is added the rich crimson of the fruit within.

The merits of the water-melon are confined to its appearance. It is never eaten except by the poorest classes. According to tradition, however, it used occasionally to be drunk—that is, its juice, well mixed with claret—by the English in former days. I remember hearing it told of one high official of that time who used to conduct his work with one of these melons propped upright on the table beside him. The upper end of the melon was cut off, the mass of seed scooped out, and claret poured in. The combined liquid used then to be ladled out and drunk as inclination prompted. That cholera did not result must be regarded as providential.

I do not know if the melon is indigenous to India; but all the finest varieties are said to have been introduced by the Mahomedans from Cabul and elsewhere. The introduction of the finest variety of all, the musk-melon, is attributed to the Emperor Babur, the founder of the Mogul dynasty. In connection with this melon, the Emperor, in his charming memoirs, relates a rather touching incident.

In the course of one of his campaigns the Emperor was encamped in a desolate tract near the banks of the Jumna. The Emperor was seated in his tent when a messenger arrived with a basket of these musk-melons from Cabul. The sight of them recalled recollections of his native country of Ferghanah, for it is there that this melon grows in its greatest perfection. The

Emperor, in his memoirs, recalls with loving recollection the scenery of Ferghanah—its snow-clad mountains, its clear running streams, its green meadows carpeted with violets. In his then dreary surroundings these memories, as they arose, so saddened him that, as he relates, he wept.

While I have been contemplating the melon-beds a line of native boats has come in sight round a bend of the river below. Clumsy, awkward structures in reality, at this distance they look picturesque. Besides, moving along each behind the others, they give some little appearance of life and animation to the landscape. They are being tracked up the river along the further bank of the main stream. The tracking ropes are fastened to the summit of the tall, thick mast, and each man of the crew, fifteen or twenty, perhaps, in number, pulls by a separate rope. From here, where I sit, neither men nor ropes are visible; but when near enough to be just in sight the effect is curious: the men appear like ants harnessed to the mast, as it were, by the section of a spider's web.

Before the days of the railways the entire heavy traffic of the country from east to west and the reverse was carried on by means of these boats, and they still convey a large proportion of it.

Formerly these boats were also much used by European families in ascending and descending the river. A boat was hired, a sort of bungalow erected on the deck, and the travellers performed the journey carrying with them their servants and all the comforts of home. The downward voyage was well enough, for the boat floated down with the current, but the ascent of the river was terribly tedious: the voyage of many hundreds of miles had to be made at the pace of a slow walk, and that only during the day-time.

Next morning, on returning from my ride, I visited the ants of the lower nest. For some few days, I fear, I have rather neglected them. I am sorry to say that I found them all engaged in fighting. From the number of dead and disabled lying about, I concluded that the battle had been going on for some time; I remained and watched it. Like the battles of Homer, it appeared to consist of an infinity of single combats. The combats having once commenced, they continued till one or both of the combatants were killed or disabled. If only one, then the victor, like Achilles, dragged the body of the defeated one away in triumph, and then returned to find a fresh antagonist.

After looking on for some little while, I discovered that the slaughter was not by any means so great as at first sight it had appeared. Many of the apparently dead were merely pretending; they were not even seriously injured. After lying for some short time motionless they would rise, look around them, and walk leisurely away. One interesting example of the resuscitation I presently witnessed.

A combat had taken place between a very large ant and a rather unusually small one. I did not witness the combat, only the result. The small ant had fallen; the large ant was dragging away his body. I had seen many apparently dead ants revive; but this poor ant, I made sure, was really defunct, he looked so utterly limp and crumpled up. The large ant was dragging away his victim along the foraging path in the direction of the pampas grass. I followed. The large ant had proceeded for the distance of about fifty feet or so; then he met another ant of much his own size coming homewards. The two ants stopped and entered into a conversation, as it seemed, through their antennæ.

The conversation continued for some time. When it had ended the victor ant released his hold of his victim, turned, and went back to the nest. The other ant also turned, took hold of the apparent corpse of the small ant by one leg, and commenced to retrace his steps, dragging the body along behind him. He dragged it to near the end of the track; then he let it go and departed.

The small ant lay motionless where it was left for some little while. Then, to my surprise, it began to move. Next it rose and commenced to clean off the dust from its head and face with its front feet. This done, it stood motionless for about the space of a minute. Then it commenced to crawl away; it moved at first very slowly and with apparent difficulty, and seemed half dazed. Presently it proceeded more briskly. Finally it broke into a trot, and ran off apparently quite well.

I now returned to the nest; the fighting was going on as actively as ever. I arrived just in time to witness the commencement of an interesting combat. Two large and equally matched ants came out of the nest together. As soon as they were clear of the entrance, they stopped, turned, and faced each other. They then commenced to shift their ground and make feints of attack with their front legs, just in the manner of two prizefighters. This went on for a minute or more; then one of the combatants made a sudden rush forward and caught the other by one of his antennæ. I am sorry to say that my notes do not record the further progress of the engagement nor its final result, but they do that of another combat.

This last combat was being waged between two very unequally matched antagonists—a large ant and a very small one. It had apparently been going on for some time; and, contrary to what might have been expected, the small ant had as yet got much the best of it. He had somehow managed to seize his large antagonist by one of his hind legs, and from this position, do what he would, the large ant was unable to dislodge him. He made desperate efforts; but he could neither shake the small ant off nor rub him off, nor could he turn his own head sufficiently far round to bite him.

I remained for some time watching the engagement, in fact till the increasing heat of the sun's rays warned me that it was time to retreat to the house. Then, as I was most anxious to see how the affair would terminate, I sent for a large saucer. I raised the large ant gently, and deposited him in the saucer, the small ant still clinging firmly to his leg. I then carried the saucer to the house, and placed it in a niche in the verandah. The edges of the saucer, I should mention, were too high and too smooth for the ants to climb over.

In the afternoon, on my return from the office, so soon as it was cool enough to venture outside I went into the verandah, very curious to see what had happened. The position of affairs was not at all what might have been anticipated. The two ants were separated, and were walking about the saucer on terms of the most perfect amiability; and, moreover, what struck me as still more singular, the leg of the large ant, notwithstanding the severe biting it had sustained, showed no sign or indication whatever of injury. To make sure on this point I examined the leg through my magnifying-glass. The glass was a powerful one. Nevertheless, though I examined most carefully, I could not discover on the leg any cut, wound, or even indentation. The small ant must have consequently retained his hold merely by the pressure of his jaws. That he should have been able to retain his hold so firmly showed how powerful a pressure his tiny jaws were able to exert.

My notes do not exactly record how long the fighting continued, but about the third morning, I think, on visiting the nest, I found that the ants had resumed their usual occupations, and had laid out an entirely new foraging track. The rapidity with which the track had been constructed showed their diligence; a portion of it manifested either their obstinacy or their extreme stupidity.

The new track lay along the bank of the terrace, not far from the edge. At one place the bank had given way. In consequence of this, for the distance of about a yard, in place of firm, level soil there was a mass of loose, crumbling sand, slanting down at a very steep inclination to a depth of nearly six feet. A bend in the track of a few inches would have avoided this rough and dangerous spot, but this bend the ants had not made; they had instead continued the track straight across it. The result was to entail on themselves an immense amount of quite unnecessary labour, and not a little danger as well. They had always great trouble and difficulty in crossing over the rough, crumbling sand, and very frequently they did not succeed in doing so: the loose sand gave way beneath them, and they rolled down to the bottom of the incline. And if they happened to be bringing home seeds, in the course of the roll they invariably lost them. Besides, even for ants the reascending the sandy incline was a work of time and difficulty. But no experience had any effect on the ants. To the last they continued to endure the labour and risk of crossing the loose sand sooner than alter the track and avoid it.

I have spoken already of how rapidly and how strongly these foraging tracks become marked. Of this, in the course of the next day or two, I had a striking example. I was strolling about the garden, not far from the house, when I came on a foraging track which I had not previously noticed. It could not, therefore, have been very long laid out. It ran for part of its distance through some short but very coarse, dry-looking grass; then it crossed the carriage drive. Where it ran through the grass, the grass was completely destroyed. The track was as clear and even as if the grass had been rooted up. Where it crossed the carriage drive, the track, besides being far broader, was also smoother, harder, and more distinct than were the marks of even the most recent and clearest of the carriage-wheels. It is possible that the feet or bodies of the ants may secrete some acid which destroys the grass; but even if so, this would not explain the clearness of their track across the firm, hard surface of the carriage drive.

CHAPTER V.

THE COMMENCEMENT OF THE RAINS

FOR the last few days the burning winds have ceased to blow. The air without has lost its crisp dryness, and the landscape its wintry aspect, while within the house the same refreshing breeze no longer passes through the tatties. The heat in consequence, though really no greater, is to the sensations far more oppressive. This cessation of the hot winds is one of the indications of the approach of the rainy season. In the afternoon, when I paid my usual visit to the terrace, I became aware of another. The appearance of the river had entirely changed.

Since that evening when I had sat and watched the passing boats, the water in the streams and pools had been continually diminishing. The stream below the terrace had shrunk in some places to half its former breadth, and it had everywhere almost entirely ceased to flow. It was now quite a wide sheet of water. The water had even submerged most of the melon-beds, and along the bank it was rushing in a rapid current full of whirls and eddies. Further beyond, where only yesterday there had stretched that dreary waste of sand, there was now a lake extending far away towards the further shore and prettily dotted over with long, winding islands. These islands were the summits of the larger sand banks. This sudden rise of the river was not due to any fall of rain, but to the melting of the snows in the higher Himalaya. This melting of the snows is generally shortly after followed by the arrival of the rains.

But a fortnight passed, and no rains arrived. We had many tantalizing disappointments. The river subsided as suddenly as it had risen. It rose again more slightly and again subsided. Several times clouds gathered; the heavens were overcast; a storm seemed imminent: but just when our expectations were at the highest the clouds mounted high in air and dispersed, and we had again the blue sky and the blazing sunshine. At length our disappointments terminated: the rains arrived.

It was about ten o'clock in the morning. It happened, as on the occasion of the dust storm, to be a holiday. I was sitting in the drawing-room, when the servants came running in to tell me that a storm was approaching. I went at once out into the verandah, the one which faced towards the river, for, while it is the west wind which brings the storms of dust, these storms of rain advance always from the east.

On reaching the verandah I saw a low bank of intensely black cloud stretching all along the eastern horizon. It rose rapidly, so rapidly that in a minute or so, as it seemed, it had overspread the entire firmament. For a brief space there was intense stillness; then came a rushing wind, a flash of lightning, and the rain descended. The rain did not fall, as with us, in a succession of drops, but in a vast multitude of continuous, uninterrupted streams. It continued thus to fall for over the period of two hours. When it ceased the face of nature was changed.

The sky that before was thick with dust was now an azure blue, clear as crystal, while the trees and shrubs, all wet with the raindrops, glistened with the freshest green. The rain, moreover, had so cooled the air that long before sunset I could walk about the garden without inconvenience.

The effect of this first fall of the rains on animated nature is all but magical. The frogs, the thousands of insects that during the intense heat have been lying torpid and concealed, now awake to life and activity. By sound and movement they seem to be making amends for their long period of silence and repose. The frogs croak, the crickets chirp, and everywhere the burrowing insects and small animals throw up their tiny hillocks.

But of all the effects of this first shower of the rains none is so striking as the sudden appearance in countless myriads of that beautiful little insect termed by the natives the "beerbhootee." Its scientific appellation I do not know. It is a small insect, seldom exceeding in size the dimensions of an ordinary pea. Seen through a magnifying-glass, its form is something that of a short, thick-legged spider. As it moves over the surface of the ground it resembles nothing so much as a morsel of animated velvet, and velvet of the richest and softest crimson.

The beerbhootee does not remain long, and its departure is almost as sudden as its arrival. After a week or so its numbers diminish; in ten days it has disappeared, and till the commencement of the rainy season of the following year it is not again beheld. Where the beerbhootees come from, whither they go, and where in the interval they remain are all mysteries, and so far as I am aware they are mysteries of which as yet no explanation has been afforded. During the short period that they remain I could never discover that they fed, or made nests, or performed any other work. They appeared to spend their time only in never-ceasing and quite purposeless wanderings.

The burrowing insects employed themselves certainly more actively. As soon as the rain had well aroused them they lost no time in setting to work. When I took my usual stroll through the garden I found all the raised earthen paths quite riddled with holes. The holes were of the most varying sizes: some would only just admit the finest wire, while others were almost wide enough to allow a marble to run down them, and between the two extremes there was every gradation.

I had a curiosity to ascertain what sort of insects some of the holes contained. I selected for first examination a hole of medium dimensions, and had it dug up. The process was very tedious. The hole was long and winding; it descended rather deep into the ground, and if its course was once lost in the moist earth it would have been next to impossible to recover it. To prevent such a misfortune, the greatest care had to be exercised, but our trouble in the end was rewarded. We at length reached the termination, and there, at a depth of about two feet below the surface, we came on an insect the like of which neither I nor any of the servants had ever before beheld. The head and body were those of an ant, but of an ant of gigantic dimensions; the abdomen, both in size and appearance, was that of a small slug.

I had the insect carefully lifted and placed on the ground for examination. Unfortunately, near where it was placed there was an ant-track, and at the time many ants were passing along it. The insect was hardly deposited on the ground before, by some instinct, the ants seemed to become aware of its presence. A party of them immediately left the track and made a rush to attack it. The details of the attack and its result were much the same as those I have already described made on the ant-lions. As the ants advanced the insect received them with its jaws; at each snap an ant was left headless. Three or four had thus fallen, and I and the servants had driven off the remainder, when the same catastrophe occurred as had happened to the ant-lion—two ants got round unnoticed behind, and now fastened themselves on the insect's abdomen.

One of the two ants I managed to brush off; the other had fixed himself too firmly, and to have torn him off might have fatally injured the insect. As the best thing to do, I had the insect removed on a leaf and placed on a patch of very soft earth, there to burrow if he desired to. This the insect did, but he only burrowed just sufficiently deep to conceal himself. I had the spot marked, and the next morning I went to examine it. On removing the earth we found that the ant was gone, the insect still there, but, alas! he was dead.

At the time when I discovered this insect I had never seen a queen of the white ants. Afterwards when I saw one it seemed to me that this insect must have been such. But later on I became doubtful. The queen of the white ants has certainly the same ant-like head and body, and the same enormous abdomen; but then none of them that I met with were able to move, much less to burrow; and, moreover, they were never found alone or in a hole, but always within the voluminous comb constructed for them by their subject ants—combs filled with eggs and young white ants in every stage of development.

I afterwards made many other explorations. The results of some I may record. One of the most interesting, however, was made previously to the commencement of the rains, a few days after the dust storm. It was the afternoon, and I was proceeding as usual to sit on the terrace. On my way I happened to notice in the side of the path a hole very much resembling that of a field-mouse; some impulse moved me to have it dug up.

At the depth of not more than a foot we came on the inhabitant; he proved to be a spider. He was an enormous creature, and of a most disgusting appearance: he had a great brown-coloured, bloated body and long, thick, hairy legs. As spiders cannot burrow, of course he had not himself excavated his residence. It was really the hole of a field-mouse; the mouse for some reason had abandoned it, and the spider had taken possession.

Although the spider had not constructed the hole, he had taken so much pains and displayed such skill in its adornment that, ugly as he was, I began to regard him quite with interest. He had lined the entrance of the hole for some short distance with a matting, most elaborately and cleverly constructed, of blades of grass, while the mouth of the hole was protected by a kind of curtain formed of similar materials. I felt quite sorry that out of mere curiosity I should have destroyed all the results of his labour and ingenuity.

A day or two after I came on the hole of another ground spider, or rather, I should say, another abandoned hole of a field-mouse of which a ground spider had taken possession. The entrance to this hole was protected by a similar but even more elaborately woven curtain. I gently lifted it. It moved on a fastening at the top, and I perceived the hole behind was not only lined with blades of grass, but that the grass was plastered over with a thin layer of mud. I was anxious to explore the hole to discover the species and appearance of its occupant, but I refrained; I had not the heart to destroy all that he had been at such pains in constructing. I may mention that I subsequently found that many species, both of insects and also of animals, occupy residences which other creatures have constructed. Sometimes the residence has been abandoned by its constructor of his own free will; sometimes the new occupant has compelled him to vacate it.

But the insects are not the only creatures which the commencement of the rains has recalled to life and activity. The frogs also have awoke from their long hot-weather slumber, and have emerged from their hiding-places in the mud. Of this fact at night I had unpleasant evidence. Early in the evening their croaking commenced. As darkness came on it grew louder; by bedtime it was overpowering. I do not know that it is then in reality louder, but it seems so. Interfering with sleep, one is more conscious of it. The croaking is so loud, so incessant, it so fills the air in every direction, that one fancies that the frogs which utter it must be present in thousands. Observation shows that this is quite a delusion. The frogs are really but very few. I do not suppose that those whose voices now so disturb me number more than half a dozen.

The Indian frogs, I may here mention, sometimes attain enormous dimensions, quite equal to those of a young duck. At another station I kept a tealery. When visiting it one morning, I noticed what I thought was one of the teal huddled up in the drain that carried off the surplus water from the tank. I went near to see if it was alive and to discover how it had got out, and then I perceived that what I had supposed to be a teal was only an immense frog. It was quite as large as the largest of the teal, larger, indeed, than many of them.

But, besides the frogs, we have at night since the rains commenced other musicians. The chief of these are the "jheengoos," a variety of cricket. Three or four of them have established themselves on the path just before the verandah which faces the river. There, each seated before his residence, they chirp the live-long night, relieving each other, so I fancy, at short intervals. At first I found their chirping a little disturbing, but I soon became accustomed to the sound; before long I even came rather to like it. The jheengoo is an interesting little creature. Later on I shall describe him, and also some other members of his species.

The weather just now at this commencement of the rainy season is very agreeable, not exactly in itself, but in its contrast to the weather that preceded it. I can remain longer out in the morning; I can leave the house earlier in the afternoon; but, most agreeable of all, it is now no more necessary to keep the doors closed and the rooms darkened. All day, as I sit and read, I can look out on the garden, on the trees and shrubs, and on the blue sky beyond. The clear, bright blue of the sky is inexpressibly lovely; even still more beautiful are its evening tints; and occasionally, though not often, we have sunsets of surpassing glory. Then, too, at night the stars shine with a brilliancy unknown in our northern climate; and words fail to describe the charm of the moonlight. Calm and bright, it bathes the trees, the garden, all nature, in one soft mysterious glow.

The season, however, has its drawbacks, and one of the greatest is the insects, in especial those that fly by night. Of these pests the pre-eminence in point of offensiveness must without question be given to the one termed by the English "the flying bug." These horrible little creatures possess a most sickening odour, an odour which they communicate to whatever they touch. When there is moonlight they fly outside, but on dark nights the lamps in the house attract them; if not prevented, they enter in swarms. To exclude them either gauze frames must be fitted to the doorways, or else the doors must be closed before the lamps are brought in.

The other evening, tempted by the pleasant coolness, I omitted this last precaution. I was soon made most unpleasantly aware of my forgetfulness. I was seated reading and drinking my tea. Of a sudden one of these little pests fell into my cup; at the same time four others alighted on my clothes, and a fifth got entangled in my hair: but these were merely the advance guard, a small party of explorers. In a minute or two after the main body arrived. They came in by hundreds, I may say by thousands: they filled the air; they covered the lamp-shade; they drowned themselves by scores in the teacup and milk-jug. I called the servants and had the doors closed, but it was too late: the insects were already in possession. I had no remedy but to go out myself and sit and watch the stars till it was time to retire to rest.

These "flying bugs" are unpleasant enough when they simply alight on one's hands or face; they are more disagreeable when they become entangled in one's hair. But it is when they fly into one's mouth and are accidentally swallowed that the full horror of their offensiveness is realized. Such an occurrence is one that does not soon fade from the memory.

Nevertheless, nauseating as is the scent of these

insects, I have heard of an instance of its being considered agreeable. It used to be said of a very high English official of former days in these parts that during the season when these "flying bugs" appear he always kept a few tied up in a corner of his handkerchief, and used to refresh himself at short intervals by inhaling their aroma, as one might salts from a smelling-bottle.

From these odious little creatures I will turn to the inoffensive and more interesting insects the crickets. Of the cricket there are here in India numerous varieties. Those most commonly seen are the small black cricket, which flies as well as hops, the larger brown cricket, termed the bhughah, another very much resembling it, known as the jheengoo, and a fourth, of still greater size and more active, named the lukhâree.

The crickets all inhabit holes in the ground. The holes are so long and so deep that I doubted at first if the crickets could themselves have constructed them. I even doubted, moreover, from the appearance of the crickets, whether they were capable of excavating holes at all. To satisfy myself on these points I made some experiments. At different times I had a cricket of each variety placed on one of the garden paths. These paths, as I have mentioned, are of earth and considerably raised. To prevent the crickets from wandering away when left, I had a large earthen pan placed over them upside down. These pans are termed nânds. They are made of the coarsest earthenware, and are very capacious. Those I used were nearly a yard in diameter and about eighteen inches deep. The crickets had consequently plenty of room to move about in and select a spot they fancied for excavation.

I tried the first experiment on a black cricket. He was placed under the pan in the afternoon about an hour before sunset. I removed the pan the next morning on returning from my ride. The cricket had dug a hole, in which he was still working. I tested the length of the hole with a stiff stem of grass. I found it to be six inches. The cricket was quite at the end of the hole, and, as I have said, still working. I remained for some little while to watch his performances. He appeared to dig away a certain amount of soil, and then to shovel it back to the mouth of the hole, and from thence to push it out unto the path. As the hole descended at a very steep inclination, the labour of thus shovelling up the earth must have been very considerable; and of course it would immensely increase as the hole became longer and deeper.

Now some of the cricket holes that I had already dug up descended to a depth of between two and three feet below the surface of the ground. The labour of excavating them must have been enormous. These, however, were the holes of the larger jheengoo.

It was on the jheengoo that my next experiment was performed. I need not repeat the details; they were the same as those already above described. On removing the pan the next morning, I found that the jheengoo had excavated a tunnel of the length of nine inches.

The other experiments I need not describe. It is

sufficient to mention that I became satisfied that the crickets of all the four varieties did not take possession of the abandoned domiciles of other animals, but that they each excavated a little subterraneous habitation for themselves.

The holes of all the crickets were generally very similar. They were long, they descended to a considerable depth and at a steep inclination, and they had no ramifications. The hole of the jheengoo, however, had two rather singular additions. Immediately before the entrance of the hole there was always a shallow, oval-shaped depression. The depression, both in form and size, very much resembled an ordinary tea-spoon. The object of this construction at first puzzled me; but I afterwards was told by my servants—those of them who sat up late—that these oval depressions were used as a sort of concert-room. At night, they said, each jheengoo came out of his hole and seated himself in the depression, and there emitted those chirruping sounds that had attracted my attention the night that followed the first fall of the rains.

I cannot clearly remember whether or not I myself ever saw the jheengoo seated in the depression. I rather think that I did; but I also think that it was not at night, but in the afternoon.

The purpose of the other addition I never ascertained, nor, indeed, can I conjecture. It is a small hole. It is situated a few inches from the principal hole, and always to one side and more or less behind. It descends straight down to the main hole, and joins it at about a depth of six inches below the surface of the ground.

It is too near the entrance of the main hole to serve as a means of escape in case of danger. And yet what other purpose it can serve I cannot imagine.

Of all the crickets the jheengoo is the most amusing to watch. When his hole is completed he sits most of the day at the entrance, his head only just within it, and there he sits gazing out at the sky and garden. He is not the least shy or timid, and remains quite undisturbed if I or the servants approach him. He has a great, round face, and it always seemed to me to wear an expression of such smiling good-temper that in the end I got quite fond of him. Of course this was only fancy on my part, for the faces of insects are mere horny masks, incapable of any expression whatever.

Notwithstanding, however, his amiable appearance, the jheengoo is an unsociable creature, leading a solitary existence. So, indeed, so far as I observed, did the other varieties of his species, with the exception of the small black crickets. I found that each of the holes of these I opened contained quite a little community.

The lukhâree, like the jheengoo, passes a good deal of his time sitting at the entrance of his hole; but he does not pass it in the same calm, contemplative manner. He is always on the alert, and will spring forward, if anything attracts him, with a suddenness and to a distance quite surprising, almost startling. Of this the other morning I had an example.

I was walking along one of the garden paths, when I passed a lukhâree's hole. The lukhâree himself was seated at the entrance. I stopped to look at him; he showed neither fear nor surprise at my presence, remaining as motionless as if in a trance. Presently, as I remained looking, a spider approached. He came on slowly, walking most leisurely. His course took him towards the hole of the lukhâree. The spider had arrived within a few inches of the hole, and was proceeding past it, when the lukhâree without warning, without any previous movement, made a spring forward. He alighted on the back of the spider, seized him, and before I had time to interfere had vanished with him back into the recesses of his hole.

In this case the distance that the lukhâree sprang was but small; it was the suddenness and rapidity of his movements that excited my surprise. The suddenness of the attack appeared also to paralyze the spider, for though he was the larger insect of the two, he made, so far as I could perceive, absolutely no resistance.

About this time I made many excavations. One of them resulted in a most interesting discovery. I was walking one afternoon along the path that leads to the terrace. Towards the end of the path I happened to notice a small hole in the surface. Something about the hole, I do not remember what, excited my curiosity. I had the hole dug up. It was not long; at the depth of some six or eight inches it terminated in a hollow space, and in this hollow space, closely huddled together, were four large toads.

The sight of these toads caused me great astonishment, and suggested many speculations.

And first, How had the toads managed to enter the

hollow? There was no passage that led to it except the hole I had dug up, and this was far too small for the toads to pass through.

Then next, How came the hollow there at all? It could not have been a natural cavity, for these raised paths are all artificially constructed. They are formed of loose earth heaped up, shaped, and allowed to settle; when finished they are therefore solid throughout. The hollow must then have been the work of some animal, but of what animal? The toads could not have excavated it, for they are unable to dig, or even to burrow, except in the softest mud. At the same time, the hollow did not resemble that of any small burrowing animal that I was acquainted with, and the size of the hole showed that the animal, whatever it was, must have been of the smallest dimensions. The hole would barely have afforded entrance to a field-mouse.

The only explanation that suggested itself to me was the following; namely, that the hollow must have been originally much smaller; that it was abandoned by the animal that constructed it; that the toads then, when very diminutive, took possession of it and there remained growing till too large to pass out again through the hole; and, finally, that their further growth enlarged the hollow by pressing back the soft earth that immediately surrounded them.

The appearance of the hollow gave some colour to this explanation, for in its shape it very much resembled the figure that the toads presented as they lay huddled together. Indeed, in some places, it almost gave the impression of a cast of their bodies taken in earth.

Whether or no the toads could have been capable of exerting such pressure I cannot say, but, supposing them capable, still a further difficulty remained: the toads could not have grown and increased in size without food, but, thus entombed in the earth, what possible food could they have obtained?

The beerbhootees are now fast disappearing. The popular belief is that they burrow beneath the surface of the soil, and there remain till the rains of the next year recall them again to the upper world. In the course of my present excavations I have made discoveries which, to some extent, confirm the correctness of this belief. In digging out the holes of various insects I have constantly found beerbhootees in the earth which was dug out. Some of those found were of full size, as large as peas; but the greater number were mere specks, not exceeding in dimension the head of the smallest pin, so small, in fact, that but for their brilliant colouring they would have been quite undistinguishable.

They were found usually at a depth of from one to two feet below the surface. It seemed to me almost impossible that such small, soft, and feeble insects could have dug their way to such a distance into the soil. I was, therefore, rather inclined to believe that these beerbhootees must have descended through the holes of some of the numerous insects. As I could not determine this point by observation of the ground, I had recourse to experiment. The point I desired to ascertain was, whether or no the beerbhootees were capable of burrowing.

My experiment was very simple. I had a large nând (earthenware pan) placed in the verandah, and then filled with earth nearly to the brim. I was careful to select earth of the same description as that in which I had found the beerbhootees. I then had two beerbhootees that we had dug up placed on the surface of the earth in the nând. They were both fair-sized specimens, about as large as peas.

The beerbhootees were no sooner on the earth than they commenced to burrow, but very slowly. They burrowed so slowly that by the end of half an hour they had not quite concealed themselves below the surface. I allowed three days to elapse, and then I had the earth very carefully removed from the surface to ascertain to what depth the beerbhootees had burrowed. I found that they had burrowed several inches. About eleven days later I made a further examination. The beerbhootees were found at the bottom of the nând. The depth of earth that they had burrowed through was between two and three feet. As I did not know how long they had been at the bottom when we discovered them there, I could not determine the exact time it had taken them to descend this distance.

I repeated the experiment two or three times on other beerbhootees; the results were generally the same. I ascertained from these experiments that the beerbhootees are able to burrow through the ordinary soil; also that they do not in their burrowing excavate holes or tunnels, but merely work their way through the sandy earth. This fact suggested another inquiry. The beerbhootees on which the first experiment was tried remained for a full fortnight beneath the soil. Owing to their manner of burrowing, during the whole of this period the earth must have closely surrounded them. This being so, how then did they obtain air to breathe or food to sustain them? Yet when found they exhibited no sign of having suffered from the want of either. They were just as plump and as active as they had been when first placed in the nând.

As the beerbhootees always appear after the first fall of rain, I resolved to ascertain if wetting the surface of earth into which they had burrowed would recall them again to the surface. For this experiment I selected very sandy earth, and earth which was also perfectly dry. I allowed sufficient time to elapse for the beerbhootees to have descended for a distance of a foot or more. I then had the surface of the earth thoroughly wetted, but no beerbhootees reappeared.

It is the general rule in nature that animals and insects that dwell in darkness are dull-coloured. To this rule the beerbhootee is a striking exception. It passes all but a few days of its whole existence in the most absolute darkness, and yet no living creature, bird, insect, or animal, has colouring of a more brilliant hue.

I have described the effect of the commencement of the rains on animated nature, of the millions and millions of creatures that the first shower calls forth to life and activity. The effect on the vegetable world is even more striking. But a few days have passed since that first shower descended. The country then, save for the trees and shrubs, had much the aspect of a desert. Everywhere it was bare, arid, and destitute of herbage, almost as the Sahara. It is now one sheet of verdure.

But particular instances will make the change more fully to be realized. There was one piece of ground in the compound which, without any exaggeration, was as absolutely bare, dry, and hard as the high-road. On this piece of land I several times made excavations, and although I looked carefully, I could never detect in the soil that was upturned the slightest appearance of either roots of grass or seeds of any description; but in the course of no more than three days after the first fall of rain the surface of this piece of land was covered with a thick crop of grass. The grass was of a deep rich green, and its average height, which I took much pains in measuring, was no less than three inches.

But I think the growth of the young bamboo shoots which now appear is even still more marvellous; one can almost see them grow. Certainly the difference in their height from one day to another is quite plainly noticeable. The point of the bamboo stems is exceedingly hard and sharp; and this and their rapid growth caused them, so I have been assured, to be used occasionally in former days, under native rule, as instruments for the execution of criminals condemned to death by impalement. The victim was securely fastened to a stake in a sitting posture. The stake was fixed by the side of a just appearing stem of bamboo. As the stem grew the body of the victim became transfixed. A death of more lingering agony is hardly to be conceived.

I may add that in one instance, under the native rule, the bamboo was utilized in a manner equally singular, but quite unconnected with cruelty. The town of Rampore, the capital of the little native state of that name, in the province of Rohilcund, was fortified by one of its former rajahs, not with ramparts and bastions of earth or stone, but by a thick circle of living bamboo-trees. Though a good deal dilapidated, this curious fortification still exists. I have never myself seen it, but I have been told by those who have that originally, before the trees were allowed to decay, the ring of bamboos must have formed a wall nearly absolutely impenetrable, one in which even the heaviest artillery could have hardly effected a breach. The ring was very wide, and narrow passages ran through it. From these the garrison could pour a destructive fire on the enemy, while themselves concealed and in perfect security. I do not, however, know whether the value of this mode of fortification was ever tested by actual attack.

CHAPTER VI.

THE RAINS

SOME days have now gone by since that fall of rain which ushered in the present rainy season, but as yet we have had no further showers. The heat in consequence has become again oppressive. At the same time, that profusion of insect life and insect activity which that first rain called forth has to a great extent disappeared.

The crickets still chirp all night as before, and as soon as darkness comes on the flying bugs are as troublesome as ever; but the swarms of insects that displayed themselves by day have mostly vanished, and I no longer notice, as then, little mounds thrown up everywhere by those that burrow beneath the soil.

The ants, however, show no diminution in either numbers or energy. Many of their communities are engaged in farming fresh colonies. I came this morning on one such colony that was in the process of establishment. The colonists were ants of the burtunga variety. The new nest was situated not far from the edge of the upper terrace. The late rain had here washed away a small portion of the bank, so that, instead of a smooth slant to the terrace below, there was now a very rough and almost precipitous descent. But, steep and rough as the descent was, nevertheless many hundreds of the ants were racing up and down it with apparently the greatest facility.

At the bottom of the descent was a small heap of what seemed very diminutive shrivelled raisins. These the ants were bringing up and conveying away into the nest. I remained for some time and watched them. The sight was very interesting. Each ant as he issued from the nest ran down the descent with quite headlong speed. Arrived at the bottom, he made a rush to the heap, seized with his jaws one of the little raisin-like bodies, and then tore up the broken bank quite as fast as he had come down it, and, it seemed to me, with not the least more effort.

Agile as the ants were, still occasionally they got a tumble. Some particle of loose earth slipped, and then away they went rolling over and over to the terrace below. These tumbles, however, seemed not in the least to discompose them. Without the delay of a moment, they recommenced the ascent just as rapidly as before, and so far as I could observe they never in the course of their tumble once lost hold of their burdens.

After watching the ants for some little while, I became curious to ascertain what these little raisin-like things they were carrying up in reality were. For this purpose I descended to the lower terrace to more nearly inspect them. I found they were the pupæ, or undeveloped young ants, still enclosed each in its chrysalis. The ants must have carried these pupæ out of the parent nest, and here deposited them, ready for conveyance into their new domicile, a conveyance they were now effecting. It was rapidly completed, for a day or two after, when I again visited the spot, the entire heap of the pupæ had been removed, and no doubt safely deposited in the recesses of the new nest.

These burtunga ants dig with almost as much rapidity as they run and climb; at least, so I conclude from the following incident. Soon after I had discovered this new colony, in the course of my strolls about the compound I came on another. It must have been a little longer established, or the number of the colonists must have been greater, for there were far more ants swarming about it. The ants, when I came up, were in the act of re-entering the nest, I suppose after foraging or roaming over the trees.

I remained looking on till the ants had all entered the nest, and then the idea occurred to me of digging out the entrance hole and discovering how far below the surface the actual nest was situated. The process had to be most slowly and carefully conducted, otherwise we might lose the trace of the hole, or come unexpectedly on the nest and injure the ants.

The process was so tedious that when we had traced the hole to a depth of some fourteen inches I gave it up. There was no knowing how much further we might not have to dig, and the sun was already becoming most unpleasantly hot. I accordingly had the earth we had dug out shovelled back, and I myself retired to the house. I had the earth shovelled back lest rain should fall, in which case, had the hole remained open, the nest would have been flooded.

In the afternoon just before sunset I visited the nest again. I wished to see if the ants had managed to open a passage through the earth that had been filled in. I felt a little remorseful lest by my proceedings in the morning I should have condemned them to a night's imprisonment, and thus prevented them from making their usual afternoon's foraging expeditions. On reaching the nest I was pleased to find that my fears were groundless. The ants had not only opened one passage through the filled-in earth, but they had opened no less than four, and not only opened these four passages, but also had used them. When I arrived the ants had just returned from foraging or wandering over the trees, and the rear guard were engaged in closing the entrance holes with the usual pellets.

It was the morning after this that I witnessed accidentally another burrowing operation. But the burrower in this case was an animal of quite another description and species.

I was strolling along a raised path of the garden. At one place as I passed I noticed a little stream of sandy earth rolling down the steep, slanting side of the path. I stopped to look. Almost immediately another small stream of earth rolled down, following the first. I looked closer, and perceived that the earth came from a small, round hole not many inches below the top of the side. I then recognized that some little animal was excavating a burrow, and was now engaged in pushing out through the hole the earth he had dug. I remained to watch his further proceedings. A minute or two passed, and then another small stream of earth issued from the hole and commenced to trickle down the side of the path, while behind the earth, and pushing it forward, appeared the point of a little black nose.

At short intervals the performance continued to be repeated, and each time as the earth was pushed forward the small nose was protruded further and further. At length, as the result of an unusually vigorous push, not only the entire nose, but also the greater part of the head it belonged to, appeared displayed. I now perceived that the little excavator was a garden rat, and that he belonged to that variety of garden rat which is long and slender, and is also, so far as a rat can be so, pretty both in form and colour.

This last push appeared to have disposed of all that remained of the earth which the rat had collected, for, though I waited for some time, no more earth issued. I presumed that the rat had gone on to the end of the burrow to dig away some more. As the morning was advancing, I did not care to wait for his return. I retired to the house, and there I endeavoured to solve a problem that rather puzzled me.

Rats dig with their fore feet, and so, of course, did this rat; but then he shovelled out the earth with his nose. He must therefore have turned himself round in his hole. The puzzle to me was how he managed to do so, for rat-holes never appear larger than just sufficient for the rat to pass through them.

The proceedings of this rat also suggested another

question, which somehow had never previously occurred to me. The holes or burrows of these garden rats extend for great distances; some that I opened were, windings included, fully seventy or eighty feet long. Now, rats do not, like moles, throw up mounds of earth at intervals as they continue their excavations; all the earth that they bring out must therefore be brought out by the entrance. There ought consequently to be a very considerable heap of the earth at the entrance of all these long burrows, but, as a matter of fact, except where the entrance is on the side of a bank, there is seldom, if ever, any accumulation of earth at all; and even when the entrance happens to be in the side of a bank, the quantity of earth thrown out is but small. What, then, becomes of the remainder?

My explanation is that these rats do not, in the ordinary sense of the word, really excavate. They simply loosen the earth before them by digging; and through this loosened earth they manage to force their bodies, leaving behind them a narrow tunnel. In the course of time this tunnel becomes enlarged by the constant passage of the rat, and at the same time its inner surface becomes firm and hardened.

That a rat can form a burrow in this way, I know from personal observation. In digging out a rat-hole, it sometimes happened that the rat was within it, but the exit not yet completed. The rat then, becoming aware of our approach, dug a passage to the surface and ran off. This new passage when we came to it, though narrow, was a tunnel quite open and distinctly marked.

At various times I dug open numerous rat-holes; they all consisted of one single, but very winding, tunnel. The tunnel, if finished, terminated in a single exit. There were no side exits for escape in case of danger nor any chambers for the occupants to lie in or to form a nest for the young, nor did I find in any of these holes or burrows any store of grain or fragments of other food. The tunnels, though long and winding, were never deep. Except where they passed under a raised path, none of these tunnels were more than six or at most seven inches below the surface.

We did not usually find the occupant at home, and this I was glad of, as on two occasions his presence resulted in a catastrophe. On the first occasion, as the rat ran out of the exit, a servant happened to be standing near with a stick in his hand. To my regret, he struck at the rat with his stick, hit and killed him. This rat was a most unpleasant-looking creature; still he was harmless and enjoying his life. I felt vexed that it should have been thus needlessly put an end to.

The fate of the other rat excited more sympathy, especially among the servants. His burrow was not yet completed, but this we did not know. There was no exit. He endeavoured to make one through a patch of very loose, moist earth. The earth was so extremely loose and wet that the poor rat became embedded in it. When in digging we reached the spot, to our great sorrow we found him suffocated. He belonged to the long, slender, and elegant-looking variety, and was prettier than usual, even for that variety. Perhaps for that reason his end the more excited our pity.

There are several varieties of garden rat. In my compound I have found three; one was the pretty variety: the other two varieties, though they differed in form and colour, were alike in the repulsiveness of their aspect. I term these rats "garden rats" to distinguish them from the field rats, which live away from human habitations, in the open fields and waste places, and which, besides, are quite different in their habits. The garden rats are solitary; the field rats live in communities, and, like our rabbits, form warrens. They usually select some piece of waste land, slightly elevated. Here, in the evenings, they may be seen sitting or scampering about in scores; they are not the least shy or timid. They will allow one to approach within a few yards without exhibiting any apprehension; on a nearer approach, they run into their holes, but reappear immediately as soon as one commences to retire. These field rats are very large, and in appearance, of all the varieties of Indian rat, they are the most disgusting. Their repulsive aspect is increased by a tuft of coarse, wiry-looking hair at the extremity of their tails.

These rats are a veritable plague to the cultivator from the damage they do to the crops. In ordinary seasons their numbers are kept down by the rains; during the rainy season their burrows are flooded, and their young destroyed in thousands; but if the rains are deficient, this fate they escape: their numbers then increase to an extent that threatens a calamity. The ingenuity of the villagers is taxed to the utmost to find means to destroy them. These field rats, though they are the largest by far of the Indian out-of-door rats, by no means equal in size the great farm-yard rats we have here in England, neither do I think that they have the same fierceness of aspect.

Besides these various out-of-door rats, there are other species that frequent the houses; but I shall defer my account of them to a later chapter.

More days have passed, and still the rain keeps off. There are indications, however, that before long it will again commence to fall. These indications as yet have been rather disappointing. The clouds gather; the sky becomes obscured; it seems as if every minute the rain was about to descend in torrents; and then, just when our expectations are at their highest, the clouds rise, separate; the blue sky again appears; and we feel that, for another day at least, our hopes must be deferred. But, as a compensation, the aspect of the firmament is always pleasantly varied, and the sunset tints are lovely.

It was one afternoon, at this time, that I sat on the terrace. Although no rain had fallen here, the appearance of the river showed that a vast amount must have descended higher up the country, and especially on the Himalaya. The whole of the river-bed, which only quite lately had been, as I have described, bare and arid as a desert, was now everywhere intersected with running streams. Many of the sand banks were entirely submerged; while the stream immediately below the terrace, instead of a narrow, half-stagnant line of water, now raced along, in itself a broad, rapid river.

All the afternoon the clouds had been gathering; they now formed a bank all along the eastern horizon, a bank which reached high up, almost to the zenith. The clouds were not, however, of the kind that indicate rain, but those which spread themselves and conceal the sky, as it were, like some vast, dark curtain. The rise of the river had been followed by the appearance of great flocks of water birds. Many scores of these were now flying above the water and the sandy beds that still remained; they were circling round and round and rising and descending in long sweeps and curves. I sat and watched them.

Some of my servants were seated on the terrace beside me, looking on, as I was, at the birds and the river. They were talking quietly among themselves. Presently one of them addressed me. He asked me to notice the dark curtain of cloud, and how prettily the white wings of the water birds, as they flew and circled, contrasted against it. The natives, like children, have but little appreciation of scenery as we understand it; they do not see much, if any, beauty in extended landscapes, nor do they at all admire even the grandest mountain views; but they are very sensitive to what I may term the smaller beauties of nature, more so, perhaps, than are the majority of Europeans.

I sat on the terrace till late in the evening. One of the servants remained with me. As sunset approached, the curtain of cloud lowered and faded away; as darkness came on, the stars shone out through the clear atmosphere with surpassing splendour. We began to talk about them. The constellations are not quite the same as those we see in England: those that in England lie far to the north are here invisible, while we look on many that in England never rise above the southern horizon.

Most conspicuous in the firmament appeared Orion. High overhead it shone with a brilliancy hardly conceivable to those who have only seen it in our northern skies. It goes here of course by a different name, and is represented, as are also many other of the constellations, by a different figure. From Orion we wandered off to gaze at and discuss other constellations, and finally the Milky Way. It is styled by the Hindoos the "Ganges of the heaven," but it is also believed to be the road which leads to the palace of Raja Indra, the king of the skies. It is along this road that Raja Indra proceeds, seated on "Indraguj," his elephant, when he repairs each night to hold court in his palace and see the "thousand fairies" dance before him. "Indraguj," far more magnificent than the elephants of earth, is also further distinguished from them by the possession of two trunks.

My servant being a Mahomedan, had of course no faith in these fables, nor had he any more in my information regarding the moons of Jupiter, the planet Neptune, and the other discoveries of our European astronomers. After listening for some time he made a remark which, coming from one of his religion, a good deal impressed me: "Your learned men say one thing, ours say another; but, after all, who can say what really exists up there?" pointing as he spoke to the stars that were glistening in their countless thousands above us.

Next day the long-expected rain at length descended. The rain commenced at about four o'clock in the afternoon and continued till past sunset. Being accompanied by a strong wind, it caused a much greater fall in the temperature than had that former first shower. It became so cold in the evening, that I not only stopped the punkah, but also put on some of my warm winter clothes.

This fall of rain was succeeded by many others. For several days the sky remained thickly overcast with clouds, and nearly every day more or less rain descended. But these latter showers, falling in a still atmosphere, had hardly any cooling influence. The temperature ere long became very nearly as high as it had been before the rains commenced; owing to the excessive dampness, it was even more oppressive.

Insects of all sorts now again appeared in profusion. They were not, however, insects called to life by the rain, but insects that had completed their various transformations, and were now issuing forth in their finally developed forms. Of the insects which thus issued none came forth so suddenly and in such vast multitudes as the white ants. Their coming forth is a sight most curious. The other afternoon I had the gratification of witnessing it.

I was walking along the path that leads from the terrace; on the side of this path, close by the mud wall that forms the boundary of the compound, there extends a line of small, thorny trees. They are a species of acacia, termed the "babool." By the side of one of these trees, and rising in the air high above it, I noticed a singular sort of haze. I approached nearer, and the haze resolved itself into a cloud of small winged insects. They were streaming forth from several holes in the bark of the tree. As they came forth the several streams of insects united and rose together in the form of a column to the height of at least thirty or forty feet. There they spread out on all sides and slowly descended, much as does the water over the rim of a fountain basin.

Approaching still nearer, I noticed that the wings of these insects were extremely narrow and enormously long. Then I became aware that this cloud of insects was a swarm of just-developed white ants, taking their one brief and never-to-be-repeated flight.

They seemed to be in the utmost eagerness to commence it. I went up to the tree; I found them crowding out of the holes in the bark with a hurry that often impeded their progress. The holes were small, hardly more than sufficient to afford exit to a single white ant; nevertheless not unfrequently two of the little creatures would endeavour to pass through together. As a result they would become jammed, and it was only after much wriggling and struggling that they managed to get disengaged and fly off.

The tree was partly dead, and where the ants were issuing the bark was dry and withered, and in places there were long cracks. I put my fingers into one of these cracks and pulled; a large piece of the bark came off, disclosing the dead wood beneath. The surface of the wood was covered with a perfect network of narrow grooves. The grooves all eventually terminated in small, round holes that seemed to descend into the interior of the tree. The grooves were now crowded with young white ants in all stages of development. In some the wings had not yet appeared ; in others they were but half formed ; but multitudes had their wings not only completely formed, but also unfolded. And these ants were hurrying along the grooves to join the flying throng outside.

I remained for some time watching the ants. So long as I remained the ants continued to issue from the tree in undiminished numbers. All as they issued joined the ascending column, mounted high in the air, and as they spread around and slowly descended, they seemed to form a thin, delicate, living veil. As the ants reached the ground they spread out their wings to their utmost extent, and shook them violently. With the shake the wings fell off, and then the little white wingless creatures crawled away, either to return to the nest, or to seek some place wherein to found a new one.

But, whatever their destination, I fancy that but few reached it. Scores of birds, attracted by the sight of the swarm, were sitting or hovering around. To them and to other enemies, no doubt, the vast majority of the ants would eventually fall victims.

The whole spectacle of this issue of the swarm was very interesting, and as regarded the upward flight and descent of the ants it was extremely pretty. It was a spectacle also that gave rise to many reflections, some of them a little melancholy.

How strange it seems that these millions and millions of wings, with all their wonderful machinery of nerves and muscles, should be thus elaborated merely to serve the purpose of one single flight, and that of only a few minutes' duration!

Then there is something sad in thus beholding how little by nature life is regarded—such myriads of creatures called into being only to be immediately destroyed.

As I watched the wingless ants crawling away, another speculation occurred to me. Such of these little creatures as escaped the birds and their other enemies would pass the rest of their existence in tunnels and underground passages into which no light can penetrate.

It was near sunset; the canopy of clouds had risen and dispersed; sky, clouds, and landscape were all glowing with rainbow tints. As I watched the crawling ants I wondered whether in their future dark abodes they would ever recall in memory the picture of that glorious outer world they were now beholding.

In all my long residence in India this was the only occasion on which I witnessed the issue of a swarm of young white ants in the day-time and in the open air. I have, however, several times witnessed their issue in the house; and then it is less agreeable. One of these issues remains impressed on my memory; I will describe it.

The house I was then occupying was a bungalow, and, as is the case with many bungalows, the inner walls were constructed of merely sun-dried bricks, and in the recesses of one wall a colony of white ants had established a nest. It was evening; I was commencing dinner. I heard behind me a buzzing sound; I turned, and from a hole near the bottom of the wall I beheld a fountain of young white ants ascending. They reached the ceiling, and then the descent commenced. They alighted by thousands on the table, and there shook off their wings. In a few minutes the cloth, the plates, the glasses, even the lamp-shades, were covered with the little white, feeble crawling creatures.

The fountain of ants continued to play for at least ten minutes. When next morning the floor was swept, the wings that the ants had shaken off filled a large basket. What became of the ants themselves I cannot say.

CHAPTER VII.

ALCHEMY

THIS morning I received a visit from one of the native merchants in the city. Our conversation happened to turn on alchemy, and then it diverged to the kindred subjects of ghosts, magic, and hidden treasures, regarding all which Orientals are firm believers. Belief in magic and ghosts does no great harm, even a little good in a way, for it heightens the interest in tales of the supernatural; but faith in alchemy and hidden treasures is very apt to lead to ruin. The result comes thus about. A reputed alchemist appears in a city; he manages to get an introduction to some man of means, a believer in his science. The alchemist is plausible; he gains the confidence of his patron, and presently offers to show him a proof of his skill. The patron provides a large amount of silver; it is conveyed away and buried in some unfrequented place, the alchemist all the while performing many incantations. The patron is then directed to return after say twenty days and dig up the deposit, and he will find that the silver has become transmuted into gold; but in the meantime neither he nor anyone else is to come near the spot, or the charm will be broken. It is almost needless to say that when the twenty days have expired both silver and alchemist have disappeared.

Some alchemists proceed in a more scientific manner. They melt a lump of lead or copper in the presence of their patron, and from it they do really appear to extract a small lump of gold. Confidence in their powers thus established, they obtain money from their patron to almost any extent.

Some years ago, when in another district, I saw the operation of extracting the gold performed in my presence and also in that of the doctor of the station, who attended to witness it. The performance took place in the verandah of my house, the time being before breakfast. The alchemist was a Mahomedan, an elderly man, tall, and, like most Mahomedans, possessing much dignity of manner. He brought with him a variety of apparatus—a pair of small tongs, several diminutive clay cups, and, what most excited our curiosity, the life-sized model of a duck, very roughly constructed of copper. The model was hollow, and at the end of the beak there was a very small, round hole.

The alchemist placed all these things on the floor of the verandah; then he requested that a "nând," a large, deep earthenware pan, might be sent for, and also an "angetee," or small, portable iron fireplace. The nând was brought, and, at the alchemist's desire, was filled with water fresh from the well, and a charcoal fire was lighted in the "angetee." These preparations completed, the alchemist produced from his waistband a small lump of lead and some copper filings. These he handed to us to examine, and then dropped them into one of the little clay cups. He next took the small tongs, and with them lifted the cup and placed it on the charcoal fire, and beside it he also placed the copper duck, and let it remain till it was thoroughly heated. Then with the tongs he raised it and dropped it into the nând of water. The heat of the fire had rarefied the air within the duck; the cold of the water now condensed it. A slight vacuum was the result, and the water was forced in by the pressure of the atmosphere through the small hole in the beak. When sufficient water had entered, the duck was removed from the nând and placed again on the fire, and we now comprehended its purpose. As the water boiled the steam issued from the beak, and formed a very powerful blowpipe. In a short time, with the aid of a little borax as a flux, the lead and copper were melted. During the process of melting the alchemist kept dropping in at short intervals various coloured powders.

The cup was now removed from the fire, plunged in the cold water, and then handed to us for inspection. The lead and copper filings had disappeared, and in their place, snugly nestled at the bottom of the cup, lay a small lump of yellow gold. It was really gold, and very pure, for I afterwards had it tested. Of course the lead and copper had been removed, and the gold substituted, but so cleverly that neither I nor the doctor had the least idea when or how the change had been effected.

At the request of the alchemist, we now left the

verandah and entered a room that opened on it, and there when we were seated the alchemist proceeded to give us a further proof of his powers. He asked us to mention any article we desired, and he would produce it, even though it had to be summoned from London. As we did not wish to spoil the performance by asking impossibilities, we left the selection to himself. He then rose, bared his arms to the elbow, extended them, the hands open, but touching at the wrists. He remained in this attitude for a minute or more, his face upturned, and all the while muttering what we presumed were incantations. Then of a sudden he jerked back his arms and closed his hands, much as a cricketer does when catching a ball. As he closed his hands we heard a clink like that of coins; he turned to us, opened his hands, and we saw displayed within them five gold mohurs.

As the gold mohurs had been so easily obtained, I proposed that they should be expended in charity; but the alchemist was equal to the occasion. He informed me that what I proposed was impossible: all that was thus obtained from the spirits must be returned to them, or calamity would ensue.

The money was returned much in the same manner that it had been obtained. The alchemist replaced the gold mohurs in his hands. He had, I should mention, handed them to us for inspection. Then he joined his hands, stretched out his arms, looked upwards, and muttered as before. In a minute he opened his hands, turned them towards us, and they were empty. Of course the whole was a conjuring trick, but

I never saw one better performed. The room was very light; the alchemist had his arms bared, as I have said, to the elbows; and both I and the doctor were sitting close by and watching attentively, and yet we neither of us perceived when or from where the coins were produced, nor how or whither they vanished.

Alchemy, except for such-like professors of it, is not a profitable pursuit. Still less so is treasure-seeking, yet, like gambling, it possesses an extreme fascination. Those who commence always continue. No experience teaches; no amount of failure disheartens. There is, of course, always a possibility of success, for undoubtedly a very great amount of gold and silver and coined money does lie concealed in India, buried in the soil or hidden away in buildings. But then the success never arrives. Treasure is not unfrequently found, but seldom, if ever, by those who are looking for it. In all the instances that I have known or heard of where treasure has been found, it has always been come upon quite accidentally. The amount found is not either generally large, but to this rule history records one striking exception. When, near two centuries ago, Nadir Shah plundered Delhi, he found concealed in a vault in the palace no less than fifty millions of silver rupees. This vast treasure had been there stored away no one knew when or by whom, and its existence was entirely forgotten.

According to native belief, however, a far greater treasure remains somewhere in the country still undiscovered. This is the treasure which, according to tradition, the Emperor Alumgire concealed before setting off for his ill-omened expedition to the Deccan. From that expedition the Emperor never returned. After years passed in the unsuccessful efforts to crush the rising power of the Mahrattas there in the Deccan, the Emperor died, and died, so the tradition asserts, without confiding to anyone the secret of where his treasure was concealed. So wherever that place may be, there the treasure still remains. To find the spot is the object of every searcher, and many have wasted their lives and means in the attempt.

Having said so much on treasure-seeking and alchemy, I should like to add a few words regarding ghosts and magic. But the subjects are too comprehensive to be here in this chapter discussed. I will return instead to the insects and animals, and describe now some of those that inhabit the house, for hitherto I have discoursed chiefly of those that live in the garden. The most conspicuous of these house animals are the lizards. They are not pretty creatures. Indeed, to a European newly arrived in the country their appearance is decidedly unpleasant. Their colour is a dull mud tint, and, with their thick, fleshy tails and rather swollen bodies, they suggest something of the toad. But this impression soon wears off. Before long one gets quite to like the little creatures, and to take an interest in watching their movements. They are perfectly harmless, and not in the least troublesome. They do not hide in the furniture, nor crawl over the floor; they confine themselves entirely to the walls and ceilings.

During the day-time they move but little. They

remain for hours on the same spot, as fixed in attitude as if they were plaster ornaments. As evening approaches they become more active; they commence to wander about catching flies and mosquitoes. Once I watched a lizard so engaged. It was near sunset, and in the rainy season. I was sitting in the drawing-room, waiting till it should be cool enough for me to take my evening drive. While thus sitting I happened to raise my eyes, and saw a large grasshopper high up on the wall. He was of the kind that fly as well as hop. He had somehow entered the house and alighted on the wall. He was there sitting perfectly motionless. On the same wall, about twenty feet distant, and equally motionless, I also noticed a lizard.

In a minute or so, as I continued looking, the lizard commenced to move, at first very slowly, then slightly faster. Next he broke into a run, and ran with considerable rapidity for about ten feet in the direction of the grasshopper. He now stopped, and remained motionless again for some minutes; then he recommenced his advance, but now with extreme slowness and many pauses, much in the manner that a cat moves when stalking a bird. The head of the grasshopper was turned in the opposite direction. He did not consequently see the lizard, nor did he apparently seem to be the least aware of his approach.

In about ten minutes, always coming on in the same stealthy manner, the lizard had arrived within the distance of a foot from the grasshopper. Here he paused, then made a dart forward; the long tongue was shot out, drawn back, and the poor grasshopper had vanished. The movement was so rapid that my eye could not distinctly follow it.

The lizards walk on the ceilings as easily as they do on the walls; but I do not think that they can run on the ceilings with quite the same rapidity. It is not very easy to understand how they can run on the ceilings at all. The lizards adhere to the walls and ceilings, so we are told, by the pressure of the atmosphere, they having the power to create small vacuums by drawing up the skin of their bodies and feet, and so forming hollows between themselves and the surfaces. But then how can these hollows be formed, closed, and re-formed with sufficient rapidity to enable the lizard to run and yet to hold on?

Occasionally the lizard does not succeed in doing so; he sometimes falls back from wall and ceiling, and when he does the result is generally a disaster. A great flop is heard as the lizard alights on the hard cemented floor, and on approaching one finds that the body and the tail have parted company; the tail has broken off at the root, and lies wriggling on the floor, while the lizard runs off and mounts the wall again apparently quite unconcerned. The tail appears almost as if endowed with an independent vitality. It will continue wriggling for a very long period, and even when it has ceased to move it will recommence its wriggling if stimulated by a touch.

The loss of his tail is to the lizard only a temporary deprivation: a new tail is developed. I have never watched the development in the same lizard; I cannot, therefore, say how long a period it occupies, but I imagine that the process is a slow one. I have, however, seen in different lizards the new tail in every stage of its growth. In its earliest stage the new tail has much the appearance of a thorn growing protruding from the end of the body. This thorn gradually thickens and lengthens into a stump. In process of time the stump lengthens into a tail. I do not think that the new tail ever attains to quite the length of the original tail, nor in form is it so symmetrical; and, moreover, there is always a mark like a ridge or scar at its base, indicating the spot where it has been protruded from the body. Sometimes, though rarely, the new tail is double. This, I imagine, is the result of an accident: the new tail when first protruded has somehow got notched or split, and each half has developed independently.

As regards this renewal of the tails of the lizards, a curious question arises, and one which I am quite unable to answer. The lizards vary greatly in size: the ordinary house lizard is not usually—I speak from memory—more than from six to nine inches in length, tail included, while the rock lizard of the Himalaya attains almost to the dimensions of a small alligator. I have seen some more than a yard long, and of proportionate girth. Now, do these great lizards also possess the power of renewing their tails? And if they do not, then at what degree of size does the power of renewal cease? For between these giants and the diminutive house lizards there are lizards of every degree of magnitude.

The lizards, as a rule, have no beauty: the house lizard is ugly; the great rock lizard is hideous. But one variety of lizard is really pretty. Its beauty, however, is less the result of its form than of its colouring, which is the freshest and brightest green.

Next to the lizards, the flies and mosquitoes are the living things most *en évidence* in an Indian house; but both are too well known to require description. The fly in no way differs from the fly of Europe; nor, except that he is smaller and more venomous, is the mosquito, to the unscientific eye, to be distinguished from our ordinary English gnat. The flies by care can be pretty well excluded, excepting during the rains, when it is pleasant to have the outer doors left open. But the mosquitoes are irrepressible. During the day they are mostly quiescent; also, being semi-aquatic animals, they confine themselves chiefly to the bathing-rooms, where there is always a supply of water. As sunset approaches they awake to activity, and commence to wander abroad. The first indication of their awakening is a low humming sound. The sound itself is not unmelodious; it is unpleasant, however, in its associations; also in its indications, for it shows that the armies of these little torments are assembling and will shortly appear.

There are two other insects always present in Indian houses; but one is rarely, the other never, seen. The first is a species of book-worm, the other a variety of beetle. The book-worm, as his name imports, bores holes through books and papers. The appellation to him of "worm" is, however, very misleading, for in shape, in colour, and in the glistening aspect of his skin, he bears the most singular resemblance to a most diminutive fish. The resemblance is so striking that among Europeans the little creature is always spoken of as the "fish insect."

The beetle confines his attention to woodwork, mostly to the doors and door frames. Into these, and also occasionally into chairs and tables, he bores little circular holes. As he bores he pushes out his borings; a tiny heap of wood dust on the floor below indicates his presence: but for this it would be almost impossible to discover where he is at work. As he bores, his jaws, scraping away the wood, give out a rasping sound. The sound is not loud, but in the midday stillness it is very distinctly audible.

The puzzle is to discover from whence it proceeds, for as soon as one rises and moves about to ascertain the beetle discontinues his labours, and the sound is no longer heard. I was once over half an hour engaged in such a search; in the end I only discovered the place by noticing the slight heap of wood dust on the floor at the foot of one of the door posts. Looking carefully upwards along the door post, I found the small, round hole from which the dust had fallen. A drop of oil caused the little workman to appear. I found him to be about half an inch in length, very slender, quite black in colour, and in shape very much resembling a narrow cylinder. I examined him through my magnifying-glass, but the glass was not sufficiently powerful to display his jaws clearly, nor consequently to enable me to ascertain how his boring of the wood was effected.

There are other dwellers in the house that do not either often display themselves. The most numerous are the bats and the rats. I shall discourse on the bats later on. The rats I have already partly discussed; I will now add a few more words. The rats reside in the thatched roof, and there they have their nests and bring up their families. They descend at night in search of food; but they do not much enter the rooms of the house, and in the day-time they are only occasionally seen. They are not, therefore, a cause of annoyance, unless food is kept on shelves in the pantry. Then the rats burrow in the walls, unless they are constructed of masonry, and become a veritable nuisance.

The rats usually descend from the roof by means of the verandah pillars, but I have known them attempt other ways. Once I happened to enter my sleeping-room in the afternoon, and there, to my surprise, I found a rat seated calmly on the top of the punkah. There was a hole in the canvas ceiling; through this he had passed, and then climbed down the punkah rope. The punkah prevented his further progress, for it was too high above the floor for him to leap, and he did not seem to like reascending the rope.

The house rat, unlike the garden rat, is an excellent climber. Indeed, he ascends a tree with almost the rapidity of the squirrel, but without any of the squirrel's ease and grace. He never leaps, like the squirrel, from bough to bough, and as he runs up the trunk he appears to cling to the bark, as if always in fear lest he should fall. Sometimes a rat will wander through the house, as it were, for mere amusement; and if he finds anyone lying asleep, he will display an inclination to partake of him. I had once experience of this. I had returned from my early morning ride, and being a little tired, I lay down, and presently fell half asleep. While thus lying I felt something very soft touch my foot. The touch was repeated, and then followed a sharp prick. I started up, and just in time to see a rat dart through the doorway.

A rat will sometimes take a fancy to some particular part of the house, and there remain, not permanently, but as long as the fancy takes him. Once, when I was at another station, a rat thus took a fancy to pass his day in my bathing-room. He dug no holes, he did no harm; he simply passed his time behind one of the doors, which was usually turned against the wall. Every evening about sunset he went away; some time in the course of the morning he returned. I was so touched at his confidence that I would not have him molested. After a month he ceased to appear.

But any account of the house rat would be incomplete without some notice of that horrible variety termed, from the odour that accompanies it, the musk-rat. This rat fortunately does not make its residence in the houses, and indeed it only occasionally enters them, and then as a rule by night. I do not know whether after all it is a true rat. In appearance it more resembles a very small, nearly hairless ferret. It is of a drab colour, and has that half-transparent look noticeable in young mice and unfledged chickens. Its presence is manifested by a squeaking cry, accompanied by an intolerably sickly odour, something resembling musk. The odour is so penetrating that, according to the European popular belief, it will pass through the glass of a bottle, and flavour the liquor within. The fact is correct, but not the explanation. Beer and wine are certainly occasionally flavoured by these rats running among the bottles that contain them; but the odour penetrates not through the bottle, but through the cork. The musk-rat is said by the natives to be blind, like our mole. I do not know if this is really the case, but certainly when running through a house these rats never leave the margin of the walls.

The house rats that reside in the thatch sometimes find unpleasant fellow-tenants in the shape of wild cats. These are not the real wild cats, but the ordinary cats that have got tired of domesticity, and have taken to finding their own living in the fields. In a house that I once occupied a lady and gentleman cat of this description took up their residence in the thatched roof, and there they reared a family. When the fancy took them they made a meal off the rats. At night, when lying awake, I often heard the chases. There would be a scamper, then a spring and a scream, and I was aware that a rat had been captured, and was now being devoured.

On one occasion the kittens, when about half grown, somehow found their way at midnight into the dining-room. The noise they made awoke me. I called for the servants; lights were brought, and the kittens found crouched together in a corner. Small as they were, they displayed the most marvellous activity and the ferocity also of so many young tigers. They ran up the doors; they flew at the servants. It was only after much trouble and with the aid of long sticks that they were driven out into the garden.

Besides these permanent occupants of our Indian houses, we are occasionally favoured with the presence of mere temporary visitors. The most objectionable of these are the snakes and the scorpions. Fortunately the visits of both are extremely rare. In the whole long course of my Indian experience I never but once discovered a snake in my house, and that once was in the Himalaya. The house, as is there usual, had a boarded floor; below the flooring there was a hollow space, and at its bottom was the uneven, rocky surface of the mountain. Through a hole in one of the boards I saw the head of a most singular animal appear; it resembled the head of no creature that I had ever seen or heard of. It rose higher, and the mystery was solved. It was a snake, holding in his jaws a frog he had just captured. Seeing a servant approach, the snake retired, and to prevent his reappearance I had the hole in the flooring securely stopped up.

I never found a snake in any of the many houses I occupied at different times in the plains, but I once discovered one at an outhouse close adjoining. The snake was not inside the building, but affixed in a most extraordinary manner to the exterior of the entrance door. The door, a very rough one, was fastened by a chain and padlock, and hanging wriggling from the padlock I saw, to my astonishment, a small snake. The snake had somehow climbed to the padlock, and had thrust his head through between it and the staple. He had thrust his head through, but was unable to withdraw it or to advance his body further. I called the servants; they ran up, declared the snake to be of the most venomous description, and at once killed it. Whether the snake was really venomous I cannot say; very probably it was, but the natives describe every snake they see to be such, even the most harmless. How the snake managed to reach the padlock was a mystery I never solved.

Scorpions are more common in houses than snakes, but they are rarely seen. They conceal themselves under boxes or hide in crevices. It sometimes, however, happens that they wander over the floor, and then should one of the servants, who all go barefooted, happen to tread on them, a tragedy may ensue. Such once occurred, but long ago, in my presence. It was evening; I was at dinner. One of the servants while passing round the table fell suddenly as if he had been shot. The others ran to his assistance, and raised him. It was found that he had trodden on a scorpion, and that the creature had stung him. The man was in great agony. I proposed to send for the doctor, but he preferred the native remedy of the "jhar," which consists in a series of something like mesmeric passes. I had no faith in the remedy; nevertheless it proved efficacious. The man presently felt easier. After the passes had been continued for something over an hour the man rose, walked about, and assured me that the pain had entirely left him.

CHAPTER VIII.

THE RAINS CONTINUED

THE rains continued till the end of August. Some few days were pleasant enough. As the rain fell the wind blew, and passing through the falling water, it diffused an agreeable coolness, while the clouds above subdued the glare. On such days I could sit by the open window, read, and gaze out on the garden with much tranquil enjoyment. But days of this description were exceptional. Between the showers there were often long intervals of most oppressive heat, and when again the rain fell, descending through a motionless atmosphere, it brought no coolness; it only added to the heat an intolerable dampness. So saturated often was the air with moisture, that clothes seemed to adhere to one's person; paper felt damp to the touch; and every article of leather—boots, shoes, the binding of books, trunks, and harness—if not continually wiped, became encrusted with mould. And yet the thermometer showed that the temperature was in reality always from three to four degrees lower than it had been during the much less oppressive heat of the preceding period of the hot winds. The damp heat, so enervating to us, seems to have an invigorating effect on the insects.

The white ants are busy day and night in erecting their long covered galleries over the floors and walls, and at no period of the year are the flies and mosquitoes more annoyingly active. The palm for energy must I think, however, be conceded to the dragonflies. These little creatures have lately appeared; they appeared suddenly and in multitudes innumerable. As I look out on the garden the whole air seems filled with them, but they cause no annoyance; they never enter the house nor even the verandahs, and they do no damage to the trees or plants in the garden. They pass their time in flitting to and fro through the atmosphere, and this they seem to do the livelong day without a moment's intermission. I have never noticed any of them to alight either on the ground or on trees. At night they depart, and, I presume, settle somewhere, but where I am not able to say. Indeed, to be quite truthful, I have as yet not made much effort to ascertain.

These Indian dragonflies are larger than our dragonflies in England, but they are not so graceful either in form or movement; they do not dart forward with quite the same rapidity, nor do they stop and reverse their flight quite so instantaneously. Still they are very interesting to watch. Unlike most other flying insects, these dragonflies appear perfectly indifferent to rain. When a shower comes on, the other insects that may be flitting and hovering in the air at once disappear; they seek shelter from the falling raindrops among the plants and trees, or under the roof of some house or shed. But unless the rain descends in a perfect deluge, the dragonflies appear to regard it with entire indifference: they fly about and dart backwards and forwards just the same as before.

It was some time early in the month of August that I received a visit from a small party of animals of a larger size, animals of a kind that do not usually much exhibit themselves when the sun is above the horizon. It was one of those agreeable days of the rainy season that I have above described. It happened also to be a holiday in the office, so that I was able to remain at home and enjoy it. It had been raining, but the rain had ceased, and a pleasant coolness pervaded the air, and there was just sufficient cloud to soften and subdue the glare. I was sitting, half reclining, in an arm-chair before the open doors. It was just noon. The servants were all in their huts or lying stretched on the floor in the entrance-room taking their midday sleep. In house and compound all was silence and repose.

I had been reading, but I had laid down the book, and gazing out on the garden, I had fallen half into a day-dream. Looking accidentally towards one of the lower terraces, I thought that I perceived some object moving. I aroused myself, looked more attentively, and perceived a jackal creeping cautiously out from among a clump of bushes. A second jackal followed, and after him a third and a fourth. They stood still for a minute, all the while looking carefully around; and then, I suppose, being satisfied that no danger threatened, they began to move towards the end of the terrace. At the end of the terrace was the poultry-house, and to this they directed their steps. Now I understood the object of their visit: they had come to plunder or to reconnoitre.

Having reached the poultry-house, they walked round it. It was most interesting to watch them, for, as I was sitting within the house, they were unaware of my presence. They moved very slowly, and with extreme caution, looking constantly around to make sure there was no danger; moving thus along, they made the complete circuit of the poultry-house, as they did so narrowly inspecting it; then they descended to the next terrace below, struck into a narrow footpath, and trotted away down to the river. Either, I presume, they had discovered that the poultry-house could not be entered, or else they had arranged their plan of attack, and intended to return after nightfall and put it into execution.

The jackals are nocturnal animals, though not entirely such; they do occasionally wander abroad in the day-time, but then they usually wander singly, and confine their wanderings to the ravines and to the margins of the rivers. Except on this occasion, I never saw a party of jackals abroad during the day-time, nor did I ever see even a solitary jackal venture during the day-time into the compound of an inhabited house, or, indeed, into a station at all.

At night the jackals hunt and move about in packs, but I am not quite sure whether they always live in communities; they do sometimes, for I have twice come across what I may term their warrens. They were both situated on slightly elevated spots, surrounded by waste land, and, curiously enough, both the warrens were almost immediately adjoining high-roads. I came on one of these warrens when walking in the evening, a little after sunset. No full-grown jackals were visible, but a number of young jackals, quite puppies, were frisking about outside. I had with me a little spaniel; he seemed to recognize in the young jackals creatures of his own kind, for he immediately ran to them and joined in their gambols. I was in terror lest they should bite him, but my apprehensions were groundless. They played with him most amicably, and so much did he enjoy their society that I had much trouble in getting him to leave them and follow me home. He brought with him evidence of their companionship in their terrible odour. It was only after a most elaborate ablution with soap and hot water that it was possible to allow him to enter the house.

The smell of a jackal resembles that of a fox, but it is more powerful and more offensive; it diffuses itself through the atmosphere to a surprising distance. The four jackals, whose visit I have above described, never approached nearer to the house than at least sixty yards, yet before they left their scent had become wafted through the air to where I sat inside at the open window, and was for some time most unpleasantly perceptible.

The odour of the jackal is not his only objectionable quality. His cry at night is very distracting; it is especially so at this season of the year, when the bed-room doors are always left more or less open. Heard at a distance, the cry is not altogether unpleasant: it has a weird, melancholy cadence, even slightly melodious, but on nearer approach the melancholy, wailing cry changes to a sharp, yelping bark of intolerable discord; it suggests almost the idea of a legion of fiends. As with the frogs, the amount and loudness of the clamour is out of all proportion to the number of the animals. These packs do not usually consist of more than five or six jackals. To judge by the noise, one would suppose them scores.

According to native belief, each pack of jackals has its chief or leader, and their cry is interpreted into a conversation between the chief and his followers. The chief calls out, "Soopna men raja hooa" ("I am the king in the night," literally "in the sleep-time"); and then the other jackals reply, "Hooa! hooa! hooa!" ("You are! you are! you are!"). With a little imagining, the cry, if not heard too near, does really appear to fit the words.

Slowly, wearily, with its damp, exhausting heat, the month of August passed away. Towards its termination some indications appeared of the approaching advent of the cold weather. The first indication was not altogether agreeable: it consisted in the torpidity of the flies. In this condition they were terrible: the waving of the fan was powerless to drive them away, and when they alighted on the hands or face the sensation of their damp, clammy bodies was something to excite a shudder even in recollection; but the annoyance did not long continue. Each day the flies were fewer; in the course of a week or ten days they had entirely disappeared; and soon after the early mornings became perceptibly cooler, and the coolness was of that fresh, invigorating kind, quite free from damp, and which is not caused by wind.

The earliest of these mornings I find noted in my diary was that of the 2nd of September. The same day was also signalized by the discovery of a new insect, not exactly an insect, but the chrysalis in which some insect was enclosed. The servants had found it in the garden, and, struck by its beauty, had brought it in to me for inspection. It was unusually large, and certainly, as far as colour went, it was a most beautiful object. Its surface resembled that of silver tissue, and had all the same lovely iridescent tints. I had it carefully placed on the mantel-piece in the drawing-room, and I visited it constantly, in the hope that I might be present when the insect within should make its appearance. My desire was gratified, and sooner than I had expected, for the event occurred on the second afternoon. I had returned from the office, and gone at once to the mantel-piece. The surface of the chrysalis appeared to be undulating, as if there was some movement going on within. As I looked the movement increased. Presently the chrysalis cracked, and split open from end to end, and with much effort and many painful struggles a butterfly dragged itself out. To my regret, as the chrysalis cracked its beauty vanished. From a silky tissue, glowing with colour, it changed to a dull white, dingy-looking film.

I am sorry to say that my diary contains no description of the butterfly that emerged. To the best of my recollection, however, it was a butterfly of very ordinary appearance, in no way remarkable, either for size or colouring. Yet it must have belonged to some rather rare species, for none of my servants had ever seen or heard of a similar chrysalis, nor did I ever meet with such another one again.

Of all the months of the year September is regarded by both natives, as well as Europeans, as the most unhealthy. The atmosphere is cloudless, and the long-continued rains have cleared it from all impurities. The sun's rays consequently shine through it unimpeded by mist or dust. So intense and brilliant are they, that, according to the native saying, they scorch the skins of even the wild deer black. They also draw out from the stagnant pools and the decaying vegetation all those unwholesome exhalations that give rise to fevers. It is during this month, therefore, that fevers are especially prevalent. Nevertheless to those who escape the fevers the month is very agreeable, that is in contrast to the months that have immediately preceded it. Each day the mornings become cooler. I can saunter longer in the garden after returning from my early ride, and I can then sit without inconvenience in the verandah till it is time to bathe and dress for breakfast.

As I sit and look out on the garden, let me describe it a little more in detail. All Indian gardens, whether native or European, are laid out on one uniform plan. The plan has been dictated by the necessities of the climate. In India cultivation depends on irrigation, and in a garden the water must be supplied to the different parts according as they may require it. The simplest way of effecting this is to divide the garden by means of raised earthen paths, crossing each other at right angles, into a series of square or oblong beds. The water is drawn up from the well by bullocks, and flows, as it is wanted, from one bed to another through earthenware pipes, which cross under the paths at their base.

This method of laying out a garden is extremely convenient; indeed, it is necessary; but at the same time it is to a European taste not at all picturesque. It imparts to the garden an unpleasant aspect of stiffness and monotony. Each bed and path is very much the reflection of all the others. In the case of my present garden, the monotony and formality are a good deal relieved by the succession of terraces and the view of the river beyond. The garden has been so long neglected that the beds are almost entirely destitute of flowers, or, indeed, of any vegetation. This bareness of the beds causes the straight lines of the raised paths to stand out with unpleasant distinctness. To some extent they suggest the idea of geometrical diagrams.

Although the garden has few or no flowers, properly so called, it has, scattered about it, several flowering shrubs, and, better still, a really beautiful line of a flowering tree termed by the natives the "babool." This line of babool trees extends the entire length of one side of the compound. Before it is a very broad raised earthen path, and it is this path which leads to the terrace overlooking the river of which I have already made mention. The babool is a species of acacia. It is a tree of no great size, hardly, if at all, exceeding that of our apple tree, nor can it boast of much beauty; its foliage is scanty, and much interspersed with thorns; and it has a dry, parched aspect, such as would befit it for the neighbourhood of a desert.

The attraction of the tree consists in its flowers; these it bears in profusion. The flowers are extremely pretty, though in shape peculiar. Each flower consists of a multitude of slender spikes, all radiating from a common centre; they form a little ball about the size of a small cherry. The especial charm of the flower is its colour and its scent; its colour is the richest golden yellow, and its perfume is hardly surpassed by even that of the rose. These flowers now cover the babool-trees in such thousands that, as I stroll along the path, the whole air is laden with their scent.

In singular contrast to the delicious odour of the flower is that of the sap of the tree from which the flower is produced: this is to the last degree offensive. A branch of the tree lopped off or broken off by the wind and left to lie on the ground will in a day or two exhale an odour hardly to be distinguished from that of the most putrid carrion.

There is another and much larger tree in the compound which also, like the babool, exhales a scent, but one less agreeable. This tree is the neem. It is what I may term a forest tree, about the size of our English elm. The scent does not proceed from the flower, but from the leaf; and then, fortunately, it is only exhaled when the leaves have been thoroughly wetted by a long-continued fall of rain succeeding a period of dry weather. I say fortunately because then, where the tree is abundant, as it is about here, the atmosphere over leagues and leagues of country is suffused with a faint odour of onions.

The leaf of the neem tree is remarkable, not only for the odour which it exhales, but also for its small size and its curious resemblance to the native saw; it is similarly curved and similarly notched: so exact is the resemblance that, according to native belief, it was from observing the neem leaf that the original carpenters were led to the invention of the saw.

The neem leaves when dried have an odour something resembling senna; it is an odour which insects of all kinds dislike extremely. These dried leaves are consequently very much used to spread over shawls and to place in valuable manuscripts to preserve them from moths and book-worms.

I will conclude this account of the scents of the neem and the babool with a few words about that queen of perfumes attar of roses. The rose from which it is made grows about here in great perfection. It is an ugly, ragged-looking rose; but the scent is unequalled. It is always spoken of by the natives as the "rose of the country"; but I am not sure whether it is really indigenous to India or if it was introduced by the Mogul emperors from Persia. But whether the rose is indigenous to India or not, it was in India that the secret was discovered of extracting from it the attar.

According to popular belief the discovery was made by the celebrated Noor Jehan, the favourite wife of the Emperor Jehangire; but the Emperor himself in his memoirs attributes the discovery, not to Noor Jehan, but to her mother. Although discovered and first made in India, the best attar of roses is now brought from Busrah, in the Persian Gulf. It is brought in small silver flasks of much the shape of a pear and about the size of a small walnut. The mouth of the neck of the flask is securely soldered; but so powerful is the perfume that it escapes through the silver of the flask. When in India I procured at different times three of these flasks. Two of them I have still; one was lost in the Mutiny. When I procured the flasks they were completely filled with the attar; they are now, and have been for years, quite empty. The soldering at the necks of the flasks is as perfect as ever, but the attar has exhaled through the silver of the flasks themselves. The flasks have been kept in a silver box lined with sandalwood; they were put among letters and various small curiosities. Although the attar has evaporated from the flasks, it remains as strong as ever among the letters and curiosities and the sandalwood of the box itself. The sandalwood, however, has imparted to the perfume of the attar a flavour rather oppressive, to our English tastes at least; for it is one which the natives of India greatly admire, and which they much prefer to that of the attar alone. The attar of roses, with which on occasions of ceremony they perfume themselves and their garments, is always mingled with a scent obtained from sandalwood.

I may add that these little flasks of Busrah attar of roses are extremely expensive, and on that account are found only in the houses of the very wealthiest natives.

The month of September passed away quite uneventfully, but pleasantly enough; I took my rides and drives morning and evening. I sauntered in the garden, sat in the verandah, and spent the rest of the day in the office. Each morning seemed cooler, and soon even the midday heat appeared slightly less oppressive. Early in October the cold weather arrived. I could dispense with the punkah in the day-time, and at night I found a blanket on the bed very agreeable. To anyone suddenly transported from England, or even from the Himalaya, the temperature would, no doubt, have seemed sufficiently warm; but to us who had passed through so many months of exhausting heat the climate was altogether delicious. In the mornings and afternoons, as I sit in the verandah and look out on the blue sky, I feel enjoyment in the mere sensation of existence.

The flies, the dragonflies, and most of the other insects have departed, but the air is not tenantless. Scores, I may almost say hundreds, of birds—hawks, kites, and vultures—are wheeling and floating throughout it. Projected against the deep blue firmament, for ever circling slowly round and round, ascending and descending in long spiral curves, they form a most beautiful spectacle. The vultures fly the highest, and their flight is of all the most graceful. They sweep round and round in immense circles, at each successive circle ascending higher and higher, till at length they are lost to view or can be discerned only as the faintest specks. There is something even majestic in their flight, it is so steady, so even, so apparently effortless. The expanded wings hardly ever appear to move; the bird seems to ascend by its own mere volition.

The kites and hawks fly lower, and sweep round in smaller circles, and their flight is less calm and even. Every now and again, as I watch them, one will drop like a stone, shoot along the surface of the ground with the rapidity of an arrow, and then as quickly re-ascend. The kite has discerned some food or prey; he has swooped down and seized it, and is now bearing it aloft.

The sight of these birds is so keen, and their downward dart so rapid, that it is unsafe to carry anything eatable exposed where many of them are flying above. Of this I once had an experience that might have had a sad termination. It was in another station, and one more to the eastward, and where the kites especially abounded. One afternoon in the cold season I walked out into the garden, carrying my little girl in my arms; she was holding a crust of bread in her hand. One of the servants immediately ran after me, and pointing to the kites hovering above, begged me to throw away the bread or return at once to the house. He had hardly finished speaking, when I heard a rushing sound, felt a blow on my hat, and saw a large kite dart by before me. The servant had waved his stick and shouted; the noise and waving of the stick caused the kite to swerve, otherwise the child might have been seriously hurt. As it was, the claw of the kite had scratched her hand; the blow on my hat was given by his wing.

But besides the birds I have other objects of interest to watch as I sit in the verandah. My compound, and still more, the compounds adjoining abound in squirrels; and many of the little creatures pass a good deal of their time about the outside of the house and in the verandahs. Never being molested, they gambol about without apprehension. They climb the pillars and the reed blinds, scamper along the floor, and when I am taking my tea some of the bolder among them will even venture on the table.

The Indian squirrel is smaller than our English squirrel, and by no means so pretty. It has not the same thick fur or bushy tail, and its colouring is poorer: instead of the rich chestnut brown of our squirrel, its fur is of a dull greyish white, varied by stripes of black running the length of its body. On the other hand, the Indian squirrels are far more numerous—they are to be seen in hundreds on all the clusters of trees—and I also think they are more active. They dart up the trunks of the trees, spring from branch to branch, and race each other to the highest summits, and this with unbroken speed and apparently without effort.

I have spoken already about scents and perfumes; I will now conclude this chapter with a few words on the kindred subject of narcotics. I am led to do so by an incident that occurred about this time in the office. Not many miles from the station there resides a Hindoo zemeendar—that is, a landowner; he is well off, and, having little else to do, he spends a good deal of his time about the different offices; he generally makes his appearance in mine two or three days in the week. He stands in the court and listens to the cases, and when tired of that he strolls outside and chats with acquaintances. He is rather a favourite both with me and the other English, for he behaved very well in the Mutiny, and is besides amusingly eccentric, both in speech and appearance. I may add also that he is extremely stout.

On this particular day, though in the court, he was not in his usual place, nor was his attendance voluntary. He was standing with several others in the prisoners' dock, and had been committed for trial on a charge of affray. He and a neighbouring zemeendar each claimed a piece of land, and they met on the spot with their followers to decide the dispute in the ancient manner with swords and "lâtees." The lâtee, I may explain, is a long, solid bamboo, often bound and tipped with iron, and in the hands of a man who can use it a most formidable weapon. The case was rather a serious one, for, though no one had been killed, several of the combatants had been more or less severely injured.

I was distressed to see my friend in such a position, but he himself seemed quite unconcerned. His face wore a drowsy expression, and he appeared to pay little or no attention to the proceedings. I remarked on his indifference, and saw a smile go round the court. Its meaning was soon explained. When called on for his defence, he was found to be incapable of making any. He had drugged himself with some narcotic, and though bodily present in the dock, his mind was far away in the land of dreams. This, when the case was over, led to a conversation. In the course of it I acquired some further information on the subject of Indian narcotics. What I know on the matter I will now very briefly relate.

There are many varieties of these drugs. The most aristocratic is opium. This, as most of my readers are aware, is the juice of the cultivated poppy. In India it is both eaten and smoked, and when used in moderation I do not know that it does any particular harm. The stories of the delightful visions it creates are, I believe, pretty much fiction. It produces an agreeable tranquillity, and pleasantly, to some degree, stimulates the imagination, but nothing more. When taken in excess its effects are very deleterious: the appetite fails; the body becomes emaciated, as the natives express it, "dries up"; loss of memory and of intellectual power next follows, death sooner or later terminating a period of most wretched existence. One of the earlier effects of opium, when taken habitually and in excess, is to impart to the eyes a peculiar dull, glassy brilliancy, and by this a confirmed opium-smoker or eater can generally be distinguished.

Next to opium, in the scale of respectability, comes the drug termed in India "bhung." This is the juice of the wild hemp, and most of it is, I believe, procured from the forests of the outer ranges of the Lower Himalaya. Bhung is neither smoked nor eaten; it is only drunk, and then largely diluted with water. Unlike opium, instead of impairing, it increases the appetite, and, so far from causing emaciation, its effect is to produce corpulence. It was to his indulgence in bhung that my friend the zemeendar, I was told, owed his unusual plumpness.

It is also said to increase the breathing power of the lungs under exertion; and on this account it is much consumed by athletes when in training, especially so by the Brahmins at the various places of pilgrimage, for these Brahmins, leading the idlest of lives, amuse themselves a good deal in wrestling, running races, and other such-like exercises.

At the same time the drug utterly ruins the nerves. The drinker of bhung, it is said, will start at a shadow, and if a bird flies by him, will shrink in terror, as from a missile thrown at him.

Two lower styles of drugs are "churrus" and "ganja." I used to know their composition, but have forgotten it. They are both horribly deleterious, and their use is regarded as disreputable. They have the effect of imparting a most offensive odour to the person and to the breath of those who indulge in them.

There was in former times a horrible drug, often mentioned in the histories, termed "poshtah." If drunk daily, after no long time it caused idiocy. On that account it was under the Mogul rule often forcibly administered to state prisoners whom it was desired to render harmless, especially to such as had been, or might be, rival claimants to the throne. An affecting story is related by the traveller Bernier in regard to one of the nephews of the Emperor Alumgire. When captured and condemned to imprisonment in the fort of Gwalior, he threw himself at the Emperor's feet and implored that he might be at once put to death rather than be compelled to drink that terrible drug.

The greatest consumers of these narcotic drugs are said to be the Hindoo fakirs. I have been told that, when by long use other drugs have ceased to stimulate, the fakirs have recourse to arsenic; that in time also loses its power, and then, if they can, they contrive to get a cobra to bite them. So hardened, it is said, has their system become, that the bite of this most poisonous of snakes, which carries death to all other creatures, produces in them only an agreeable drowsiness. I have been told this frequently, and by natives of respectability, and who were themselves entirely convinced of the truth of what they asserted. Whether the statement is really correct I am unable to say.

I will conclude these remarks on narcotics by the mention of a circumstance regarding the cultivation of opium which has always puzzled me. The opium cultivation and sale is a Government monopoly. Of late years the Government had been desirous of extending the cultivation in these upper provinces. It is a cultivation in itself very profitable, and, in addition, especial advantages were offered by the Government. Nevertheless, so strong were the objections to the cultivation on the part of the Hindoos, that it was only with extreme difficulty, and by the exercise of all its immense influence, that the Government could succeed in inducing them anywhere to undertake it.

What the objection was I never could ascertain. It was not in the least a moral one, for the same people who objected to planting the poppies had no objection whatever to eat the opium manufactured from their juice. Nor was the objection the result of any caste prejudice, for in other parts of the country opium has been cultivated from time immemorial, and by Hindoos of the same castes.

CHAPTER IX.

THE STATION

THE station is one of the oldest in Upper India. It dates indeed from the time of Warren Hastings. It was at first, and for long after, a mere military outpost, advanced a hundred miles and more beyond our then frontier. The houses, such at least as remain of that period, were those of the officers. They are all bungalows, not large, and surrounded by only very moderate-sized compounds. Perhaps their occupants, so far away removed from their fellow-countrymen, found it pleasant to dwell near together.

I often try and picture the kind of life they led, very tranquil, very calm, no doubt, but terribly monotonous—few letters, fewer papers, rarely a traveller—but a life nevertheless in after days perhaps not unpleasant to look back to; and then what a dim, far-away country England must have appeared to them!

At the commencement of the present century these provinces passed under our English rule; and the station, as I have already mentioned, to some slight extent became a seat of government. It was made the headquarters of several of the chief civil depart-ments. The high officials of that day drew immense salaries, and kept up great establishments. Their houses which they erected here were of corresponding magnitude. In size they approach to palaces, and they stand in grounds fully equal in extent to the smaller of our English parks. Years go by, and the station begins to decline in importance. One by one the high officials are transferred elsewhere, and of the houses they erected many are left vacant.

As the century grows older the intercourse with England becomes more rapid and frequent; and, as a consequence, the tone of Indian society is more influenced by that prevailing at home. One of the results is the erection of the church. It is an ugly building, designed by an Engineer officer in a style meant to be classical.

A long, quiet period now ensues. Regiments and officials come and go, but the station remains much the same. Then occurs the Mutiny. The ruins of the church are its memorial. A new church and lines of barracks and stabling mark the restoration of order and the increase of troops that accompanied it; and, as regards the new church, its appearance shows the improvement in architectural taste that had taken place since the previous one was erected.

After this account of the station, I will say a few words regarding my office. According to tradition, it was originally a private residence, one of those left vacant when the chief officials departed. The grounds around it are extensive and dotted over with trees. When the office is open, the grounds present a most animated appearance. They are crowded with people, many of them picturesquely attired. There are numbers of horses, bullocks, and ponies, besides palanquins and those quaint little dome-shaped vehicles so bright in colour, and so Oriental in aspect.

The office I will leave unnoticed, for, except that it is more untidy, it does not much differ from an ordinary house. Let us pass through to the vernacular record room. This is a later erection, and bears testimony to the powers for destruction of those little creatures the white ants. To protect them from their ravages, the records are tied up in bundles of cotton cloth, and placed on broad stone shelves. Tier over tier of these shelves extends round the walls up to the very ceiling. But even this precaution does not always ensure security. Occasionally, when a bundle is opened, a portion of its contents is found converted by the ants into a powdery earth.

To facilitate reference, the documents relating to different subjects are tied up in bundles differently coloured. The Indian dyes are brilliant; the shelves in consequence have something of the gay appearance of the beds of a flower-garden.

In India all official proceedings, even the most trivial, are conducted in writing. Hence the rapidity with which the records accumulate is something appalling. During the Mutiny every scrap of paper that this room contained was either burnt or thrown into the river. Not so many years have since passed, and yet the shelves are now again filled to overflowing.

The English records are kept in another room. Compared with these, they are in amount insignificant They consist merely of letters and tabulated statements. They are bound up in large volumes, and, except to anyone desirous of statistical information, are the very driest of reading. The earlier records, those of the years that followed the commencement of our rule, were, on the contrary, often extremely interesting. They were full of incident, and described occurrences that threw so much light on the then condition of the country and mode of life and habits of the English of that long-past time. Unfortunately, except in a very few districts, these early records were all destroyed in the Mutiny.

Among the records that escaped were those of a district where, not very long ago, I was stationed. It was one of the eastern districts, the part of these provinces where our rule had been earliest established. The records extended far back into the last century. Looking over them one day, I came, to my surprise, on a paper drawn up by no less a person than Warren Hastings. It was a printed narrative of his proceedings towards the then Raja of Benares—proceedings which were afterwards made one of the charges against him on the occasion of his state trial. I was aware from the histories that some such proceedings had occurred, but I knew nothing of their details. I commenced to read the narrative from mere curiosity; but I soon grew deeply interested. What had been a mere bare historical statement now rose before me with all the life, colour, and movement of a chapter of romance.

The narrative which so much interested me may

perhaps also prove interesting to my readers. I, therefore, give a brief summary of its contents. The summary, I should mention, is drawn up from mere recollection, and from the recollection of a perusal at a time long gone by.

Warren Hastings, then Governor-General of India, set out, so the narrative records, on a progress through the western provinces of our then dominions. He intended also to extend his progress to the adjacent half-tributory territory of the Nawab of Oude. We may infer that he moved with all the state and splendour at that time regarded as befitting his high position, with tents, horses, elephants, and an army of attendants. He was also, as we learn from the narrative, accompanied by a strong military escort.

There were many political matters of high importance to be arranged, and among others the affairs of the Raja of Benares. The Raja had of late been occasioning trouble, chiefly, if I remember correctly, by evading the payment of his revenue, for, notwithstanding his extensive domains and his royal sounding title, the Raja was in reality no more than a tenant of our Government. He held his lands by virtue of a lease granted him by our Government, and he had engaged to pay for them a certain rental. This is a point on which the narrative strongly insists, but of which I confess that till I perused it I was entirely unaware.

Warren Hastings left Calcutta, and in due course arrived at Benares. He there halted his camp in the neighbourhood of the city, and entered into communications with the Raja. He hoped, it would seem, that by this means the differences between the Raja and our Government might be amicably arranged. This expectation was not realized. The Raja remained unyielding, and Warren Hastings then decided to exert authority. He issued an order to the commander of his escort to march a force into the city, to arrest the Raja and bring him back a prisoner to the camp.

It would appear that no resistance was anticipated on the part of the Raja, and certainly no arrangements were made to meet resistance should any be offered. Only a small party of Sepoys were despatched, and, what seems extraordinary, they were sent off with unloaded muskets and, moreover, without any ammunition to load them should the necessity for doing so arise. Thus equipped, the party reached the palace. They found the gates closed. The summons to open them was answered by a fire of matchlocks from the roof and the narrow windows. This fire the Sepoys, with their unloaded muskets and without ammunition, were, of course, unable to return. They had no course but to retreat.

As the news spread the city rose, and then the adjacent country. Matters appeared so serious that Warren Hastings thought it prudent to hurriedly strike his camp and to march away further to the west. He proceeded for some distance along the banks of the Ganges; then he crossed the river and, with his escort and attendants, took refuge in the old native fortress of Chundalghurrie, or, as it is termed by us Europeans, Chunar.

This fortress, since modernized, crowns the level

summit of a hill. The hill is of no great elevation, but its sides are steep, and it rises abruptly from the margin of the river, and this in those days rendered its position a strong one. The hill forms the termination of a low range which stretches away to the westward, and rising continually in altitude, unites at length with the mountains of Central India.

Warren Hastings remained shut up in the fort of Chunar till the arrival of a force sent from Calcutta to relieve him; and, from the slow manner in which affairs in those days were conducted, this was not till after the lapse of a considerable period. Meanwhile throughout all the adjacent country there was much the same condition of things as in the present century followed the breaking out of the Mutiny. There were, to be sure, no massacres and but little disorder, but everywhere in a similar manner the British authority at once, as it were, disappeared.

As far as I remember, the narrative does not mention the punishment awarded to the Raja of Benares. That, perhaps, was a matter for later determination. I rather think that eventually it was thought sufficient to impose on him a heavy fine.

In reading the narrative two things particularly struck me. The one was that Warren Hastings did not issue his orders for the arrest of the Raja through any of his secretaries. He wrote himself a letter to the commander of his escort directing him to march down a party of Sepoys, to arrest the Raja in his palace and to return with him to the camp. In later times such action on the part of one so exalted as the Governor-

General of India would have been regarded as very unusual, even undignified.

The other matter that impressed me was this: when the news of the disaster at Benares reached the Nawab of Oude, instead of taking advantage of it to throw off his allegiance to the English Government, he at once collected his armies and set off to march to Chunar to afford it assistance. The very different behaviour of the population of Oude towards us during the Mutiny certainly affords grounds for reflection.

I will follow this account of my office and its records with a short description of the gaol, for that institution is also, to some extent, under my authority. The gaol is situated a little beyond the station. The building is merely a large, square-walled enclosure. In the centre of the side that faces the high-road is the entrance gateway. It is a large, solid, very plain, two-storied structure. To pass through it would hardly repay one, for the interior contains only smaller enclosures and a variety of long tiled sheds, in which the prisoners sleep and work. There are, however, besides, some smaller rooms for the accommodation of guards, and for the confinement of prisoners who have proved refractory; but a visitor would be most struck by the order and cleanliness everywhere apparent, and the total absence of that oppressive gloom characteristic of our prisons at home.

The gaol as a building has certainly no beauty; but then it has been a good deal altered and added to. There are other prisons built on the same plan that, in a way, are really pretty. One I especially remember. It stood alone on the open plain. At each of the four angles of the wall was a quaint-looking little domed turret, which served as a sentry-box. The gateway was surmounted by a parapet, and the whole building, walls, gateway, and turrets, was painted a cheerful yellow; also the head gaoler had planted rows of flowers, chiefly marigolds, before a portion of the front wall. Altogether the edifice looked so gay, bright, and Oriental that a picture of it might have served to illustrate an Eastern tale as the castle or residence of some jin or enchanter.

The inmates of our gaol are in harmony with their surroundings. They are well fed and not overworked; they look plump and contented. They spend most of their time outside the prison in the open air, chiefly working on the roads. So far as the position of a prisoner can be agreeable, theirs is such. One thing about them is very noticeable: their countenances rarely, if ever, have that expression of brutality, ferocity, and moral degradation that, according to description, is so often found among our own criminal population. Indeed, but for their prison dress, they are not in any way distinguishable from ordinary labourers: they have the same quiet manner and placid expression.

Nevertheless, they are at times capable of acts of savage violence. In my time the guards were always instructed never for an instant to lay aside their swords; and I remember that one of the first lessons impressed upon me when I was given partial charge of a prison was that I should never, under any circumstances whatever, make the round of the wards unless accompanied by a strong armed guard of several men. The neglect of these precautions led, even within my experience, to many disasters, and once resulted in a sad tragedy; but this last occurred a little before my arrival in the country.

A magistrate—I forget his name—visited his gaol in the course of his morning drive. He entered one of the wards escorted by only a single attendant, and this attendant was unarmed. The prisoners, from some reason, were discontented, and had planned an outbreak. The appearance of the magistrate thus unprotected seemed to offer them the opportunity. They surrounded and killed him, beating in his skull—so I heard the story—with the heavy brass pots they carried for the purpose of drawing water. A circumstance added pathos to the tragedy. The magistrate had driven to the gaol accompanied by his wife. While he was being thus murdered within, she, all unconscious, was sitting in her carriage at the gateway quietly awaiting his return.

From gaols to robbers the transition is easy. So I will make it, and relate one or two stories that may interest the reader. I should mention that they occurred long ago, soon after my first arrival in the country.

In order to render the first story quite clear to the English reader, I must make a short preliminary explanation. Indian houses — I mean those of the natives—have no outer windows, save those over the entrance, or perhaps some small square aperture high aloft. The rooms receive their light from the courtyard within. The houses being thus constructed, thieves can only effect an entrance by digging a hole through one of the outer walls. This they do with a short, sharp-pointed iron bar.

Now about the time I speak of a party of thieves had thus one night broken into the house of a banker; it was, I think, in this very city. The thieves had collected their plunder and were departing, when the banker awoke, heard a noise, and ran down. He entered the room just in time to see the last of the thieves crawling out through the hole; his legs were still inside. With great presence of mind, the banker ran forward and forced himself between them. The thief was now caught: with his legs separated he could not get out, and, with his arms and shoulders beyond the wall, neither could he force himself back.

The banker summoned his servants and sent for the police. Meanwhile he remained exultant: through this thief the rest would be apprehended, and his property recovered. But in this he was disappointed. So soon as the other thieves found that their comrade was fixed in the hole they took measures to prevent his betraying them. They drew their swords, cut off his head, and carried it off, together with their plunder. The police on their arrival found only a bleeding neck protruding from the hole, and a body that no one could identify.

The next story, I think, is even more ghastly. I was on a visit to my brother. He was the subordinate, or, as it was then termed, the "joint," magistrate of a rather wild district. A band of dacoits—that is, armed robbers—had lately infested it. The band had been dispersed, but the leader had escaped. A reward had been offered for his apprehension, dead or alive.

It was the hot weather. We were returning from our evening drive; darkness was just setting in. As the carriage drew up at the house a man rushed forward. By the light of the lamp that hung in the porch we could see that he was a policeman, and that he held something in his hand wrapped up in a cotton cloth. My brother stepped out. The policeman drew aside the cloth, and we saw a human head. The eyes were open and staring, and the countenance all smeared over with dried, clotted blood. It was the head of the leader of the dacoits. He had been discovered, had resisted, and been slain. His head had been sent in as proof of his death, in order to claim the reward.

Everyone has heard of the Thugs. I will add a story about them. One of their haunts was the old city of Canouje. Not far from the city there was a well; it was known as the well of the "Bhuttyarah," from having been constructed by a man of that caste. A bhuttyarah, I may explain, is the man who cooks food for travellers in a caravanserai. The well was a very large one, and lined with masonry; it had long been disused, and was half choked up. Some seventy years ago, when the Government commenced to put down the Thugs, many of them turned informers. One of these informers pointed out this well as the place where the Thugs about Canouje hid away the bodies of their victims.

I was once encamped near the well, and I heard the finding of the bodies described by many persons who were present when, in consequence of the informer's statement, the well was searched. They told me that the human remains were many yards in depth—scattered bones, skulls, whole skeletons, and, at the top of all, many bodies not yet altogether decomposed.

From robbers and Thugs it will be a relief to return again to the insects and animals. I will first conclude my remarks on snakes, and then I will say a few words regarding the locusts.

Snakes, as I have mentioned, are but very rarely seen near English houses; nevertheless I once came on a large collection, not, however, of snakes themselves, but of their eggs. It was some years ago, and at another station. One afternoon the servants came running in to inform me that they had discovered a "bombay" in the garden. This, they explained, was a place where snakes of the same species collected together and deposited their eggs. I proceeded with them to the spot. It was in a large, round flower-bed, not a hundred feet from the front of the house. The eggs were lying all near together, about sixty in number; but whether they were beneath the soil, or lying exposed on the surface, or covered with leaves, I do not remember.

The eggs were nearly round in shape, a greyish white in colour, and with shells almost as hard as stones. They were not much larger than walnuts, and felt quite cold to the touch. The servants declared that they were the eggs of the cobra, but I do not think that really they in the least knew.

The prettiest snake I ever saw was one that I came suddenly on in an open space in a forest below Mussoorie. It was very slender, not more than eighteen inches in length, and in colour the very brightest emerald green. It was so extremely pretty that I wished to catch it; but before we could make arrangements for doing so the snake took alarm. It darted into a clump of grass, and was lost to view. The servants declared that it was a snake of the most deadly kind; possibly it may have been, but then the natives say the same of nearly every snake.

One snake, however, they do admit to be harmless. This is the "dâman." It is a snake most peculiar in appearance: it seems to have no eyes nor any mouth, and excepting that its skin is covered with scales, it almost exactly resembles a gigantic worm. The natives declare that it possesses two mouths, one at each extremity of its body, and also that it has the faculty of moving backwards and forwards with equal facility.

The "gerait," or, as it is termed by Europeans, the "whip" snake, is really deadly, even more so, it is said, than the cobra. It derives its English designation from its extreme slenderness, which gives it very much the appearance of the thong of a whip. I only once saw a gerait, but when and where I do not recollect.

Those who have merely beheld snakes in confinement can form no idea of the rapidity with which they can move when at liberty and in their native haunts. I will give an example. I was once descending a broad, bare track that led down to a river; on each side of the track there were bushes and tall, coarse grass. Suddenly a large snake shot out from the grass on my left; it crossed the track with the rapidity, so it seemed to me, of a horse at full gallop. It moved so rapidly that before I could well discern its figure it had disappeared among the grass and bushes on the other side. As far as I could judge, it must have been at least six feet in length.

The villagers, who work all day in the fields, see snakes of course far more frequently than do Europeans, and they are certainly occasionally bitten by them; but the statements made of late in England of the thousands of natives who perish from snake-bites each year I regard with entire incredulity.

So much for the snakes. I will now speak of the locusts. I ought to have done so earlier, for those I am about to describe made their appearance soon after my arrival at this station. I was in the office one day, when I heard a shouting outside. I inquired the cause, and learnt that a swarm of locusts had appeared, and that the shouts arose from a mob of children who were running after them.

I went at once into the verandah, and there, sure enough, I beheld the locusts. They filled the air; they dimmed the light; they quite hid the sun; they flew with a heavy, slow, undulating motion that gave to the swarm as it passed something the appearance of dark, falling snow. As they flew on thousands of them continually alighted on the ground, on the trees, and on the garden crops. The mob of children were busily engaged in running about and catching them, all the while shouting, "Tidhi! tidhi!" the native name of the locust. They were catching them for food, for the natives eat the locusts, and regard them when fried in oil as a delicacy. Some Europeans also eat them curried, and I have heard their taste described as agreeable; I never, however, had the courage myself to test the correctness of the statement.

The swarm passed by in about an hour. Notwithstanding the myriads and myriads of locusts it contained, I found that the swarm was regarded as no more than a small one. It certainly by no means occasioned the devastation which has often been described as accompanying the passage of these insects; still there was a good deal of injury done to the crops, more especially to those of the gardens.

The natives have an idea that the locusts are bred in the Himalaya. The idea is, I believe, quite erroneous; still, according to my experience, flights of locusts are more common among the lower ranges of those mountains than in the plains. When seen among those ranges their appearance even more strikingly resembles that of dark-coloured, slowly falling snow. Filling the valleys, obscuring the great mountains, they impress the mind with an extreme sense of gloom and of grandeur.

Towards the end of October it was full moon; I never remember moonlight more beautiful; I used often in the evenings to sit outside to enjoy it, there was something so soothing, so delicious, in its soft, mysterious glow. The air, besides, was in itself agreeable, not exactly cold, but sufficiently cool to make a shawl or an overcoat pleasant.

This mention of the moonlight reminds me of another appearance peculiar to Eastern nights; it is what I have heard described as the "mirage of the dark." I first witnessed it when crossing the desert of Suez on the occasion of my first journey to India. We were a small party, and crossed the desert riding on donkeys; we had ridden for many hours, and were all very tired when night came on; we had then still some miles to travel. There was no moon, and, in the darkness, the desert seemed full of shadows. Presently, as we journeyed on, the shadows seemed to take shape and assume the form of hills and gentle undulations; next, figures appeared passing by or approaching.

They were all such as I had seen during the day: camels and men on horseback wearing turbans and flowing robes, and carrying in their hands long lances; they were so distinct that at first I supposed them to be real. It was only as they came near and vanished that I perceived that they were illusions. Presently, as I became more tired, I seemed to behold buildings and lights. It was past midnight before we arrived at the station; there during supper we talked over our journey, and I found that nearly all the party had had much the same experience of the mirage as myself.

On some few occasions I have witnessed the same phenomena in India. The objects that I then appeared to see were similarly those that I had beheld in the day-time: carts drawn by bullocks, palanquins, men in native dresses, and, perhaps, a string of camels or an elephant; also, when very tired, I thought that I saw lights and houses. The conditions necessary to give rise to the phenomena seem to be a dark night, an open country, allowing an extended surface to be indistinctly visible, and on the part of the beholder extreme fatigue.

The ordinary day mirage is also sometimes to be seen in India, but only during the hot weather, and in a very bare, open tract of country. I myself have only once beheld it; its appearance then was not at all striking. There was none of that beauty and illusion of trees and buildings which, according to description, accompanies the mirage as seen in the deserts of Africa and Arabia; there was only in the distance what seemed a sheet of water, nothing more.

With the above description of the October moonlight my diary for the time abruptly closes; it commences again after an interval of several months, and then in a station further to the north, to which, in the meantime, I had been transferred. The house I now occupy is not, as before, on the bank of the river, but then it has the compensating advantage of an extremely large garden, and a garden, moreover, in excellent order. The first entry in my diary of any interest records my making the acquaintance of a community of extremely small ants of the red variety; but the particulars of this acquaintance I will relate in the next chapter.

CHAPTER X.

WHITE ANTS

THIS morning—it was towards the end of September—on returning from my ride, I took a stroll through the garden. Half-way down the central path I came on a small mound of earth very much resembling in appearance the crater of a volcano. The mound in shape was circular, about four inches high and eight inches in diameter, and in the centre there was a saucer-like depression; and in the centre again of this depression there was a small hole. From this hole a number of the minutest red-coloured ants were coming out and returning. Each ant that came out carried in his jaws a grain of sandy earth, deposited it on the top of the mound, and then ran rapidly back again into the hole.

Although the mound in itself was small, yet, compared with the size of the ants, it was gigantic; and yet it must have all been constructed within the very brief period of two, or at the most two and a half, days. I made sure of this because during the third day previous there had been a heavy fall of rain, and if the mound had then existed the rain would certainly have washed it away. However, not to rely on conjecture, I determined to ascertain by direct observation the rate at which these little creatures could erect their mound. For this purpose I had a small stake driven into the path, to mark the position of the nest; and then I had the entire earth of the mound very carefully removed. I took particular care that none of the ants should be hurt, nor any of the earth get swept into the hole, which, of course, was the entrance to the nest. This done, I sent for a chair, and sat in the shade of a tree to observe what would ensue.

In a minute or two the ants commenced to reappear. Each ant, as before, carried in his jaws a minute pellet of sandy earth. This he deposited on the ground, at a distance of about six inches from the hole. Each ant deposited his pellet in a different spot, but always at the same distance from the hole; and thus they presently formed a small ring of pellets, that completely encircled the hole. They worked with such diligence and speed, running out and racing back, that while I sat and looked on the ring of pellets had become as high and broad as a piece of cord; and the ring, I noticed, was a nearly exact circle.

The next morning the ring was considerably broader and higher. By the fourth morning a new crater appeared completed; and this new crater was broader, loftier, in all its dimensions very much exceeding in magnitude the previous crater which I had removed. And it is to be remembered that at this season of the year the ants work outside their nests only during the early hours of the morning, and for a shorter period in the afternoon. This for them immense mound represented therefore the labour of little more than one entire day.

The mound having reached this size, it ceased to be added to. I presume that the subterranean galleries which the ants were excavating were now finished, and that consequently there was no more earth for them to bring up. While the galleries were being excavated it was, of course, necessary that the earth which was dug away should be brought out; but why it should have been deposited round the entrance, in the form of a circular mound, was a matter which remained to me a puzzle to the last.

The mound, so far as I could see, was not only of no use, but, on the contrary, it was a constant inconvenience and a possible danger. If rain fell, it would cause the nest to be flooded, and as it was the mound formed an obstacle which every morning and evening, when the ants went out to forage, they had repeatedly to surmount. I made a rough calculation that the mound was to these little ants what a steep ridge sixty feet high would have been to an average-sized man. Agile as the ants were, the crossing the mound must have required some exertion. It also entailed some little risk. The earth of the mound was so loose and sandy, that it often gave way even beneath their light tread. Then down they rolled to the bottom; and if returning with seed, the seed was lost.

It was not very long after the completion of this second crater that the commencement occurred of the Hindoo month of Kuer, and, to the great delight of the natives, a shower of rain fell in the course of the afternoon. Their delight was due to a belief that the rain which falls on the first day of that month possesses especial fertilizing influence on the soil. The clods of earth which it moistens, according to popular belief, never again grow dry. It is also believed that the drops of this rain which fall in the ocean, should the oysters receive them, form the pearls within their shells.

The climate here is much moister than it was at my previous station, and, as a consequence, the white ants far more abound. They are very numerous in the garden, and I have lately occupied my early mornings a good deal in watching them. I was induced to do so by coming unexpectedly the other morning on one of their nests. The nest was below the ground, and the ants were busily engaged in erecting one of their great, conical-shaped mounds on the surface above it. The ants were issuing in great numbers from several holes in the path. The holes were all near together, and round each hole the ants were erecting what I may describe as a tower. These proceedings were quite new to me. I sent for a chair, sat down, and watched them with extreme interest. Two or three of my servants remained standing beside me, but neither my presence nor theirs appeared in the least to disturb the ants; indeed, they did not show any indication that they were aware we were near them.

The towers had already been raised to the height of six or seven inches; they were from two to three inches in diameter, and in shape very irregular circles;

their elevation was equally defective. Instead of rising perpendicularly, they curved from side to side like an ill-constructed chimney. The walls were extremely thin, not thicker than a sheet of ordinary drawing-paper; they were formed of very minute pellets of earth, which the ants had evidently kneaded and fashioned in the nest below. The pellets were not only moist, but also slightly glutinous. The towers had certainly been erected during the morning, for the walls were still damp; they had much the appearance of moist brown paper.

Thin and damp as the walls were, they were, nevertheless, evidently very strong, for they supported the weight of the numerous white ants that ran up and down them without yielding or bending in the least. The towers were all erected near together; several even touched, forming little groups, affording each other mutual support. One of these groups, which consisted of several towers, rested against the stem of a shrub that grew on the side of the path.

The ants worked only inside the towers; they worked with extreme rapidity: they came running up the nearly perpendicular wall at full speed, and without apparently any effort. Each ant carried a pellet in his jaws. On reaching the top of the wall he adjusted the pellet very carefully; next he seemed, I thought, to lick it with his tongue; and that done, he ran down the wall again with the same rapidity that he had ascended it.

The towers were sufficiently large to enable five or six white ants to ascend and descend at the same time.

The ants worked so fast that during the half-hour that I sat watching them the towers had all risen in height at least an inch. The ants must have continued thus working the whole of the day and perhaps for some part of the night as well, for when I visited the nest the next morning the towers had all risen to the height of two and three feet, and several of them had also been arched over. In others the process of arching over was just commencing. I remained for a long time and watched it. The process was most interesting to observe, but owing to the extremely minute size of the pellets, it was a process not easy to observe correctly. So far as I could make out, the process was as follows:

The circumference of the tower was first reduced by placing the pellets so that they overlapped a little inwardly. The overlapping in each successive row was so slight as to be hardly perceptible. But after several rows of pellets had thus been laid the circumference appeared decidedly smaller; next the wall commenced to bend over inwardly, and presently it became nearly horizontal. The pellets were now clearly kept in position by some glutinous substance, which caused each successive pellet to adhere to the one against which it was placed.

I noticed now that the white ants placed the pellets in their positions with extreme care; they also appeared to moisten the pellets repeatedly with their tongues, both before and after they were deposited. The process of arching over was completed while I looked on. The summit of the tower had now the appearance of a very flat but very rough and uneven dome.

For some reason or other, I did not visit the nest again for two or three days, and then I found, to my extreme regret, that the towers had all disappeared. I had omitted to give orders for their preservation, and the gardeners had swept them away as disfiguring the path. It was an untoward event which I have always since much deplored, for I never again saw these towers in course of erection, and in consequence many matters in regard to the use and mode of construction of the great ant-hills of which they were the commencement, and which I had hoped to ascertain, remain for me still enigmas.

The white-ant hills when completed are tall, roughly conical structures; they are mostly from four to five feet high, and have many very narrow but far protruding buttresses. The earth of which they are composed is extremely hard, so hard that it can only be broken by a pickaxe, and even then with much difficulty. When cut open they are found to be nearly solid. They contain only some winding passages, and a few large, hollow spaces, into which the passages lead. The hollow towers that I saw in course of erection must, therefore, be subsequently filled up, and also the spaces between them. The use and purpose of these mounds is to me a mystery, for the actual nest, so far as my experience goes, is always beneath the surface of the soil.

With this notice of the white ants my diary for a time again closes. It recommences after a lapse of nearly two years, and in a station still further to the north, and within not much more than thirty miles of the outermost of the lower ranges of the Himalaya. The climate is very much cooler than at my last station, and it is also far more moist and damp. As a consequence the white ants are proportionately more numerous. They are so numerous that for some time after my arrival they were the chief subjects of my observation, and my diary for that period is almost exclusively occupied with notices regarding them. Such of these notices as appear to me to be sufficiently interesting I will place before the reader.

On the 18th of August I dug up a white ants' nest. It was situated near the edge of a bank; the digging it open was, therefore, comparatively easy. It contained thirty chambers. Each was about the size and very much the shape of a large sponge; that is they were round above, while their floors were flat with a slight rising in the centre. They all communicated by passages. The passages ran below from the centre of one floor to the centre of the next. Some few of the chambers, however, had second, but smaller, passages. These second passages ran above. The openings into them were in the centre of each roof. The chambers were all tolerably near together, perhaps from one to two feet apart, and they were mostly situated on different levels. The uppermost chamber was not more than twelve inches below the surface, and the lowest about a yard.

Nearly all the chambers contained combs. Some were fresh and full of eggs, pupæ, and young white ants; others were old, long disused, and dry. They were so dry that on a slight touch they crumbled to powder. A few of the combs had crumbled away of themselves, and formed a layer of dust on the floor of the chamber. The fresh combs were most unpleasant-looking objects. Both in colour and shape they almost exactly resembled human skulls. Indeed, as they lay about on the ground they might easily, at a little distance, have been mistaken for such just disinterred from a cemetery.

These combs consist of a multitude of large, flat cells placed over each other in very irregular layers. Flat shells the size of a shilling, and arranged in the shape of a sponge, would give some idea of their construction. The cells are formed of a material which has much the appearance of brown paper. It is, I imagine, merely earth kneaded together with the glutinous liquid which the ants secrete from their mouths.

I had two of these fresh combs placed under the shade of a tree, that I might further observe them. In order to protect them from injury, I caused them to be carefully covered with soft, dry earth. This measure of precaution had, however, an unfortunate result. Next morning, when the earth was removed, the combs were found covered with a green fungus, and their inhabitants, the young ants and pupæ, were all dead.

About a fortnight afterwards I dug up another nest, and made a discovery, for in one of the combs we came on the queen. At first sight she had the appearance only of an enormous grub, some three inches long and at least an inch and a half in circumference; but on closer inspection I perceived that this apparent grub was in reality merely the queen's abdomen. Affixed to it in front were the body and head. These were those of an ordinary white ant, only slightly larger. The surface of the abdomen had a curious undulating appearance. On examining it through a magnifying-glass I found that this appearance was caused by the alternate contraction and expansion of the different rings of which the abdomen seemed to be composed. The movement went on incessantly without a moment's intermission. Its purpose, I concluded, was to expel the eggs; but although I watched for some time, I did not perceive that any eggs were ejected.

When I had finished my observations, I placed the queen again gently on the ground. In a few minutes a number of white ants approached, and commenced to crawl over her. As I could not determine whether their intentions were friendly or hostile, I thought it prudent to brush them away, and also to place the queen in a place of security, for, if attacked, she appeared quite incapable of defence. After some consideration she was deposited in the hollow between two empty combs; there she lay as in a little cave, and, to make her more secure, the combs were covered with a small mound of fine earth.

In the afternoon, on my return from office, I went at once to the mound to release the queen, and to restore her to her nest. But when the earth was removed, and the combs separated, to the astonishment of myself and the servants, the queen was found to have disappeared, where and how to the last remained a mystery, for the earth of the mound showed no sign of having been disturbed, and the queen herself appeared incapable of movement.

The following week I opened a third white ants' nest. In this nest there was a great number of fresh combs, all full of eggs, pupæ, and completely developed young white ants. These young ants had their wings all ready to be expanded, and seemed waiting for the moment when they should make their exit from the nest, take their one short flight, and have their one brief view of the glories of the world above. I noticed that the bodies of these young ants were of a milky whiteness and appeared half transparent. The colour of the adult ants is more of a yellowish brown, and their bodies are quite opaque.

I had two or three of these fresh combs placed under the shade of a tree for subsequent observation. Warned by previous experience, I was careful to have no earth put over them. On visiting the spot next morning I found that each of the combs had been encased by the adult white ants of the nest with a thick coating of their own prepared earth. The inmates appeared alive and vigorous, and the combs will, no doubt, become the nucleus of a fresh community.

The number of white ants in this neighbourhood is enormous. The whole country appears honeycombed with their chambers and passages. They answer, no doubt, some wise purpose in the economy of nature, but what that purpose may be is not very apparent. I thought at one time that the empty chambers might serve in some degree as storehouses for the rainwater, and so give moisture to the soil, but experience showed me that this idea was incorrect. Out of the many chambers that I opened, I never found one that contained water, or whose walls were in the least degree damper than the ground elsewhere.

Not only are the ants more numerous here than at my previous stations, but the mounds they throw up are larger and loftier. Some of them just now present a most picturesque appearance; they are covered with a fungus of a pretty green colour, and what with their conical summits and wide flanking buttresses, they do really very much resemble those steep, forest-covered mountains that one sees represented in Chinese pictures of their gardens and landscapes.

Small, soft, and feeble as the white ants are, yet by their numbers and powers of destruction they have influenced to some extent both the architecture and also the civilization of the country. To their ravages, which prevent much the use of timber, is in a great measure due the massive solidity of the grander Indian edifices, and by their devouring of papers and documents they have restricted the cultivation of literature; they have rendered the preservation of books difficult; they have continuously destroyed the records that would have thrown light on the history of the past.

It is providential that the white ants do not attack the living as they do the dead vegetation, for otherwise they would soon reduce the country to a desert. They do, however, occasionally attack and destroy both plants and trees. They eat away the bark of the tree, and then when the wood is dry they excavate their chambers and galleries in the trunk. The plants they appear to devour simply as food. On this matter I will mention a curious circumstance. It was told me about this time by a very respectable landowner. We were talking about sugarcane. He informed me that the large variety, termed by the natives the "poundah," had been introduced into this part of the country about forty years previously by the English Government. Then he added that on its first introduction it was with the utmost difficulty the cane could be grown, the white ants attacked it so systematically; but as time passed their attacks grew less frequent, and after a few years they entirely ceased.

My observations of the white ants were not very prolonged, nor in the least scientific; they have left unsolved two problems. One, as I have already mentioned, is the use and purpose of the tall conical mounds which with such infinite labour these little creatures erect; the other is by what means the eggs which the queen lays become deposited in the cells of the combs. Either they must be conveyed to the cells by the other ants, or else the queen must after all be capable of movement. I will conclude my notices of the white ants with the remark that in Upper India they are not found at the height of more than four thousand feet above the level of the sea.

The damp climate of this station, which so promotes the increase of the white ants, is favourable also to the development of another and more picturesque insect; this is the firefly. In most parts of these provinces the fireflies are not often seen, but here they abound. They especially frequent a low-lying tract of ground not very far from the entrance of my compound. The other evening they there afforded me a most interesting spectacle. I was returning from my drive rather later than usual; there was no moon, and the short twilight had faded away. This piece of land, which is overshadowed on one side by trees, was enveloped in darkness; but scattered everywhere in the darkness were to be seen little specks of soft, bright moving light. They were rising, falling, advancing, retreating, for an instant vanishing, then again reappearing. The sight was so pretty that, though it was late, I remained for a long time quite interested in watching it.

The firefly is not the only flying insect that has the power of emitting light. There is a species of beetle that also possesses this faculty. I only once met with it, and that was many years ago, and in a station much lower down the country. I was sitting in the drawing-room one evening during the rainy season, when I noticed a small dot of light moving to and fro in the air towards the further end of the room. I saw that it proceeded from some insect. The insect presently alighted on a table, and I succeeded in securing it under an inverted tumbler; then I carried it to the lamp for examination.

I found that it was a beetle, rather small, but, both in form and colour, exceedingly pretty. The light did not proceed, as in the firefly, from the tail, but from two circular spots, one on each side of the head. Whether these spots were its eyes or not I could not determine. The light they emitted was greater than that of the firefly, and also more beautiful; it was softer, and was, besides, faintly tinged with green. My examination being concluded, I carried the little captive into the verandah, and there released him. His soft light flitted for a minute or so in the darkness, and then disappeared. Either he had extinguished it, or he had himself become concealed among the shrubs of the garden.

But of all the Indian insect lights the palm for beauty must, I think, be conceded to that of the glow-worm. I can only, however, remember but once beholding it. I was on leave at Mussoorie. Riding out one evening, I passed a rocky bank much overgrown with bushes and long grass. At one place near the bottom of the bank I noticed a glow of light; it was so large and soft that I stopped to examine it. I found that it issued from a small hollow, where a piece of the rock had loosened and fallen out. A curtain of long grass hung over in front, giving to the hollow the aspect of a little cave. It required but slight imagination to picture some small fairy seated within it, so clear, so soft and beautiful, was the light that filled the hollow and shone through the veil of grass. It was a disillusioning when I drew aside the grass and found behind it only a large grub of a most unpleasant appearance.

From insects I will now turn to animals. In a former chapter I stated that I should presently say a few words regarding that variety of them that can fly, namely, the bats. An incident that occurred the other evening reminds me to do so. I had finished tea, and was sitting reading, when I felt a wave of air against my cheek, and at the same time some dark object shot swiftly by. It was a bat. Attracted by the lights, it had entered the room, and was now circling about it. When a bat thus enters a room it is farewell to peace till it has departed. With short intervals of rest on the walls and cornices, it sweeps round incessantly, and there is something in its noiseless flight that is most unpleasant; besides, it occasionally extinguishes the candles; and there is always the dread that it may alight on one's person, or if a lady is present, get entangled in her hair. But to drive out a bat is not easy, it flies so rapidly, conceals itself so readily, and then the rooms are so large and lofty. It was more than half an hour before this bat was got rid of. At length it was chased to one of the open windows, passed through it, and departed.

The bats that thus enter houses are mostly those of the smaller varieties. Their bodies do not much exceed in size that of a mouse. From these smallest of bats there is every gradation of magnitude up to those enormous creatures known among Europeans as the "flying foxes." These great bats are, however, rarely seen in these provinces except in the eastern districts, those that are nearest to Bengal. I was once stationed in that part of the country, and often beheld them, but only when flying. Soon after sunset they used to appear, and in great numbers, but each always flew alone. They flew at immense altitudes, and always in the same direction. High as they were above, they still appeared as large as vultures. But their flight was different; it had in it something very majestic. They never rose, never descended, never swerved to right or left, never increased their speed nor diminished it; they moved on always at the same even rate, in the same direct, undeviating course, their wings beating with the regularity of machinery. Their flight was very swift, though, from its evenness, it did not appear so. It was only when I noticed how quickly they passed out of view that I realized how rapidly they flew.

The natives regard the bat as the very type of impurity, and I think that those who have ever entered the upper domes of the ancient mosques and tombs will incline to the same opinion. In these places the bats especially congregate. Hanging head downward, they form a complete lining to the walls. Their droppings make a layer inches deep on the floors; their hideous aspect, their sickening odour, excite a feeling of intense repulsion.

Nevertheless the bats, notwithstanding their offensive odour, are clean feeders. They devour insects certainly, but they subsist chiefly on fruits. They will travel great distances to obtain such as they fancy. Some years ago, at another station, a tree grew in front of the house I occupied. The tree bore in great profusion a kind of uneatable fruit. The fruit ripened towards the end of the rains; and then as it ripened a species of bat came in multitudes to devour it. They used to arrive soon after dark. They first flitted round the tree; next they attached themselves to the branches and commenced to devour the fruit. The tree then presented the most weird appearance. The bats were very large, the size at least of half-grown kittens; and from every branch and spray capable of supporting the weight hung one or several of them head downwards. Beheld thus in the half-darkness, the tree resembled one of those I have seen represented in old pictures as growing in the lower regions on the bank of the Styx.

Now the curious thing was that this was the only tree of the kind in the station; and this species of bat, I was told, was not found anywhere in the neighbourhood. By what instinct, then, did they discover the existence of the tree and the time when its fruit ripened? As soon as the fruit was all devoured, the bats departed.

CHAPTER XI.

THE EARLY COLD WEATHER

THE garden attached to this house is very large and extremely pretty. It is indeed, I think, one of the very prettiest of the English gardens in Upper India. It abounds in orange, lemon, and pomegranate trees; and also, due to the more northerly latitude, there are grapes and peaches as well. Roses in profusion border the paths, and scattered over the lawn there are many oleanders and other flowering shrubs. In the centre of the garden there is a very large thatched summer-house; and the water by which the garden is irrigated is raised from the well by means of to me the novelty of a Persian wheel.

I had returned from my drive the other morning, and was sauntering through the garden. When near the summer-house I came on a grasshopper, one of that curious variety termed by Europeans the "praying mantis." He was on the path, seated on his hind legs; his long body was erect, and his front legs raised with the feet joined, exactly like the arms and hands of a man in an attitude of devotion. The little creature allowed me to approach quite near, even to touch it. Then of a sudden it gave a spring, shot high into the air, alighted on a small shrub close by, and as it alighted it disappeared.

I had seen the mantis alight, and I had noted the branch, and also the part of the branch, on which it had descended; and yet, look as I would, I could not discover it. I looked long and carefully. The branch was rather bare; there were a few leaves on it, and some twigs, but nothing more. Of the mantis there was no sign. Suddenly, while I was still looking and wondering what had become of it, one of the twigs moved, sprang into the air, alighted on the path; and there was the mantis again, seated erect on the ground, with its legs raised in the same devotional attitude as before.

There are in India many varieties of insects that, when they place themselves in certain positions on plants or shrubs, appear to be a part of the vegetation. Many of them have been described, but to realize their wonder they must be seen—one moment a twig, a leaf, or a flower, the next moment a moth or a grasshopper.

The most marvellous of these transformations that I ever beheld was at the commencement of the ascent from the valley of the Doon to Mussoorie. For the first thousand feet or so the road zigzags up the steep face of the mountain. The lowest portion of the road is exceedingly bare, hot, and dusty. Along its outer edge there grew a row of extremely small shrubs, hardly much more than half a yard in height. The shrubs were always covered with a profusion of white flowers, much resembling "immortelles." In appearance they seemed as dry and dusty as the road itself.

I had often noticed these flowers, and one day I inquired of my servant what was their name and where else they grew, for I had never seen any exactly like them before. The man looked surprised at my question, and inquired what flowers I referred to; for, he added, there were none there. I pointed to the shrubs. He smiled, walked to one of them, and touched it with his stick. Instantly the flowers vanished; I saw a tuft of bare twigs, and the air was filled with a perfect cloud of small white moths. They flitted about for a time, gradually alighted, and the twigs were covered again with white flowers as before.

The transformation was so sudden, so entirely unexpected, that at first I could hardly believe that it was real. It was not till I had myself touched another shrub, and with a similar result, that I could feel quite satisfied that these seeming flowers were actually insects.

It was about this time when, as above related, I met with the mantis, that I discovered a colony of wild bees. These wild bees are not common in the plains. I had never seen a collection of them before. I was strolling through the garden, when I noticed a large protuberance on the lower side of a branch of a very tall tree. Looking more attentively, I saw that it was the comb of a wild bees' nest. It seemed full of honey. I had a curiosity to taste the honey. I told the gardeners, if they could manage it, to get me a piece of the comb for breakfast next morning. Somehow or other they succeeded in doing so, and, moreover, as I was very glad to learn, without any of them getting stung.

The honey was not at all nice; it was dark in colour,

and had a degree of unpleasant acidity underlying its sweetness. The natives regard this honey as very unwholesome. My experience confirmed their opinion. I did not eat much of it, but what I did eat made me feel for some hours after very uncomfortable. I noticed that the cells of the comb were extremely small, hardly more than half the size of the cells of an English honeycomb. The natives say that these bees of the plains collect the honey from the flowers during the fourteen days when the moon shines at night, and that they eat the honey they have collected in the course of the other fourteen days when the nights are moonless. This, I imagine, is a mere fable; but why the bees should store up honey at all in this winterless climate does seem rather surprising.

Having mentioned the bees, I will say a few words on the wasps. The Indian wasp is larger than the wasp of this country, and different in appearance. The body is quite smooth and entirely destitute of hair or down. In colour it is a bright yellow, very much the tint of the yellow of our carriages. The colour is not a becoming one; these wasps look very much as if they had been painted. Although they are larger than the English wasp, their sting is not by any means so painful. This I can certify from experience.

A great attraction to me in the garden is the Persian wheel. For the benefit of those readers who have not seen one, I will briefly describe it. Though called a wheel, it is really a very roughly made wooden drum, a yard or more in diameter, and at least six or eight feet long. It is fixed horizontally across the open mouth of the well, and near each end there hangs suspended round it, in the fashion of a necklace, a long rope ladder, and to each step of the ladders there is fastened a small earthen pot.

As the drum revolves it carries round the ladders with it; the pots descend, mouths downward, dip into the water, and rise filled on the other side. As they reach the top and pass over the drum, they become again reversed, and discharge their contents into a wooden trough. The trough conveys the water to a small reservoir, and from thence, by means of shallow trenches and earthen pipes, it is distributed, as required, over the garden.

The drum revolves by means of a pair of bullocks yoked together. They move round and round an upright post some few yards from the well. As the bullocks go round they turn the post, and the post again, by means of a cog-wheel, turns a long beam, and the beam, by means of another cog-wheel, turns the axle of the drum. With the exception of the earthen pots, the whole machine, drum, cog-wheels, post, beam, and all, is composed entirely of wood and rope. No machine could be more clumsy or more wasteful of labour, nor, at the same time, more picturesque.

The bullocks move leisurely round. The driver sits on the yoke between them, the image of calm. The cog-wheels creak, the drum as it revolves gives out a monotonous droning hum, while as the earthen pots ascend and turn at least a third of the water they have brought up falls again back into the well. It falls with a gentle splash, pleasant to the ear. The machine itself and all its sounds and movements are suggestive of quiet, of meditation and repose.

The Persian wheel can only be used where the water lies very near the surface. Twelve or fourteen feet is, I think, the extreme limit. Beyond this limit the weight of the pots when filled with water becomes too great for the ropes to bear, or for the drum to raise. It is a curious fact that in all Upper India it is only in the immediate neighbourhood of this station that the water does lie thus near to the surface, and consequently it is only here, and in the small tract of land just around, that the Persian wheel is found.

Elsewhere in Upper India the wells are deep, and the water is drawn up in great leathern bags. The bag is attached to a rope; the rope passes over a wheel, and is hitched by a hook at the end to the yoke of a pair of bullocks. The bullocks walk down a long incline, and as they do so they draw up the bag. To raise the water in this manner, two men are required. One man drives the bullocks, the other man stands at the mouth of the well, receives the bag as it reaches the summit, and empties the water it has brought up into the reservoir: from the reservoir it flows into the field or garden.

In this part of the country the man who receives the bag sings as he works. His song is a monotonous chant. When heard at a little distance it is not unpleasing. The origin of the custom is accounted for by a pretty legend. Once in former times a traveller, so the legend states, was found lying dead in a field. It was the hot season, and he had perished from thirst;

for, although a well was near, it was concealed by trees and bushes, and the traveller had not perceived it. When the raja of the country heard the story he gave orders that the men at the wells should in future sing as they drew the water, that travellers suffering from thirst might know where they could find water to assuage it.

Usually immediately outside every village there is a large well, and near it one or two great shady trees, and, perhaps, a small white temple. The scene at sunset is then very picturesque. The children play about, the women assemble to draw water and converse; Indian rural life appears in its prettiest aspect.

These wells are, however, a great cause of accident and of mortality. The mouth of the well is always left open, and the margin unprotected by fence or wall. It not unfrequently happens that in drawing the water a woman overbalances, or her feet slip, and then she falls. The wells are deep. In most cases, before the woman who falls is rescued, she is drowned. The number of deaths thus caused each year in these provinces must be enormous. I once roughly calculated it, taking the amount in my own district as the standard. I forget the exact numbers, but they amounted to many thousands. The wells certainly cause a far greater mortality than either the snakes or the wild beasts.

The wells also, I am sorry to say, afford great facilities both for murder and suicide. The flinging children into wells, after robbing them of their ornaments, was in my time a crime not uncommon, and the leaping into a well and there drowning was the mode of terminating one's own existence the most frequently resorted to.

Disused wells and wells in lonely and unfrequented places were, I may add, much used in former days by Thugs and robbers for the concealment of the bodies of their victims. Occasionally they are even now still so used.

I find in my diary nothing more of interest to record during the remainder of the rainy season; I will, therefore, pass on to the cold weather. Owing to the higher latitude, the cold weather commences here earlier than at my two former stations; it lasts longer, and while it lasts it is cooler, more bracing and agreeable.

It is now the middle of October; the mornings are delicious. After returning from my early ride, I can walk about the garden till the sun is quite high without any inconvenience; then I sit in the summer-house, read, and drink my early tea. The blue sky is above, the flowers around, and, softened by the distance, there falls pleasantly on my ear the monotonous droning hum of the Persian wheel.

The garden presents a pretty scene, but beyond it lies one far grander. I pass the belt of trees that encloses the compound, and see stretched before me the long, glistening line of the far Himalaya. During the rains the mountains were nearly always concealed behind a thick bank of cloud; now at morning and evening they stand out clear in all their sublimity. The mountains run from north-west to south-east; and, seen from here, they appear to form a boundary round nearly a fourth of the horizon. They rise in successive ranges: the lowest, comparatively near, is dark, and clothed with forest; the next, loftier and more distant, stretches steep and bare; while behind it towers the long white wall of the range of perpetual snow.

The sunrise at this season of the year is a beautiful spectacle. First the atmosphere above the snow assumes a rosy tint; the tint deepens, and occasionally beams of light issue from it and spread high into the firmament. Next the sun appears; the higher peaks for an instant glitter like crystal; then they and the entire line of mountains disappear in a luminous mist. The mist fades as the sun mounts higher, and presently the lower mountains and the white, snowy range come clearly into view.

The other morning the sunrise was peculiarly beautiful; the beams of light stretched over the entire heaven, and met again on the opposite horizon; and at the point where the beams met there was the same rosy tint in the sky as at the point above the mountains from whence they issued. The effect was that of a double sunrise: a sunrise to the east over the Himalaya and a second sunrise over the boundless plain to the west.

The similar appearance of a double sunset is not at all unfrequent during the rainy season; but this of a double sunrise is of extreme rarity. It is so rare, that, except on this one occasion, I never beheld it; and yet, during my long residence in India, I must have seen the rising of the sun many thousand times.

The especial beauty of this sunrise was the breadth, the brightness, and the many tints of the beams of light that stretched across the heavens. The one that passed through the zenith was of a blue so intense, that the sky on either side, deep blue as it really was, appeared pale, almost white, in contrast.

During the last few days, when in the garden in the morning, I have been struck by the number of flocks of wild ducks, wild geese, cranes, and other aquatic birds that have passed by overhead. At this season of the year they can hardly be migrating to colder regions, and yet they have all been directing their course more or less to the north.

The flocks have never been large; the largest have been those of the wild ducks, but even these have seldom consisted of more than twenty or twenty-five birds. From the height, however, at which they fly, it is not easy to quite correctly ascertain their numbers. The wild ducks, and indeed most of the other aquatic birds, fly in two converging lines; the lines unite in front, forming a figure resembling the letter V. The reason for this arrangement usually assigned is that it enables the flock to pass most easily through the air, just as a sharp-prowed boat does through the water.

I am not quite sure that this explanation is correct; but one fact appears to support it. The foremost bird, the bird at the point of the V, never for very long retains his position; after a short interval he drops to the rear, and some other bird succeeds him. From this it may be inferred that the foremost position is the most laborious, as having the greatest resistance of the air to overcome; and if so, the resistance of the air must be lessened for the birds that follow.

I have often watched the birds making this change of position; it is a sight most pretty to witness. The change is effected so quietly, so easily, without pause, confusion, or even the least diminution of speed.

In regard to the two converging lines in which these birds fly, it is curious that they are never of the same length, one line being always considerably longer than the other. The difference is occasionally very great. I have seen the one line consist of no more than two birds; the leader and the bird behind him; while in the other line the number of the birds amounts to as many as six or even eight; and what is more curious, if I remember correctly, is that the longer line is invariably the line on the right.

The flight of these aquatic birds is very different to that of the vultures, kites, swallows, or indeed any of the purely land birds: they do not sweep round nor circle, nor rise nor fall, nor augment nor diminish their speed. They proceed on always in the same direct course, and at the same uniform pace. The most striking to observe are the great cranes; they flap their large, pointed wings so leisurely; their long necks stretch out in front, and their still longer legs behind, in a manner almost laughable. Far prettier, however, to watch are the flocks of the wild ducks; they fly with extreme rapidity, and the beat of their wings, in its force and regularity, reminds one almost of that of the paddles of a steamer. It seems to require great effort, and yet it can hardly do so, for these birds thus travel through the air for immense distances, and that without ever alighting or at any time diminishing their speed.

As the cranes and the geese pass by overhead, they often utter their shrill, screaming cry. High as they are aloft, their cry is still quite distinctly, loudly heard; and yet, when uttered by the birds on the ground, I do not know that it seems louder, or is heard further, than that of many other animals.

I think, but am not sure, that when the flocks of wild ducks happened to fly lower than usual, that I have sometimes heard the beating of their wings against the air.

The weather is now so cool that I often walk instead of riding in the early morning. To-day I returned home by a footpath that led across the open fields. I had, as usual, a servant with me. We presently came on a large party of labouring women, at least thirty or forty in number; they were walking over the fields a little to our right. They were singing as they went, and I noticed that most of them carried small sheets of coarse cotton cloth, such as the poor in harvest-time use to hold their gleanings. As there was then no harvest being gathered, I was curious to know where the women were going, and sent my servant to inquire.

The man went, the women stopped, and a long conversation ensued. Presently the servant returned and informed me that the women were on their way to a tract of fallow land about a mile in front, where a wild grass grew. The seeds of this grass were now ripe, and the women were going to gather them to grind up with their flour.

The late rain crops had been deficient in quantity, so much so, indeed, that there were some fears of a scarcity, for it is on these crops that the poor chiefly depend. I supposed that it was on this account that the women were going to gather the grass seed. My servant, however, told me that the badness of the harvest had nothing to do with the use of the grass seed. This seed, he said, was in itself nutritious, and was always thus ground up with their corn by the poor, however abundant the harvest might be. He informed me also that the grass which yielded this seed was found only on land left fallow, and on which wheat or some other similar cereal had been previously grown.

This account of the servant excited my interest, for, long as I had been in India, I had never previously heard of a grass of this description. If the account was in all particulars correct, the existence of such a grass might possibly throw some light on the problem of the origin of cereal grains. I resolved to visit the place and obtain some specimens of the grass and its seed. I am sorry to say that, for some cause or other, I never carried this resolution into effect. That the seeds of this grass are ground up by the poor with their corn may be accepted as a fact, but as to whether the seeds are in themselves nutritious, or in any way resemble wheat or other grain, I am unable to express an opinion.

The meeting with these women and the purpose for which they were going brought before me the simplicity and also the unchangeableness of Eastern life. The oxen tread out the corn, and the winds winnow it, and the women of each household grind it to-day, just as they did in the times of the patriarchs. The women, as they grind the corn, sit face to face, the light handmill between. It must have been to women so grinding that our Lord alluded when He said that of the two the one should be taken, and the other left.

The handmill is to the Indian household much what the distaff and spindle were to the household of mediæval Europe. It is always associated with the careful housewife, the industrious maiden. It must be confessed, however, that it does not suggest to the minds the same poetical images. Nevertheless it has been made the subject of a pretty verse—a verse composed, according to tradition, by a fakir, one Kubbeera Doss, who lived some three centuries ago. The verse, if I remember it correctly, is as follows :—

"Chultee, chuckee, dakhekar
Dea Kubbeera ro :
'Do patan ke beech âkar
Sabit gia neh ko.'"

It may be thus rendered :—

"Seeing a handmill grinding,
Kubbeera gave a sigh :
'Who come between the two discs
None unbroken pass.'"

The millstones suggest the earth and the heavens, the grains of corn the human race, all of whom are destined to death and decay.

I have mentioned that the women I met were all singing. To a European ear nothing could be more discordant than the sound ; even distance did not soften it. I inquired of my servant what were the words of the song. He listened for a minute or two, and then repeated them. The song consisted of a single verse. The following is a nearly literal translation :—

> " My husband has ridden away,
> On his horse he has strapped the saddle :
> If I had known his intention
> [*Lit.:* If I had known this word],
> I would have snatched away his whip."

About three miles beyond the station there is a small tract of waste land. Scattered over it are some clumps of a species of giant grass; the central stem of each clump is as thick as a bulrush, and grows to a height—I write from memory—of from thirteen to fifteen feet: the stem terminates in a feathery tuft. I often pass this waste tract in my morning walk, and I had noticed that the tops of many of these stems bent over till the tufts at the end hung down nearly perpendicularly, and suspended from each there was a large pear-shaped lump nearly the size of a cocoa-nut.

This morning I had the curiosity to examine these lumps. I found that they were birds' nests, and birds' nests of the most singular construction. The pear-shaped lump was the actual nest; it was attached to the feathery tuft by a pendant of blades of dry grass most ingeniously entwined; and, what was even more curious, there projected from the side of the nest, near the bottom, where the nest was broadest, a sort of spout. This spout curved downwards, and descended in very much the form of a trumpet for the distance of at least half a yard. This, my servant told me, was the passage which led up to the entrance to the nest.

The nest was so curious that I was anxious to closely examine it, but on the spot this was not possible, for it hung high out of reach. However, on my return home I sent and had two of the stems of grass cut and brought to me with the nest attached; I felt that I could do this without unkindness, as the young birds had long ago been hatched, grown up, and departed. One of the nests I kept as a curiosity; the other I partly opened to examine.

The more I examined the nest the more I became impressed with wonder that a bird could have constructed it. The trumpet-like tube was a marvel of delicate weaving; the long neck by which the nest was suspended was as strong almost as a rope, and the blades of grass of which it was composed were so elaborately entwined into the feathery tuft that I in vain endeavoured to undo them.

The nest consisted of a little chamber within the pear-shaped mass; it was domed above, and, if I remember correctly, was also partly divided by a sort of partition; it was lined with pieces of cotton-wool that had been manifestly plucked from the growing plants, bits of cloth, and a variety of other soft substances. For a hibernating animal in the far north the little chamber would have been a paradise, but how in this climate the young birds could have endured it seemed astonishing, for, exposed the livelong day to the blazing Indian sun, its temperature must have approached to that of an oven.

I may add that the bottom and lower parts of the sides of the nest were extremely thick, and it was this that gave to the nest when seen from without its pear-shaped appearance. The nest was so firmly constructed that it was with the greatest difficulty that I could partially open it without tearing the whole fabric to pieces.

On examining one of these nests the feeling excited is one of wonder and admiration at the skill and patient labour displayed in their construction; then the question presents itself as to the purpose for which all this skill and labour has been exerted. The explanation usually given is that the nest is suspended to protect the eggs and young birds from snakes, and that the long, hollow tube is added as an additional security, but this explanation has never appeared to me at all satisfactory. The nest would be as safe in a tree, for snakes do not ordinarily climb trees, while, as to the hollow tube, no snake could reach the nest as it is, and if one did the lightly woven tube would certainly afford no protection.

A day or two after examining these nests I was strolling through the garden. I passed a bush. Something brown darted out of it; I thought it was a rat: then, as it ran, I perceived it was a bird. It ran on and joined its companions who were under another bush a little further on.

These birds—I forget their name—are very common in the Indian gardens. They are about the size of a thrush, and with plumage almost exactly the colour of dust; they rarely, if ever, fly, always run, and this they do with outstretched necks and extreme rapidity. Their size, their colour, their mode of running, and the sudden way in which they dart out of the bushes give them a most disagreeable resemblance to rats.

They have also a singular habit of always associating in groups of uneven numbers, either five or seven. The natives have a pretty legend accounting for the habit. I am sorry to say that I have forgotten it.

The plumage of these birds is certainly unusually dull; but, contrary to what is generally supposed, the colouring of the Indian birds is rarely brilliant. The peacock, indeed, in his gorgeous tints has no equal; and the munâl, the pheasant of the Himalaya, may bear comparison with the golden pheasant of China; and the bright green of the parrots is extremely pretty. But, with the exception of these and those occasional visitors the flamingoes and the mango-birds, I cannot, at the moment, call to mind any bird in Upper India that is really brilliantly arrayed.

The flamingo I have already described. I will here say a few words of the mango-bird. It is a species of oriole. It is termed by the English the mango-bird, from the circumstance that it makes its appearance at the time when the mango fruit ripens. As regards both form and colouring, it is a beautiful creature. Its back and wings and long, graceful tail are of the smoothest velvety black, while its breast is of the richest golden yellow.

I have mentioned the parrots. About here they abound. They fly in flocks, screaming as they fly. Heard out of doors, their scream is not unpleasant, and it is charming to watch them; their flight is so rapid and graceful, their form so pretty, and their colouring so bright. In their colouring, however, they are surpassed by their brethren in the Himalaya, for the parrots of the Himalaya, in addition to the green plumage of their wings and body, have their necks encircled by a crimson band.

The country now looks extremely pretty. The young wheat of the next spring harvest is just appearing. For miles and miles the fields, hitherto bare and brown, now display a surface of the freshest green. Interspersed among them are plantations of cotton and sugarcane, and occasionally patches of the taller rain crops, which, though long ripe, for some reason or other have been left still standing. These crops are magnificent in appearance. They rise to a height of nine or ten feet, and, their stems growing close together, they form an impenetrable screen. A whole army might conceal itself behind them. During the Mutiny this actually occurred.

A mutineer force lay hidden among these tall crops for three whole days, and that within a mile of the fort of Agra. Their presence was only discovered when they opened fire and charged out on General Greathed's column, which had encamped on the parade ground close adjacent.

The prettiest of the crops—I mean of those full grown—are the sugarcane and the cotton plants. The sugarcane, tall and green, resembles a patch of the wildest jungle. A tiger might have his lair within it. The cotton field, on the other hand, is the perfection of neatness. The plants, straight and slim, of but moderate height, with bushy crowns, might be walking canes that blossomed into life. Each plant is now covered with ripening pods, most of which have burst, and display the little white bundles of cotton that have developed within them.

Many of the fields contain several varieties of crops, all growing up intermingled together. In one field the other morning I counted no fewer than five distinct crops, all thus growing together. They were as follow: (1) wheat; (2) a kind of barley; (3) a grain called kussum; (4) another called seeson; and (5), last, one called tilsee.

This practice of growing several varieties of crops intermingled was in former days regarded by some English writers as showing the agricultural ignorance and backward civilization of the Hindoos. The practice is now recognized as the outcome of the accumulated experience of centuries. The practice has in this climate many advantages, among others that the young shoots of the later-sown crops are protected by the taller and earlier grown from the scorching heat of the Indian sun.

In connection with Indian agriculture there is one circumstance which must always excite curiosity. Except in the immediate neighbourhood of the towns, the soil is never manured, and yet it continues year after year to yield these abundant crops. How then are the constituents which the plants withdraw from the soil again supplied? Is it by means of the irrigation, or by the dust which during the hot weather is deposited by the winds in such abundance?

When walking over the open fields, one can understand why the Levitical law so denounces those who remove their neighbour's landmark. The fields here, as generally in the East, are separated by neither hedges, ditches, nor stone walls. A low, narrow raised line of earth alone indicates their limits, and where the fields of two different proprietors adjoin, small conical-shaped mounds of earth at either end of the line show that the line forms also the boundary of the two properties.

These earthen mounds can be easily removed and re-erected, and they often are. One of the proprietors comes to inspect his fields some morning; he discovers that the field on the border has diminished in area, the position of the boundary pillars has been altered, and a strip, perhaps a large one, of this field now appears to belong to his neighbour.

This removal of boundary pillars is a most fertile source of litigation, and the cases, owing to the unreliability of the evidence on either side, are some of the most difficult to justly determine.

CHAPTER XII.

A COLD WEATHER TOUR

I HAVE occasionally to visit some outlying offices, and one of them is situated beyond the first range of the mountains in the valley of the Doon. The weather being now so pleasant, I decided to make the journey by marching with tents. It was about the middle of November when I set out. The tents, horses, servants, and the carts with the baggage left in the morning; I followed on my pony in the afternoon. The march was a long one, and I rode leisurely. It was near sunset before I reached the camp. I found it pitched on the margin of a grove of mango-trees, close adjacent to a village. Before the village there stood a great peepul-tree, and not far from it a small white temple and a well.

The open space between my camp and the village presented a most animated appearance. The sugar-cane crop had just been cut and carried, and the juice was now being pressed out in a mill and boiled. The mill was a machine as simple and clumsy as the Persian wheel, and almost as picturesque. It consisted of a round block of wood, apparently the lower part of the trunk of a tree. The block was fixed firmly in the ground; its upper portion was hollowed. The hollow was filled with pieces of the sugarcane cut in short lengths, and from the midst of them, standing nearly upright, there projected a long, thick pole. The pole was made to turn round and round by means of a horizontal shaft, to which were yoked a pair of bullocks. As the pole turned it crushed the cane, and the cane juice flowed out through a hole lower down in the block. A rough wooden trough received the juice, and conveyed it to a shed at a little distance; there it fell into a cauldron, and was boiled by a fire below.

The bullocks moved placidly round, the man that drove them sitting half asleep on their shoulders. The shaft and pole creaked and groaned as they turned. The cane juice as it boiled hissed and bubbled, and at the same time diffused through the air a pleasant aroma; while from the fire, fed with thorny brushwood, there issued at short intervals loud crackling sounds.

The pressing and boiling employed the services of several men. Some chopped the canes; some fed the mill; others attended to the fire and the boiling. But these formed only a small portion of the people assembled. Half the men of the village seemed to be present, looking on. Most of them were comfortably seated on the ground, but several were standing; and these appeared to have just returned from their labours in the fields, for they had with them spades and hoes and their light Indian ploughs. Besides the men, there were women at the well, chattering and drawing water, also a multitude of children, running and playing about, and most of them were munching pieces of the fresh sugarcane, as, indeed, were a considerable number of the men. It was a pretty scene of rural enjoyment.

As the day faded the villagers gradually retired, but the mill continued working, and the cane juice boiling, till well into the night. It soon grew dark, and then the fire in the shed sent out a bright ruddy glow. I remained watching it, and listening to the sleepy droning of the mill, till I was summoned away by the announcement that my dinner was ready. My ride had given me an appetite. I ate my dinner with much enjoyment. Then I sat and read, and had tea, and soon after I went to bed, for at earliest dawn the next morning we were to strike the tents and to commence our second march.

It would be tedious to describe my tour day by day. I will, therefore, mention only such incidents as I think will prove interesting, and some of these, I should explain, occurred on former occasions, when in earlier years I had held office in this part of the country through which I am now proceeding.

We marched at first in the direction of the Ganges. We had crossed the canal, and were proceeding along its further bank to the northward, when there fell on our ears a murmuring sound, like the humming of insects. As we went on the sound grew louder, and presently it began to resemble that confused noise which arises from a great assembly of people ; but no such assembly was in sight, nor were there any large towns or villages in the neighbourhood. Both I and my servants were greatly puzzled.

Presently there appeared before us a grove of trees. We passed the grove, and the mystery of the noise stood revealed. About a mile away, on the other side of the canal, we beheld a collection of tents and booths, and around and among them a vast concourse of people. It was from this concourse that the murmuring sound proceeded.

The mystery of the noise thus explained, another enigma presented itself. What was the cause of the assemblage? No great fair was ever held in these parts; and yet what else could have ever drawn so many people together? While the servants were making all sorts of surmises we reached one of the many bridges that cross the canal. A small party of villagers were passing over it from the other side. We stopped, pointed to the crowd, and inquired its meaning. One of the party stepped forward and answered. He told us that a very wealthy banker had lately died in a town not far distant. By his will he had directed that a sum of one or two lacs of rupees should be bestowed in charity on the poor of the neighbourhood, and this spot, for some reason or other, had been selected as the place of distribution.

The man added that the whole country far and near had flocked in for a share, and, among the rest, himself and his companions. To their extreme disgust, the money was distributed, not in silver, as they had expected, but in copper, and that of coins of the very smallest value. He and his party had received not more than a few pennies altogether, a sum which, he exclaimed with much indignation, was not worth the trouble of the journey they had made to receive it.

This sort of almsgiving was common in former days, but under our rule it has fallen very much into disuse. It is certainly opposed to all our conceptions of beneficial charity, and no doubt it was often the result of mere ostentation or superstition. Still it tended to inculcate unselfish ideas regarding wealth and to promote kindly feelings between the rich and the poor, while not unfrequently the money was distributed from very pure and sincere feelings of religion.

I proceeded onwards to near the head of the canal. From there I retraced my steps, and, after marching for two or three days to the westward, I reached the margin of the great forest that stretches along the base of the Shewalic mountains; and here we halted for the night. Next morning after breakfast the tents were struck and laden, and sent on with the rest of the baggage, the horses, and servants. I strolled about and sat under a tree. Early in the afternoon I mounted my pony and followed. Our march lay through the forest, and our halting-place was to be at the foot of the mountains.

The first sight of this forest is a little disappointing. There is no silence, no gloom. The trees do not meet overhead; many of them are small: while, interspersed among them, there are frequent patches of brushwood or tall grass. The scene does not at all realize one's conceptions of a primeval forest. It rather suggests a gigantic copse.

I have been told by those who have seen them that the forests far to the east are much grander. The trees there are of enormous size. High aloft their branches interlace, and form a canopy of foliage—a canopy so thick, that through it even the rays of the Indian hot weather sun can but faintly penetrate. Above the forest there is dazzling sunshine; the burning wind sweeps by, carrying with it clouds of dust. Below there is gloom, half twilight, motionless air, and a silence broken only by the faint murmur of the wind that roars above.

In great contrast to those eastern forests was the forest through which I was now proceeding. There was plenty of sunlight, abundance of sound. The birds twittered, the insects hummed, and the tall grass and the leaves waved and rustled in the wind. Also I did not want for society, for the road along which I was travelling was the high-road to the Doon and Mussoorie, and carts, cattle, and foot-passengers were continually passing along it. Once or twice also I met camels.

For the first few miles I enjoyed the ride. The forest was a pleasant change from the monotonous aspect of the cultivated country I had left behind. But after a while the forest itself became wearisome. There were no streams, no glades, no habitations, for ever the same straight road, on either side the same scattered trees, and between them the same patches of tall, coarse grass and copse-like brushwood. The sameness of the scene was not either diversified by the appearance of any wild animals. The forest swarms with game of every description, yet in the day-time but few display themselves. Once a small deer trotted across the road, and further on I caught sight of three jackals; but as to the multitude of the other forest inhabitants, neither by sight nor sound did they give evidence of their existence.

It was a relief when at length I reached our encamping-ground. It was a small, open space not far from the entrance of the pass which leads through the mountains to the Doon. The carts and servants had already arrived, and the tents were being pitched, and the baggage unladen. There was still an hour or more of daylight remaining; so, to pass away the time, I strolled up to the dâk bungalow, that is, the small house erected by the Government for the accommodation of European travellers. In those days one such bungalow stood at the interval of a few miles along all the great roads in Upper India.

This bungalow was situated on a small, level spot on a spur of the mountain. It stood about eighty feet above our encamping-ground. The ascent to it was by an easy zigzag path. At the bungalow I met with an old acquaintance in the person of one of the two servants. I had known him for many years, first as a "bearer"—house attendant—in the service of an English family. He was then a Hindoo, meek and placid, and in demeanour very deferential. He had since embraced the Mahomedan faith, and both in manner and appearance he exhibited the influence of his new religion.

He had adopted of course the Mahomedan dress,

and with it, and in an exaggerated and rather an aggressive degree, the Mahomedan independent demeanour. Also he had grown a beard. The cause of his conversion was the usual one. He had formed an attachment to a Mahomedan young lady, not one, I am sorry to say, of the most irreproachable character, and being in consequence ejected from his own religion, he had no option but to embrace hers.

I had last seen him at the dâk bungalow in the open waste land that extends all along the margin of the forest. He was then, he informed me, very unhappy; the desolation of his surroundings utterly depressed him, and certainly the place was very lonesome and dreary. He added that he had applied to be transferred elsewhere. The result of his application was my finding him here; but in this case success had not brought contentment. At first, he said, he had liked the change, for he had arrived at the commencement of the hot season, when there were plenty of travellers. Now he rather regretted the waste. "That," as he expressed it, "was a jehunnum" (hell); "but this was a 'dobarah jehunnum'" (a double hell). At this time there were few or no travellers, and what troubled him more, in consequence, no perquisites; and, besides, at night he and his fellow-servant went in fear of their lives. All around there were bears, wolves, and hyenas, and lately they had heard a tiger; and, as if this was not enough, only three days ago a whole herd of wild elephants had crossed the mountain just behind the bungalow, and these having come, it was only likely that others would follow.

Now I knew that the herds of wild elephants did wander into the Doon, but then I had always understood that they made their way through the passes. It appeared to me utterly incredible that these enormous, clumsy creatures could climb mountains that it was difficult even for a man to ascend. My friend, however, insisted that he was speaking only the exact truth. The tracks of the elephants, he said, were still quite plain, and if I would accompany him he would take me at once and show them. I thought it rather too late to venture unarmed into the jungle, with so many wild animals about, and so I made an arrangement to visit the place with him the next morning. This matter settled, I had a chair brought and placed on the little terrace before the verandah, and sat down to contemplate the landscape.

The view was very striking. During the whole day's march we had ascended. The ascent was gentle, but it was continuous; it had conducted us to an elevation of many hundred feet above the place from whence we had started. Foreshortened by the distance, concealed by the higher trees, the patches of grass and brushwood were no longer visible. The mountains rose abruptly behind. Before me, so far as the eye could reach, there stretched one long, wide slope of verdant forest.

All along the horizon the forest was bounded by a yellow band of mingled dust and haze. As the day declined the yellow band assumed a purple tinge. Presently the sun disappeared within it, a deep red, glowing ball.

I remained a short time watching the sunset tints; then I rose and descended to the encamping-ground. So quickly in these latitudes does night succeed to day that by the time I reached the ground the short twilight was already beginning to fade. I found my tents now pitched; and during my absence several travellers had arrived, and also carts laden with goods and produce. Some had come from the Doon; others were on their way there. What with men, carts, and animals, the camping-ground presented a most cheerful appearance.

The cattle and ponies were reposing or eating their grain or fodder; the travellers were preparing their dinners. Each traveller or each small party cooked their dinner at a separate fire. As the darkness came on the multitude of these little fires had a most cheerful and pretty appearance; but I did not remain long to observe it, for my own dinner was now ready, and I was too hungry to delay going into the tent to enjoy it.

Dinner over, I had logs and brushwood collected outside, and a fire lighted; and then, well wrapped up, I left the tent and sat beside it, for here, with the mountains behind and the forest in front, and at an elevation of more than two thousand feet above the sea, the night was really cold. The glow of the fire soon attracted the servants, and before long some of the travellers as well. One by one they crept cautiously up, standing at a respectful distance; then, on my inviting them, they approached near, and sat down.

We had presently quite an assemblage round the

fire. Soon we began to converse. The situation suggested the subjects. We spoke of the inhabitants of the forest, and also of those of the mountains. I listened to tales of the elephants, the tigers, the bears, and the other many wild beasts, also to those of evil spirits and the fairies. The tales related were often very marvellous; but the time, the darkness, and the surroundings imparted to them a reality. The forest was in front, close behind us rose the mountains, and from both forest and mountains sounds continually fell on our ears which showed that the animals about which we were conversing were not far distant, also that they were awake and wandering around in search of prey.

Every now and then we heard the barking cry of the deer, the melancholy wailing yelp of the troops of jackals, and occasionally that most fear-inspiring of all the forest sounds, the dull roar of the tiger; and once we all paused in our talk to listen to a crashing among the trees that told us that a herd of elephants were passing, and were not very far distant.

The stories of the supernatural beings were, perhaps, the most exciting. To many of our assembly they were also the most alarming, for in the reality of their existence the natives are firm believers; and it is in the mountains that the fairies mostly reside. The Indian fairy, I may explain, unlike our English fairy, is of more than human stature, and though marvellously beautiful, is yet perfectly malignant.

We continued to chat till the fire sank low, and then

one by one the travellers retired. Most of the servants did the same; and I also, after sitting a little longer, entered my tent and went to bed. I was tired, and soon fell asleep, and slept that delicious sleep that is only in tents to be obtained, for though the canvas walls exclude the draughts, the pure, fresh air still for ever passes through them.

Our march next day was to be through a defile in the mountains into the valley of the Doon. As the march would be a long one, I breakfasted early. The meal over, the tents were struck, and the servants commenced to load the carts; and I, in fulfilment of my engagement, walked up to the bungalow to see the tracks of the elephants. I found the servant waiting to conduct me. Immediately behind the bungalow there projected a small spur of the mountain; a narrow footpath led round it. On reaching the other side I beheld, to my astonishment, plain and unmistakable, the tracks of evidently a large number of elephants.

The tracks extended from the base of the mountain to the summit of the spur, a height, I should say, of nearly three hundred feet. The slope was throughout extremely steep. Towards the summit it was indeed so steep that I could only ascend it on my hands and knees, and not unfrequently I had also to draw myself up by catching hold of the stems of the coarse grass and the brushwood.

The appearance of the track explained the mode by which the elephants had ascended. Where the soil was sandy there were numerous impressions of their feet; but generally the track presented only a tolerably smooth, bare surface, with the grass and brushwood crushed flat or torn away, much as if a large block of stone or a mass of timber had been dragged up the mountain. It was evident that the elephants must have knelt on the knees of their hind legs and worked themselves up the ascent, their bodies resting on the surface.

The smoothness of the track and the multitude of their droppings showed that many elephants must have passed, but as to how many the bungalow attendant could give me no information. Indeed, I do not think he had been in a position to observe, for I gathered that on first becoming aware of the approach of the herd he had made his way back to the bungalow with as much haste as he could, and I think that most other persons would have done the same.

The inspection of the elephant tracks had occupied some time. When I returned to the camping-ground I found that the carts and servants had already departed. I waited for an hour or two to let them get well on their way, and then I mounted my pony and followed. Just at the end of the encamping-ground there lay a wide expanse of bare sand, thickly strewn with stones and boulders. This sandy expanse is the entrance of the pass; I proceeded along it.

For some distance it continued tolerably wide and nearly straight. A succession of hollows along the centre marked the course of what in the rainy season was the bed of a torrent. In some of the hollows water still remained. For a mile or so the pass continued so wide and straight that the slope of forest beyond its entrance remained still visible. Then the pass narrowed and turned, and the forest became concealed by the spurs of the mountains. The scenery of the pass was for some time very interesting. But before I describe the pass I will give a short account of the range of mountains through which it leads.

These mountains, known among the English as the "Shewalic," issue from the Himalaya some ten miles or so to the eastward of the Ganges. They run for a short distance in a south-westerly direction, and then follow a course nearly parallel to the Himalayas to a point a little to the westward of the Jumna. There they spread and widen, and again reunite with the Himalaya. Although the Shewalic mountains appear to form a portion of the Himalaya, they are in reality entirely distinct. They are of a different geological formation, and are considered to be of far greater antiquity; also, as compared with the Himalaya, they are both in extent and in altitude altogether insignificant. Their entire length is not much more than a hundred miles, their average breadth does not exceed fifteen miles, while their highest peaks do not quite reach the elevation of three thousand two hundred feet above the level of the sea, and hardly that of a thousand feet above the plains that lie immediately below them. Between the Shewalic mountains and the Himalaya lies that valley of the Doon to which I am now proceeding.

The term Shewalic, as applied to these mountains, has only come into use among the English within quite recent times. It is a term altogether incorrect; properly it is the designation of the entire Himalaya, snowy and lower ranges and these mountains included, that lies to the westward of the Ganges. As such it is used invariably by the native historians, and was by the English themselves up to the early years of the present century. By the natives these mountains are termed the "Mountains of the Passes." They are so termed from the circumstance that it is through the passes among them that the roads run which lead to the Doon and Mussoorie.

The term Shewalic is stated by one of the native historians to be a combination of the two Hindee words "sewa" and "lâe," the word "sewa" signifying one and a quarter, and the word "lâe" being the term which expresses the number of one hundred thousand. The historian further states that the compounded word "Shewalic" has been used to designate the mountains of the Western Himalaya, from the belief that these mountains consisted of one and a quarter lae—that is, of one hundred and twenty-five thousand—separate peaks.

I may here mention that the name Himalaya is used equally incorrectly by the English, and indeed by all Europeans. The name signifies the "Necklace of Snow," and applies, strictly speaking, only to the highest line of mountains, on which the snow never melts, and not to the lower ranges.

The Shewalic mountains—I mean the range now

so designated by the English—are perhaps the wildest in the world. Although hardly more than hills in elevation, they display in miniature all the features of the grandest mountains. In passing through them one beholds an endless succession of sharp, towering peaks, nearly perpendicular precipices, and a very maze of little valleys; and during the season of the rains through each small valley there runs a little mountain torrent.

This singular appearance is the result of the geological formation. That formation is sandstone, and for the most part sandstone so soft as hardly to deserve the name of stone. Easily cut by the falling rain or running water, flaking off from exposure to the atmosphere, it has in the course of ages been moulded by the elements into its present fantastic forms.

After this brief description of these mountains, I will continue my account of my ride through them. For the first few miles, as I have said, the scenery was very interesting. It was especially so in contrast with the monotonous level of the plains through which I had been previously journeying. As I advanced the pass narrowed. On either side rose precipices; they were not very lofty, but almost absolutely perpendicular. Composed of bright yellow sandstone, their appearance was exceedingly picturesque. At short intervals tall peaks rose behind them, and also long, slanting ridges; and these ridges were often interspersed with small, grass-covered slopes or little patches of green forest. Occasionally these patches of forest consisted of fir trees, and their green was of the darkest hue. It formed the prettiest contrast to the bright yellow of the cliffs.

The cliffs themselves, too, were a source of constant interest. Composed always of the softest sandstone, they were frequently interspersed with rounded stones of a harder formation. These stones were of all sizes, from that of a cricket-ball to quite large boulders. Some few of the cliffs were so thickly interspersed with these stones as to suggest the idea of a gigantic currant cake, from which a perpendicular slice had been cut.

Occasionally the larger stones were not round, but long and narrow, and they projected from the face of the cliff exactly as might the tusks of some fossil elephant. The resemblance was so exact that on the first occasion when I traversed the pass I did really imagine, when I came in sight of these projecting stones, that they were fossil tusks. It was only on nearer approach that I became aware of my mistake.

Interesting, however, as the scenery was, after a time it became wearisome—always the same narrow valley, the same steep cliffs, and the same ridges and peaks rising behind them. The valley turned and wound, but each turn only disclosed a repetition of the same scenery. One longed to come on some open space, some stream or waterfall, some field, garden, or human habitation. It was a relief when at length, after a steep ascent, we reached the summit of the pass. Peaks and cliffs there vanished, and we commenced to descend through a long green slope of forest.

After a mile or two the forest ceased, and I beheld

stretched before me, broad and verdant, the beautiful valley of the Doon. Beyond it, bounding the horizon from east to west, like a vast unbroken wall, rose the Himalaya. Presently we came to the cultivated country; and there on the margin of a fallow field, and close adjacent to a small village, I found the carts unladen and the tents erected. The next morning I marched on to the little town of Dehra, where I remained for some few days.

CHAPTER XIII.

DEHRA

ALTHOUGH the town of Dehra is well known to the English in India, I imagine that but few persons in this country have ever heard of it or of the valley in which it is situated. A short description of both may, therefore, be interesting, and this will be a convenient opportunity for introducing it.

The Doon, or, to give it its full appellation, the "Dehra Doon," or "Valley of the Tent," is, as I have already stated, that tract of level ground which lies between the Himalaya mountains and that offshoot from them now known among the English as the Shewalic range. Across the eastern end of the valley flows the river Ganges, and across it, near to its western end, flows the Jumna. The space between these two rivers constitutes the Dehra Doon. The two small tracts beyond the rivers at either end go by other designations; but being mere uninhabited waste and forest, they do not call for any special mention or consideration.

The Dehra Doon is about fifty miles in length, and from twelve to fifteen in breadth. It contains an area of a little over four hundred thousand acres, of which, in my time, rather more than half were forest and jungle. The valley takes its name from its capital, the little town of Dehra, which is situated at about the centre of its length; and the town is so called because it was on a spot near adjacent to it that "Gooroo Nanuck," one of the founders of the Sikh religion, set up his "dehra," or tent, when, over two centuries ago, he sought refuge in the valley from the persecutions of the Mahomedans of the Punjaub.

The valley and a portion of the adjacent mountains came into the English possession at the conclusion of the Nepaulese war in 1818. The Nepaulese had themselves then only recently acquired it. The valley had previously formed a portion of the territories of the hill raja of Srinugger. The Doon, when it then came into our possession, was little more than a wilderness. What cultivation existed was confined to the immediate neighbourhood of Dehra and to a narrow strip extending along the centre of the valley to the westward. The villages were mere grass huts, and even Dehra, the capital, with the exception of the tomb of the Gooroo and the buildings attached to it, did not possess a single masonry structure. The Doon of to-day presents a different aspect, and one that speaks eloquently to the benefits of English domination.

In beauty or grandeur of scenery the Doon can bear no comparison with Cashmere. Still it is exceedingly pretty, especially all that part that surrounds its capital of Dehra. Embosomed in mountains, lying at an elevation of over two thousand feet above the sea, it possesses a climate in which the vegetation of the tropics and some of that of the temperate regions can equally flourish. Rice, sugarcane, wheat, and red pepper are cultivated in the fields, while the rose and the white raspberry grow wild in the hedges. The mango tree attains a height and girth unknown elsewhere; and on the slopes of the mountains are to be found the walnut tree and the wild apricot. In the spring-time the fields near the forests are literally carpeted with a flower much resembling the English primrose, but larger and of a richer and more brilliant yellow.

The town of Dehra is ideally pretty. The grass huts of former days have given place to the neatest of houses. Many of them are gaily painted, and most are coated with the beautiful white Indian chunam. A canal of mountain water flows along the principal street, falling at intervals in miniature cascades. On the east of the town there extends a grove of mango trees, reputed to be the most extensive in Upper India; it is said to have consisted originally of no less than a tenth of a million of trees, and on that account is known as the "Lâci Bagh," or grove of one hundred thousand; but of the correctness of this tradition I was always a little doubtful.

Within the town itself there is a smaller grove; it surrounds the tomb of his Holiness the Gooroo Nanuck. The white dome of the tomb, rising above the trees, contrasts most pleasingly with their deep green foliage. Close adjoining the town, on the north, are the cantonments and the English station, with its white houses and pretty gardens, and beyond them, like a protecting rampart, rises the long line of the Lower Himalaya.

The especial charm of the town is its smallness and extreme neatness. Both the town and environs, the houses, the streets and canal, the parade ground, and the English gardens and residences have something of the prettiness of a miniature or a model. The impression of smallness is heightened by the vastness of the mountains beneath which the little town seems to nestle for protection.

Bright and pretty as are the houses of Dehra, there is only one building in the town that has any pretension to architectural beauty, and this one building is the tomb of Gooroo; it is a building of no great size, and of the ordinary form of Indian mausoleum; that is, it consists of a square block placed on a terrace and surmounted by a dome. The block contains a single vaulted chamber, and on the pavement of the chamber rests the monument beneath which the ashes of the saint repose. In the plains of India the building would attract but little attention, but situated in this secluded valley, it becomes an object of interest; also, being surrounded only by the smallest of edifices, it gives to the beholder by contrast a certain impression of size and grandeur.

The first time that I visited the tomb was many years ago, when I was in charge of the Doon. The garden that surrounds the tomb is enclosed by a high brick wall; the principal gateway faces the east, but there is a small doorway on the northern side: this doorway opens on a bare, dusty space where native travellers usually put up. One day near noon I happened to be crossing this tract; it was at the end of the cold season, and the rays of the sun at midday were becoming powerful. Though protected by a thickly wadded umbrella, I found them unpleasantly warm; also there happened to be a rather large concourse of travellers. The open space was crowded with men, carts, and animals, and there was much dust and noise.

As I passed the doorway, I noticed the trees that rose above the wall. In contrast to the dusty camping-ground, they looked invitingly green and shady. I had often intended to visit the tomb; I now resolved to do so. One of the attendants of the garden was standing by; he opened the door, and I entered. As I did so, I seemed to have passed into another region: the glare, the heat, the dust, were left behind, and the noises without only fell on the ear as a gentle murmur. The branches of the trees met overhead; their foliage formed a green canopy: the sunbeams passing through it diffused only a soft, misty light. Here and there, through some opening, there shone a stronger ray which illumined the thousand motes that floated in the air.

Accompanied by the attendant, I passed along a straight raised path; it presently brought us to an open space. In the centre of the space, raised on a broad, high terrace, stood the tomb; it was a pretty building, coated with beautiful white chunam, that quite glistened in the sunshine, and much of the surface was gaily decorated with paintings representing conventional foliage and geometrical designs.

On the terrace, cross-legged, sat three of the priests of the shrine. Two of them were motionless as statues; the third had a large volume lying open on his lap. From it he was reading; he read in a sort of chant, and as he read he swayed his body backwards and forwards as if to give emphasis to his words; he read in a droning tone, but the sound fell on the ear with a cadence not unmusical; so also did the humming of some bees that were lazily flitting in the sunlight. The shady trees, the pretty building, the chanting of the priest, and the humming of the bees seemed all in harmony; they suggested a place designed for contemplation and repose. The impression of the tomb and the garden that I then received I have always since retained.

The tomb occupies the centre of the garden, which is square. Around the tomb, but near the four angles of the garden, are four smaller tombs, tombs, indeed, so small, that they are mere cupolas. These four tombs are those of the four wives of the Gooroo Nanuck. Three of them are decorated with paintings; the fourth is simply overlaid with white chunam. This last tomb is that of the Gooroo's chief wife. According to tradition, it was left undecorated by her own express injunctions, and as a mark of her widowhood, white being in the East the colour of mourning. For the same reason, the tradition also relates that after the death of her husband, the Gooroo, she abandoned the use of jewels and wore no coloured garments.

This cupola, though small, and possessing no especial architectural beauty, is interesting on another account.

It illustrates, and in a most curious manner, the singular effects sometimes occasioned by earthquakes. On the occurrence of the great earthquake that took place in Upper India towards the close of the last century, this cupola was cracked completely through horizontally; and not only was it thus cracked through, but the part of the tomb above the crack was also twisted round, and that to the extent, if I remember correctly, of nearly half a yard. It is not easy to understand by what succession of movements of the ground this result could have been effected, nor why the movements that thus split this cupola should have left the other three cupolas and also the tomb of the Gooroo entirely unaffected.

The tomb of the Gooroo, like many other of the Indian mausoleums, is a shrine as well as a place of sepulture; services are performed in it daily at various hours: they consist in the reciting of prayers, the ringing of bells, and the reading aloud of the "Grunth," or sacred book of the Sikh religion. It was from this volume that the priest was reading, as I have above described, on the occasion of my first visit. If I remember aright, the services also include the offering of flowers and the burning of incense.

The services appeared to me to be very scantily attended; often there was no worshipper beyond the priest himself: but then I ought to add that it was but very rarely that I happened to be in the garden at the times when the services were going on. Once each year, however, at the commencement of the hot season, a religious fair is held; and then the pilgrims and worshippers flock in by thousands, most of them coming from the Punjaub.

Having described the tomb of the Gooroo, it remains to say a few words regarding the small monastic establishment to the members of which the custody of the tomb is confided; but this I will reserve to a later occasion. I will now give an account of what then was regarded as the most interesting of the sights of Dehra, namely the Government tea plantations. They were situated about a mile from the town of Dehra, on the other side of a large watercourse, one of a kind nearly peculiar to the Doon, and there known by the designation of "roas." For the greater part of the year these "roas" are mere deep dry gullies or wide expanses of sand and rounded stones. Along the centre of some of the broadest, perhaps a tiny stream may trickle; but during the rainy season, when a storm occurs in the mountains, then presently the roas become each a raging torrent.

I shall presently give some further account of the "roas," but just now I will proceed on to the tea plantations, and will conduct with me in imagination the reader as well.

The plantations—I am describing them as they then existed—were very large, extending over an area of several hundred acres; they were also exceedingly pretty, so pretty, indeed, that they always seemed to almost realize one's childish conception of fairyland. There were fruit trees of all kinds, green lawns, hedges of aloes and hedges covered with roses, beds full of the gayest of flowers, long, low white buildings that glistened in the sunshine, and everywhere small canals and water-courses, through which flowed the clear, sparkling water of some mountain torrent. Furthermore, to complete the resemblance, not far away, though out of sight, ran a little river, in whose sandy bed were mingled grains of gold. I did not on the present occasion encamp in the plantations, but many years ago, when in charge of the Doon, I had once done so; and I look back to that time as one of the pleasantest of all my Indian life. The climate was so delicious, the scenery so charming, no wind, no dust, no unpleasant heat or glare, always bright sunshine and a clear blue sky.

The superintendent of the plantation was absent, and had allowed us to occupy his bungalow; our camp was pitched on the lawn before it. The lawn was very spacious, and was dotted over with mango trees, the remnants of what at some former time had been an extensive grove. These trees were of great age and of enormous size; the largest of all stood near the centre of the lawn, and in the afternoons we used often to sit and have our tea beneath it. I had the trunk of this tree carefully measured; the measurement was made a good yard from the ground, and well above the projections of the roots: the circumference of the tree was there more than twenty-two feet. From thence the trunk rose in a clear unbroken column to the height of about twenty-five or thirty feet, when it threw out in all directions its massive branches. The branches and foliage formed a wide, spreading canopy, through which neither sunshine nor any but the most long-continued rain could penetrate.

This mango tree was the largest I ever beheld. In the adjacent groves, however, there were many that in girth and spread of branches were but little inferior. One I especially remember. It grew in a field about a mile distant; its trunk, well above the projections of the roots, measured some inches over eighteen feet in circumference; and it towered up without curve or bend, almost as straight as a pine, to the height of near forty feet, I should say, before it threw out a single branch.

Of all the Indian trees the mango as it here appears is beyond compare the most beautiful. Its form is so graceful, its bark so smooth and clean, and the green of its foliage so deep and rich. In the early spring the beauty of the foliage is enhanced by its variety of tint, for while the matured leaves are of the darkest green, the young leaves just expanding are in colour of a reddish brown. The contrast of colour, perfectly harmonious, is most charming. I should add, however, that it is only in the Doon that the mango tree is seen in this perfection. The mango tree in the plains is, both in size and beauty, much inferior, though still, there as here, the queen of the groves.

Although the mango tree is so characteristic of India, and is found everywhere in such profusion, I have always been assured by the natives that it is not indigenous to the soil, at least of Hindostan, and also that it never here grows wild, and that of all the millions of mango trees now existing each one has been separately planted.

I may explain, for the benefit of the reader, that

the large mango tree of the groves, the tree that I have been describing, is quite distinct from the small mango tree of the gardens, which bears the celebrated fruit. This last, the fruit tree, is a grafted tree, and does not exceed in size the lemon or orange tree. The large mango tree of the groves also bears a fruit, but it is one of a very inferior description — small and suffused with a flavour resembling turpentine. Though to a European taste almost uneatable, the fruit is much appreciated by the poorer classes of natives, so much so, that the sale of the fruit yields a considerable income to the proprietors of the larger groves.

But to return to my stay at the plantations.

Most pleasantly the time went by. In the early morning we rode or walked; in the day I had my office work; towards sunset we strolled about the gardens or sat on the lawn. The view was one which I was never weary of contemplating. Behind us rose the great wall of the Himalaya; before us lay the valley, just then an expanse of ripening crops, prettily dotted over with groves of trees and small villages; beyond, and bounding the horizon, stretched the long green forest slope that led up to the Shewalics. It was behind the slope that the sun set; but for long after the sun had set for us he continued to shine on the Himalaya. Slowly, gradually, the shadows crept up the mountains, so slowly that the highest peaks still glowed with ruddy light when all the valley around us was wrapped in twilight gloom. With the dark the air grew cold. We left the lawn for the bungalow, dined, and spent the evening by a fire of blazing logs.

It was when thus encamped in the plantation that I made acquaintance with the tea-plant, and witnessed the process by which its leaves are prepared. Some account of the plant, of its leaves, and the mode of their preparation may perhaps be interesting to the reader. The tea-plant is one of the prettiest of shrubs. The stem and branches are so smooth and clean, the leaves so green and glossy; and then in the spring-time it bears a delicate white flower, something resembling a miniature camellia. If allowed to do so, the plant will grow to a height of ten or twelve feet; and there were several of this size then in the plantation, but these formed separate clumps, and were kept for seed or for ornament. The ordinary plants, those whose leaves were to be made into tea, were kept by clipping to a size not much exceeding that of gooseberry bushes.

The leaves were picked in the spring, that is towards the end of the cold season. The picking occupied a period of some weeks, and while it lasted the plantation presented a scene of the busiest activity. The leaf-pickers, I may mention, were mostly women, and they were employed by hundreds, certainly by many scores and scores. The leaves were picked in succession, according to their size and age, for on the age and size of the leaf depended the quality of the tea it would produce: the finest tea was that prepared from the youngest, and consequently the smallest, leaves; the coarsest tea was that made from the leaves which were the oldest and largest. After a certain age and size the leaves were no longer fit for manufacture at all.

Between the finest and coarsest qualities there were several gradations. All were indicated by different Chinese-sounding designations. The coarsest and most inferior tea, that prepared from the largest leaves, was the Congo; the tea of the first excellence, made from the very youngest and smallest leaves, was that termed "fine Souchong." As the leaves were picked they were carried away in baskets to the factories, those long white buildings I have already alluded to. There they were piled in great heaps on the floors, each quality of leaf having a heap or heaps of its own. The leaves being now picked and piled in heaps, next followed the operation of drying, or, as it was technically termed, of "firing," them. The operation was thus conducted.

Down each side of the long building was a row of small, square masonry structures. They were built close against the wall, a few feet apart from each other, and, with their flat tops, they had much the appearance of altars. A large iron bowl was let into the surface of each, and in the recess below was a fire that heated it. Into these iron bowls the leaves were emptied, and allowed to remain till perfectly dry, all the while being constantly moved and stirred by an attendant with a long, thin iron rod. When the drying was completed the leaves had assumed that curled, shrivelled appearance with which all drinkers of tea are familiar.

The process of the drying seemed to the last degree simple and easy; nevertheless I was told that it required for its proper performance much experience, skill, and also a certain amount of manual dexterity, besides extreme care and attention. If the firing was too quick or too slow, or too long continued, or in any point defective, then, however excellent the leaf, the flavour of the tea would prove defective.

When the plantations were first established the operation of "firing" was performed only by Chinese, who had been brought from China for the purpose. It was now, at the time I am describing, done almost entirely by natives of India, whom the Chinese had instructed. A little of the "firing" was, however, still conducted by Chinese, and then as they bent over the bowls in their long robes and quaint-looking caps, slowly stirring the leaves with the thin iron rods, they had much the aspect of necromancers in the act of performing incantations.

I used often to stroll into the factories when the preparation of the tea was going on, and in the course of my visits I learnt the answer to a question that in former days used to be much debated in England. It was whether black and green tea were produced from the leaves of the same or of different plants. I learnt that the leaves are the same. The difference in the teas is the result of the difference of preparation. The black tea leaves are simply fired; those of the green tea are previously damped and allowed to slightly ferment.

When the firing was completed the tea was carried to another building and there stored; it was subsequently packed in tin cases and boxes of various sizes. The boxes were covered with yellow paper, ornamented with characters and designs of Chinese appearance.

The tea when packed was kept in store for three years before it was disposed of, for till that period had expired it was not considered to be fit for consumption.

Having described the process of "firing" the tea, I must say a few words regarding the bowls in which it was conducted. They were always pointed out to visitors as great curiosities, for, though made of cast-iron, they had all the appearance of being formed of the finest beaten copper; they were equally thin and delicate, and with surfaces similarly smooth and even. They were imported from China, for neither in India, nor even in England, was the secret of their manufacture understood.

The plantations had been established, and were carried on, by the Government, not for profit, but with the object of introducing the cultivation of tea among the natives of the Doon, and elsewhere where the climate was favourable. The establishments were consequently conducted with a liberality and at an expense which for private firms would have been hardly possible. The result was the production of a tea not now, I imagine, easily attainable. The tea when made much resembled that described by former travellers as made especially in China for the Emperor and the highest nobles.

In colour it was a pale yellow, and when poured out diffused all around a most agreeable aroma. I must add, however, that till one had become accustomed to it the flavour to an English taste was not agreeable. The tea was also extremely dear. The price at the plantations for the very finest qualities was as much as three and a half rupees, equivalent then to seven shillings a pound.

The endeavours of the Government to introduce the tea cultivation among the natives, though long continued, proved entirely unavailing. The inducements held out were extremely liberal. The Government offered to supply seed to all who would accept it, and that without charge, and also to purchase the leaves at a fair price when the plants were grown, and themselves manufacture the tea, but all in vain. The natives of the Doon and the surrounding hills had no religious or caste objection to the cultivation, but it was new, and it would involve trouble; and the profit, they thought, might not be sufficient to compensate them for the trouble. So they preferred to continue to till their lands as had their fathers before them, to sow the same seeds and to gather in the same harvests.

Some few of the larger landowners accepted the seed that the Government offered, but they did so merely as an act of deference and respect. They had no intention whatever of seriously undertaking the cultivation; they planted the seed so carelessly that much of it never came up, and that which did they so neglected that the young plants all sooner or later withered and died. Others—but this was in the hills further to the east—ensured the failure of the cultivation in a simpler and surer manner: before planting the seeds they previously boiled them.

I endeavoured to overcome their objections by showing them that tea would grow on the waste lands, where there was at present only coarse grass and brushwood.

With this object I had three or four small patches of land cleared and dug up in different places on the slopes of the hills, and in these I had tea seeds planted. As far as the tea was concerned, the experiment was a great success. The seeds all came up, and not only that, but they produced plants so strong and healthy as to call forth the high approbation of the superintendent of the plantations. But the success of the experiment had no influence on the landowners.

They possessed hundreds and thousands of acres of such waste land, but they preferred that it should remain waste sooner than they should have the trouble of planting it with tea. The Indian tea cultivation, now so extensive, owes its development entirely to European energy.

But though the natives would not cultivate tea, they were very partial to drinking it, especially the Mahomedans. When I left India a large portion of the tea produced in the Doon was purchased by native merchants, and exported to the Punjaub and Cashmere. The tea most preferred was the green.

I have mentioned that the road from the town of Dehra to the plantations crosses the bed of one of those singular watercourses termed raos. Of these raos I will now continue my account.

The base of the Himalayas for the entire length of the Doon is everywhere broken by recesses. Many of these recesses are the openings of what may be termed valleys or gorges, running high up the mountain-side: others are little more than mere indentations; but at the mouth of every recess—whether it be valley, gorge, or mere indentation—there is a "rao," and the size and form of the "rao" is always in proportion to the smallness or magnitude of the recess.

The raos at the mouths of the valleys and larger gorges are wide and shallow, and along them a stream trickles, or even a small river flows. On the other hand, the raos before the mere indentations are deep and narrow, and, except after a fall of rain in the mountains, their beds are dry.

At the immediate base of the mountains the small raos are very numerous; I should say—speaking, however, merely from memory—that one occurs at a distance of every two or three hundred yards. These smaller raos, however, rapidly unite, and eventually merge into the larger raos; and these larger raos, after traversing the slope of the valley, merge into the beds of the rivers which flow along the length of the Doon to east and west, and empty their waters into the Ganges and the Jumna.

The narrow raos, though usually dry, occasionally, especially during the rainy season, carry along an immense body of water, for after a storm in the mountains the rain that has fallen on miles and miles of steep hillside is suddenly poured into the rao at the base; and owing to the slope of the land, this volume of water is borne along with extreme force and rapidity. Dashing alternately from side to side, it eventually cuts portions of the banks away; these narrow raos are in consequence continually widening.

They widen in a singular manner: the torrents do not so much cut away the banks as undermine them.

The first indication of the undermining is the appearance of a crack in the ground on the side of the rao. The crack is sometimes quite close to the edge; occasionally it appears at a distance of several yards; but, whether near or distant, the crack generally runs more or less parallel to the bank. The appearance of the crack is followed by a slight subsidence of the ground between it and the rao; the subsidence increases; eventually the whole mass of soil slides into the rao and is swept away by the torrent. Owing to the nature of the ground, the new bank is nearly always precipitous. The area of the soil thus carried away is not generally of any great extent. I have, however, known of cases where it must have amounted to nearly half an acre.

As this process goes on continuously, it follows that in course of ages the present surface of the slope of the Doon at the base of the Himalayas will be entirely swept away; but the ground below the present surface is composed of coarse gravel, sand, and boulder-stones. It may take centuries before these, after disintegration by the elements, become capable of supporting a vegetation. During this long period, in place of the present verdant forests, there will appear only a dreary expanse of sterile, stony desert.

I have spoken of the violence of the torrents that at times sweep through these raos and of the suddenness with which they descend. Of their suddenness and violence I will give two examples.

Once during the rainy season, at the time when I had charge of the Doon, I set off one afternoon to visit a village some few miles from Dehra. As the road lay partly through a forest, I went on an elephant. Presently I came to a rao; it was deep, and had precipitous sides, but was tolerably wide; it was also nearly dry. I crossed it, visited the village, and returned. About an hour and a half had elapsed when on my way back I reached the rao; but in the meantime there had been a heavy downpour of rain in the mountains. I found the rao now half filled with water; the water was at least five feet deep, and was flowing with a force that only an elephant could have withstood.

The other case was even more remarkable; it occurred in the rao I have already mentioned as lying between Dehra and the tea plantations. Lower down this rao widens considerably, to the extent, I should say, of over a quarter of a mile. At this part the high-road from Dehra to the Jumna crosses the rao. Now it happened one morning during the rainy season that a small covered cart drawn by two bullocks was proceeding along the road over the rao; inside the cart were a woman and a child. When the cart entered it the rao was nearly dry, but before the cart reached the other side a rush of water from the mountains came down. The cart was overturned, and, with its occupants and the two bullocks and their driver, it was swept away and carried down the rao for the distance of about half a mile, and there left stranded as the flood rushed on. The driver, the two bullocks, and the woman and child were all drowned.

After these examples of the violence of the torrents in the Doon during the rains, I will give an illustration of the rapid growth of vegetation during the same season. Towards the end of the cold weather one year we were encamped by a village not far from the tea plantations. Our camp was pitched on a smooth tract of ground close adjoining to a small strip of forest. Not more than four or five months afterwards, in the course of the ensuing rains, I had occasion to pass the spot. To my astonishment, I found that what had so lately been all open space was now a tall, thick copse, so tall and thick that, had I not been mounted on an elephant, I should have been hardly able to pass through it.

CHAPTER XIV.

THE DOON

WHILE encamped in the plantation I was waited on by all the chief inhabitants of Dehra. As in duty bound, they called at intervals to pay their respects. Among the rest who presented themselves was the "mohunt," the head of the little monastic establishment founded by the Gooroo Nanuck, and to whom the care and custody of his tomb had been confided.

The mohunt paid his first visit in state, and with all observance of the prescribed etiquette. He sent notice the previous day of his intention to call, received my permission to do so, and then at the hour appointed he arrived on his elephant, accompanied by his confidential priest and one or two other attendants. His next visit was less ceremonious. But before I describe the visit or the events which occasioned it I must give a short account of the mohunt himself and the establishment over which he presided.

The society consisted of about twenty monks, but there may have been more. At the head of them, of course, was the mohunt. Next to him in rank and authority was his heir apparent. The heir apparent, like the mohunt, had a designation, but what it was

I do not remember. There were four other officials of inferior dignity who also bore the title of mohunt; the remainder were ordinary priests. The fraternity did not reside together. The mohunt had a rather fine dwelling, close adjacent to the garden of the tomb. The rest lived where they pleased in the city. Their houses, however, mostly belonged to the establishment, and were passed on, as each monk died, to his successor.

The religious calm that had so impressed me at the tomb did not extend to its guardians. The community was full of quarrel and dissension. Want of discipline was partly the cause, but chiefly the distribution of the revenues. The mohunt was rich, at least as riches were then regarded in the Doon; and so in a less degree was the heir apparent. The four lower officials were in just comfortable circumstances; the rest of the monks were poor, many of them in absolute indigence. This state of things naturally caused discontent, and the more so because it was not believed to be in accordance with the intentions of the founder.

In a Christian monastery any monk may hope to be abbot, but by these monks no such expectation could be indulged in. The mohunt was succeeded by the heir apparent, and the heir apparent was chosen when a lad from the outside, something in the manner as is the Grand Lama of Thibet. The rules for the selection were never explained to me; the area for it was wide. The then mohunt was a native of some village in the Himalaya beyond Mussoorie. The heir apparent had been brought from the further confines of the Punjaub.

The revenues of the monastery were derived partly from lands bequeathed by the Gooroo, but principally from the offerings made by the pilgrims at the great annual fair. This fair was held at the end of the cold season, and was attended by many thousands of persons, chiefly from the Punjaub. All who came made an offering, and those who were rich offered largely. The amount received must have been considerable. I have heard it estimated, when the attendance was exceptionally large, at a lac of rupees; but this was a mere guess, for it was a subject on which both the mohunt and his subordinates maintained an extreme reticence.

The mohunt was a man of about sixty years of age. He was very homely in appearance, quite illiterate, and, notwithstanding his sacerdotal position, not in the least devotional. The spiritual concerns of the monastery he left to the priests; the secular affairs he mostly allowed the heir apparent to manage. Although on bad terms with his monks, he was greatly liked by the people in general. Indeed, in his amiability and extreme simplicity of character there was something very attractive even to Europeans.

The heir apparent was less popular. He was better educated than the mohunt, but not in the least more spiritual. He was said—rather an inappropriate occupation for a priest—to carry on privately a money-lending concern, and as the interest he charged was high, and he was rigorous in exacting it, the belief did not add to his popularity. He had at one time also acquired the reputation of being too gay; but the attendance of the pilgrims, and with it the amount of the offerings, falling off in consequence, he had since conducted himself with more decorum. He was then about thirty years of age, and, in the Sikh style, very good-looking.

The mohunt, the heir apparent, and the other members of the fraternity all wore a peculiar-looking head-dress. It was a tall, conical cap, in shape much resembling an extinguisher, and having, in like manner, round the base a similar raised border. The cap worn by the mohunt was of the same shape as the rest, but was distinguished by its superior materials and its ornamentations of gold embroidery. The mohunt also wore on his wrists a very massive pair of solid gold bangles. The rest of his attire was extremely plain, and also, cap included, not a little shabby. The gold bangles had descended to him from his predecessors, and judging from its appearance, so, I think, must have the cap as well. The gold embroidery was black with age, and the material beneath dirty and faded to the last degree. I often, but unsuccessfully, endeavoured to persuade him to provide himself with a new head-dress. At length, as I shall subsequently relate, I had one prepared myself, and presented to him as a mark of my regard.

The disputes in the monastery had been going on for years. Now, at the time I was encamped in the plantation, they arrived at a crisis, and it was this that caused the mohunt to pay me the second and unannounced visit. It was not long after breakfast; I was in my office-room, when a servant came in and informed me that the mohunt had arrived, and that he had arrived on foot, and desired to see me on a matter of great importance. The servant had hardly finished speaking when the mohunt entered. He entered leaning on the arm of his confidential priest, and followed by an attendant.

The mohunt's countenance wore an expression of much distress. The priest and the attendant conducted him to a chair. Sighing deeply, he sank on it, and then by a motion of his hand he signified to the priest to address me. On this the priest, standing by the chair, commenced a most elaborate and complicated narrative. The narrative was rendered the more complicated by the mohunt's many interruptions and suggestions. In the end, and only after considerable questioning, I made out the following story.

There was a dispute between the mohunt and one of his monks as to the ownership of a house in the town, one of those houses that belonged to the monastery. The mohunt had gone that morning to claim the rent or to perform some other act that would indicate possession. The monk presently followed for a similar purpose. As a matter of course, an altercation ensued; other monks and some bystanders joined in. Both sides became excited. The monk had a stick in his hand; he raised it and struck the mohunt a violent blow with it on the side of his head. The mohunt had come to me for redress.

At this point of the narrative the mohunt directed towards me an appealing look; his eyes filled with tears, and with one hand he slightly raised his cap. As he did so, the priest pointed out the place where the stick had alighted, and called my attention to the bruise and swelling which had resulted.

I consoled the mohunt as best I could, and suggested that he might prosecute the priest, or sue him for damages; and then, as his return on foot was hardly consistent with his dignity, I had him conveyed home in my own palanquin, and accompanied by a becoming escort of my own guards and attendants.

After much hesitation—for natives of position dislike extremely entering the criminal courts—the mohunt decided to prosecute, and, the case being proved, the monk was punished. His punishment had the effect of procuring for the mohunt a little more outward deference from his subordinates; but the dissensions and ill-feeling continued the same as before. It was at this time, and as a sort of consolation, that I presented the mohunt with the new cap.

When completed it proved exceedingly handsome; the materials were of the best, and I had taken especial pains that the embroidery should be worked with thread of real gold. Before ordering the cap, I obtained from the mohunt an assurance that he would wear it, and this assurance he carried out: he wore the cap so long as he lived, and after his death it descended with the gold bangles to his successor, the then heir apparent. Some years afterwards, when I had long left the Doon, I received a visit from him when I was staying at Mussoorie. He had on his wrists the gold bangles, and on his head, the brilliancy of its embroidery a little softened by time, I recognized the cap I had presented to his predecessor.

I will conclude my account of the monastery by remarking that, though Gooroo Nanuck was himself the husband of four wives, neither the mohunts, his successors, nor the monks who represented his disciples were permitted any. This obligation to celibacy was, however, from all I heard, but very lightly regarded.

Having now described the tea plantations, the town of Dehra, and the monastery, I will give a short account of the Doon itself, and first of its history. Of this, previous to the arrival of Gooroo Nanuck, next to nothing authentic is known. It has been supposed by some Indian archæologists that a great city once stood within the Doon near the banks of the Jumna. The idea is based on the statements of a Chinese traveller who visited India about the period of the Christian era, but as to its correctness I am very incredulous. There are no traditions of such a city, nor any remains, nor any indications whatever of its having ever existed.

On the further side of the river there is, however, a curious relic of remote antiquity; it is a large boulder stone, completely covered with inscriptions. The stone is of roundish shape, and of considerable size, some six or seven feet perhaps in diameter; it lies not very far from the river, in a tract of ground covered with stones and drift and overgrown with jungle. The inscriptions are in some unknown character; in appearance they something resemble those on the column of Feroze

Shah at Delhi. Nothing is known of the history of the boulder, nor is there any tradition as to when, why, or by whom the inscriptions on it were engraved.

Although there is no tradition of the former existence of any large city in the Doon, there is a universal belief among its inhabitants that the valley was at one time much more thickly populated than it is at present. The tales related are manifest exaggerations; whether there is any fragment of truth underlying them I cannot say.

Since the time of Gooroo Nanuck the Doon has had a recorded history, but it is a history very eventless. Cut off by the forests and mountains from the world beyond, the inhabitants passed their days in a sleepy calm; the seasons came, the seasons went; the villagers sowed their crops and reaped their harvests: only the annual fair broke the monotony of their lives. Two centuries thus passed away, and then came the Nepaulese invasion. The story of the invasion, as I had heard it, always impressed me as full of romance. The Nepaulese army burst suddenly into the valley of Sreenugger. Driven from his capital, the Raja, Shudershun Suhai, took refuge in the Doon; there he collected his scattered troops, fought another battle, sustained another defeat. Accompanied by a few horsemen, followed by the enemy, he made his way along the valley to one of the western passes; through this he escaped, and reached the English territory. Then followed long years of dreary exile, embittered by penury and for ever disappointed hopes; in the end, unexpected restoration to his dominions and a remaining life of wealth and prosperity.

But afterwards, when marching among the villages, I arrived at one where I was told that a very aged man resided who had witnessed all these events, and would be able to describe them. I sent for the old man, and, with a good deal of questioning, obtained his story. I am sorry to say that, if correct, it took from mine much of its poetry. The Raja, he said, left Sreenugger as soon as he learnt that the Nepaulese were approaching it. When he reached the Doon he summoned all the villagers; none of them wanted to go, but some did, and he among them. When the Nepaulese appeared they ran away. There was some fighting, but very little, and he did not know that the Raja took any part in it; he went away quite leisurely, and nobody pursued him. But perhaps the old man's account was as much too prosaic as in my fancy the events had been overcoloured.

The old man's recollections went back well into the last century, but he could tell me very little that was interesting; his memory was almost entirely occupied with petty events that had occurred in his own and the neighbouring villages. I asked him when he first heard of the English. "Oh, that was when he was very young; they were then far away down at Benares." Then I inquired what he had heard about them. The answer was unexpected and amusing. "People said," he replied, "that their horses had no tails, nor their swords any handles." The tailless horses were, of course, the closely docked ones of that day; and the swords, I imagine, must have been the dress swords then worn, whose handles had no guards.

The old man went on to tell about the first Europeans he had seen, and here he grew animated, and his recollections were really interesting. Once, he said, when he was a very young man, a Mahratta army suddenly entered the Doon through one of the western passes; they marched on to near Dehra, and there they encamped. In the camp there were two European children; they were very fair, and had long light, curling hair; they were so pretty that all the villagers far and near flocked in to see them, and brought pieces of sugarcane to give them. He went among the rest. The Mahratta army remained encamped for some days, and then it left as suddenly as it had entered. Why it came and where it went to he did not know, neither could he tell me to whom the two children belonged.

But to return to my history. The Nepaulese, or, as they were then more generally termed, the Goorkhas, held possession of the Doon for some years; then, in the same manner as they had driven out the Raja of Sreenugger, so were they in turn driven out by the English, but not without a struggle. The English army was commanded by Sir Rollo Gillespie, a most gallant soldier, and regarded also as a capable general. A little to the eastward of the town of Dehra a long, low spur of hill runs out from the Himalaya. On the extremity of this hill the Goorkhas had erected a fort. When the English army entered the Doon into this fort the Goorkhas retired. Sir Rollo Gillespie advanced to attack it.

The attack on Kalunga—for so this fort was named—

was in former days an event very celebrated in the annals of our Indian wars; it is now almost entirely forgotten. A very brief account of it may therefore, perhaps, prove interesting. I describe the occurrences as I have heard them narrated by officers who had themselves been present and taken part in them.

It was arranged by Sir Rollo that the fort should be attacked at the same time by three different divisions and at three different points. The signal for the attack was to be the firing of a gun, and the gun was to be fired from the head of the division which Sir Rollo himself was to lead. The time fixed for the attack was the early morning. The morning dawned, the gun was fired, and Sir Rollo's division commenced to move, but it seemed doubtful if the other divisions had heard the report of the gun; it turned out that they had not. Sir Rollo was entreated to fire a second gun and meanwhile to delay his own advance. He would do neither.

His division, headed by English soldiers, moved on unsupported. There was other mismanagement. On reaching the fort the troops found themselves in front of a wall which they had no means of ascending; there they stood exposed to the fire of the Goorkhas above, and this fire from their position they were unable to return. I was told that, in their rage and despair, the soldiers beat at the wall with the butts of their muskets and dug their bayonets into it between the joining of the stones. It was a position where courage could avail nothing. There was no course save to retreat; but before the retreat was ordered many had fallen, and among them Sir Rollo himself. He fell shot dead by a ball from a matchlock.

A second attack was arranged, but in the meantime a discovery was made which rendered it unnecessary. There was no spring or well within the fort. The Goorkhas depended for their supply of water on a stream at some little distance without; the stream was conveyed to the fort by a small channel cut in the hill-side; this channel was accidentally found, and the stream diverted. Without a supply of water the fort was untenable. In the course of the night the Goorkhas abandoned it; in the morning the fort was found empty, and the Goorkhas in full retreat and already far away among the mountains.

The English officers and soldiers who fell in the attack on the fort were buried in the plain before it. The white monuments erected over their graves can be seen from some of the houses at Dehra. Connected with these graves there is related a rather ghastly story. The dead were buried hastily and without coffins, wrapped only in their cotton quilted bed coverlets. In the hurry their graves were dug none too deep. A few days after it was noticed that the ground all around the graves was strewed over with small white fragments. An examination was made, and it was then discovered that some animals had burrowed down to the bottom of one of the shallow graves, had dragged up the corpse or portions of it, and devoured them. The white fragments that had attracted attention were those of the cotton wool of the coverlet in which the body had been wrapped. The animals were a species of badger, styled among Europeans, from its habits, as the gravedigger.

Sir Rollo Gillespie was a man of extreme courage, and also of unusual bodily strength. Of his courage and strength I have either heard or read the following story. At some fair in Bengal a tiger that was being exhibited had escaped from its cage. There was wild confusion. Sir Rollo happened to be present. He was riding an Arab horse, which he had trained to perfectly obey him; he had in his hand a spear—one of those short-handled, exceedingly sharp-bladed spears used in wild boar hunting. The tiger lay crouched on the ground; Sir Rollo rode up and made his horse leap over it. As the horse rose in his leap Sir Rollo dug down his spear, and with such force that the tiger rolled over dead, pierced through and through.

CHAPTER XV.

THE DOON CONTINUED

THE war with Nepaul, like most mountain wars, was long and tedious. It ended in the defeat of the Nepaulese, and the territory they had recently acquired in the Himalayas passed under the English rule. The greater part was restored to the various rajas whom the Nepaulese had driven out; but some portions our Government retained in its own immediate possession, and among these was the Doon, that first range of the Himalayas which bounds it on the north, and also a small mountain tract which has always been connected with the Doon, and which lies just beyond the Jumna to the west.

The climate on this first range of the Himalayas approaches in coolness to that of England. It is singular, therefore, that, though so easily accessible, these mountains remained for fully ten years in our possession before any English thought of resorting to them for either health or relaxation. The reason, I have heard, was this. The mountains of Central India, covered with wood and jungle, were known to be deadly unhealthy. It was supposed that these mountains, similarly forest-clad, would be the same; the discovery that they were not was due, so I have been told, to the potato.

The Doon was then under charge of the colonel who commanded the regiment at Dehra. The colonel was an Irishman, and fond of potatoes. He had received some of superior quality, and was considering where to plant them. Some men from the hills were present. They recommended the upper part of the range, for all about there, they said, the potatoes grew remarkably well. The colonel ascended the range to select a spot, and there he found a climate so cool and delightful that he remained and erected a house. His example was followed, and the stations of Landour and Mussoorie presently arose.

The potato at first flourished extremely well in the Himalaya; but it afterwards underwent a curious change. Its shape from oval became long and irregular, and its skin thick, dark, and rough, and its taste slightly sweetish. In short, it appeared as if it was approximating towards that native root termed by Europeans the "yam," or sweet potato. It was remarkable that no such change occurred among the potatoes cultivated in the plains. On the contrary, they gradually improved very much, both in size and quality.

The introduction of the potato has been one of the many benefits which our rule has conferred on India; but it is a benefit that at first it was by no means certain that the Hindoo part of the population would accept. The potato was new; doubts were entertained if it would be lawful to eat it. To determine the point, so I have been informed, a conference of Brahmins was assembled, and, fortunately for the country, after much debate a decision was given in favour of the potato. The turnip, introduced about the same time, was less successful. As an article of food its use was prohibited; and yet for what reason, in all my long residence in India, I never met a Hindoo who could inform me, or indeed who was himself aware.

The potato has certainly only come into use among the natives of India under our rule. It is curious, therefore, that it should be mentioned by Terry, the chaplain to the embassy sent by our James I. to the Emperor Jehangire. Terry was present at a dinner given to the Ambassador, Sir Thomas Roe, by the then Prime Minister, Asof Khan, brother to the celebrated Lady Noor Jehan. Terry describes the various dishes that appeared rather elaborately, and among others he mentions potatoes, and he remarks that they were exceedingly well cooked. Possibly Terry mistook for the potato that somewhat similar-tasting root, the "yam."

Hindoo prejudices suggest Hindoo customs. And this leads me to mention a very singular custom that here prevails, not in the Doon itself, but in that small mountain tract which, as I have mentioned, is attached to the Doon, and lies beyond the Jumna. I first became aware of the custom when I was encamped just at the base of the mountains, and was holding a trial. A witness in the case mentioned his father. The writer who was recording his deposition inquired, "Which father?" The witness replied, "My eldest father." Seeing my look of surprise, the head of the office then explained. He informed me that in that region the brothers of a family have among them but one wife. The woman whom the eldest brother marries becomes also the wife of the other brothers, and the children who may be born regard all the brothers as equally their fathers, distinguishing them according to their age, as thus: eldest, second, or other father.

This custom of "polyandrism," as it is termed, prevails in other parts of the Himalaya, also, I believe, in some places in Southern India; and it is supposed to have prevailed in past ages even in Europe. Many theories have been advanced to account for the existence of the custom in these mountains and elsewhere in the Himalaya, but none of these theories are satisfactory, for they leave altogether unexplained one remarkable fact. It is this. The custom prevails only in small isolated tracts such as this, but it is utterly unknown in all the extensive regions by which these small tracts are surrounded, and yet the populations where the custom exists, and where it does not, are of the same race, of the same religion, and live under precisely the same conditions of life.

It might be supposed that the custom, to our ideas so repellent, would have a deteriorating moral effect on the people among whom it prevailed; but, so far as I saw and heard, this did not appear to me to be the case. The people of this small tract were not more criminal, nor, so far as I could ascertain, in any way inferior, either in behaviour or in character, to the populations around them.

The existence of this and of other dissimilar marriage customs in the same country, and among practically the same people, afforded a curious spectacle, and one that suggested many reflections. We had, though this was afterwards, a nurse for our little girl; she was a woman from these mountains. She was quiet and modest in manner, by her fellow-servants well thought of; yet she had five husbands, and all were brothers. The head of my guard was a Mahomedan, a man of excellent character, much esteemed, but he had four wives. Then among the office establishment there was a native Christian, to whom but one wife was permissible.

Here then in this small territory, among people of the same race, and living under the same general laws, there were on this subject of marriage three different codes of morality prevailing, and codes not only of morality, but of law. That which in the case of one person was innocent, consistent both with self-respect and public esteem, was in the case of another person sinful, reprehensible, even by law criminally punishable.

Having described the custom, I will say a few words regarding the small mountain tract in which the custom prevails. The scenery of this tract is no way remarkable. Like nearly all the rest of the Lower Himalaya, it consists of long, winding ridges, rising into peaks or eminences, and separated by deep, narrow valleys. Two of these eminences, however, are worthy of notice. One is the mountain of Daobun, or "Wood of the Gods"; the other, of lower elevation, is that of Bârât.

The mountain of Daobun is really beautiful. It rises to a height of about ten thousand feet, and it is clothed with forests to its very topmost crest. It has also, what is very rare in the Lower Himalaya, precipices of limestone. Nearly perpendicular, and standing on either side of a narrow gorge, these cliffs tower upwards above the forest like gigantic gateways, with an aspect of extreme grandeur.

On the northern slope of the mountain, a little below the summit, there is a broad, deep dyke. It is artificial, and has been quarried out of the rocky soil. The tradition is, that it was excavated to hold the frozen snow which in former days the raja of the region had, during the hot season, to send to Delhi to cool the water and sherbet of the Emperor. The tradition is scarcely one to be accepted. Carried on men's shoulders, the snow would hardly have reached the plains unmelted, let alone the long journey to Delhi beyond.

The mountain of Bârât possesses no beauty; it is noticeable only on account of the ruins of a fortress that crown its summit. The ruins are insignificant, but they are interesting as being almost the only example of a fortress so situated in all this region of the Himalaya. I may add also that from the summit of this mountain is to be obtained a distant view of the plains of the Punjaub.

It remains to make a brief mention of the capital of this small region; it is situated in the Doon below, not in the Dehra Doon, but in that prolongation of the valley which lies to the west of the Jumna. There, not far from the river, the little town, hardly more than a village, stands picturesquely nestled below the mountains, with forests all around; it is itself almost hidden among groves of mango trees, planted by the ancestors of its present inhabitants. Lying low, surrounded by vegetation, it is during the rainy season extremely unhealthy, indeed, a very abode of fever, but during the cold season the climate is pleasant enough, by day bright warm sunshine, at night sufficiently cold to make sitting round a fire of logs outside the tent very agreeable.

The enjoyment of the fire is, however, a good deal interfered with by a wind which soon after nightfall commences to blow down the valley of the Jumna. This wind, termed by the natives the "dadhoo," is one of the peculiarities of the Himalaya; it occurs at the mouths of all the larger valleys, those that lead up toward the snow; it is thus accounted for: after sunset the air of the higher portion of the valleys becomes chilled, and becoming in consequence also heavier, it sweeps downwards to the plains.

At night are heard the usual forest cries, but mostly the bark-like call of the deer and occasionally that sweetest of all the forest sounds, the note of the night-hawk; this, heard only in the mountains, resembles nothing so much as the sound of a musical glass or the softest of bells. It is uttered once, and presently replied to, then after the interval of a minute again repeated, and so continued the livelong night. The note is sweet in itself, and heard among the mountains, it seems to express all the wildness and poetry of its surroundings.

The forests round here have also by day-time a special charm, at least at this season of the year. A creeper grows among them, now in flower, and the flower exhales a scent faintly resembling that of honey. For miles around the atmosphere is laden with the perfume.

I have mentioned the mango groves; they are very extensive, so extensive, indeed, as almost to form forests. Though rather monotonous, they are still pleasant to stroll among, especially towards sunset, when the light streams soft and mellow through the canopy of foliage. One of the groves raises sad recollections. Scattered about it are small white buildings, something resembling those diminutive temples which the Hindoos often erect near wells or beneath some adjacent tree; but these small edifices are solid, and are not temples, but memorials, and memorials of sacrifice. Each marks the spot where in former days some widow was immolated on the funeral pyre of her deceased husband, in other words where a suttee was performed.

The number of these memorial edifices astonished me, for the population of the town is but scanty, and its foundation does not date back much above a century and a half.

Everyone has heard of the practice of suttee, but very few Europeans even in India are aware that the practice was not confined to the Hindoos, but to some extent prevailed also among the Indian Mahomedans. On this point the histories leave no doubt. The Emperor Jehangire, in his memoirs, records that in the course of one of his progresses he came on a town or place where a Mahomedan wife had been thus immolated at the funeral of her husband. The Emperor expresses his horror and indignation at the proceeding; his indignation was the greater on account of the extreme youth of the victim. The wife who was thus sacrificed was, the Emperor learnt, of no more than twelve years of age.

The incident caused the Emperor to make further inquiries, and he ascertained, to his surprise and further indignation, that the practice of suttee prevailed among the Mahomedans in various other localities.

The Emperor issued edicts prohibiting the practice among Mahomedans under the severest penalties; but, nevertheless, the practice appears to have continued; it continued, indeed, till within less than half a century of the commencement of our rule, for it is stated in the histories that at the funeral of the celebrated Syud Abdoolah at Delhi, about the year 1725 of our era, several of his wives were burnt to do him honour. Now Abdoolah, as a syud, or descendant of the Prophet, was among Mahomedans an object of religious veneration; and, moreover, he held the very highest secular rank, for he and his brother, under the title of ministers, had been for some years the actual rulers of the empire.

I have spoken of the grandeur of the line of the Himalaya as seen from the Doon, and the enormous height to which the mountains appear to rise. I will conclude this chapter with some further observations on the subject. The impression of the height of the mountains is the most striking when they come suddenly into view, as, for example, at some opening in the forests or some bend in a ravine; then the higher peaks seem to pierce the very firmament.

The mountains, however, convey this impression of extreme elevation only in the day-time. When seen at night, even at the distance of a few miles, they appear to rise but very little above the horizon, so little that when encamped on the further side of the Doon I have had, even in the brightest moonlight night, great difficulty in distinguishing them at all.

This contrast between the apparent elevation of the mountains when seen by day and by night is very singular. I think that it may be thus explained: the mountains, although so lofty, do not in reality rise more than a very few degrees above the horizon; they consequently conceal only a narrow strip of the lower zone of the sky, but it is to this lower zone that during the day-time our eyes are almost entirely directed, for in the day-time we seldom gaze except on the surface of the ground and on objects that rise but slightly above it. Seeing, therefore, that the mountains do conceal a very appreciable amount of this lower zone of sky on which we gaze, we forget how narrow, as compared with the entire firmament, this lower zone really is, and hence we form an exaggerated conception of the altitude of the mountains.

But at night these conditions are reversed. Our gaze is then chiefly directed towards the zenith; we look almost entirely on the moon or stars. In order to observe the mountains, we have to direct our eyes downwards, and, in doing so, to traverse with our gaze the whole expanse of the firmament; then, when at length the mountains come into view, we perceive how insignificant is the space they occupy in comparison to the expanse above them. Moreover, small as the space they occupy actually is, it appears to be even smaller, for, owing to the indistinctness of the light, the line of horizon is but vaguely defined. Much, consequently, of the lower portions of the mountains appears merged in the surface of the ground.

While on the subject of the mountains, I will mention another optical illusion connected with them, which is still more singular, and also less easy to explain.

The plains immediately below the outer ranges of the Himalaya slope upwards, and at a considerable angle; nevertheless the impression conveyed to the traveller approaching the mountains, always provided that he is mounted, either riding or driving, is that he is descending. This impression is the strongest when the road is straight and is bordered by trees.

The first time that I witnessed this illusion was in approaching the line of mountains around Nynee Tal. The road was straight; it ran through the forest in a direct line towards the mountains. I was not then aware of the illusion, nor of the upward slope of the ground. Judging from appearances, I was under the impression that the road descended, and, moreover, that the descent was steep.

Presently we came to a little stream; it flowed along the margin of the road. To my amazement, the water was running towards us, racing and foaming, so it seemed, up the steep incline. So perfect was the illusion that, though my companion informed me that it was such, it was not till I had dismounted that I could altogether dispel it. Then, on walking a short distance, the exertion which the ascent demanded convinced me of its reality.

CHAPTER XVI.

TIGERS, LEOPARDS, AND BEARS

THE Doon, as I have said, swarms with wild animals. I have spoken of them generally; I will now describe some of the best known a little more in detail, and first that most masterful and dreaded of all, that lord of the forests, the tiger.

Tigers abound in the Doon; nevertheless, except by sportsmen who search for them, they are but very rarely seen. I myself, though I marched much about the valley, never saw even one. But once, though I did not see him, a tiger paid me a visit; that is to say, in the course of the night he came and remained some time just on the edge of my camp. It was the cold season; we were in tents, and the tents were pitched close adjacent to a large patch of tall, coarse grass, and immediately beyond the grass was a wide ravine, full of jungle. It was about ten o'clock. We were all in bed; I was falling asleep, when there burst on my ears a very babel of noise. The horses were neighing and stamping, the elephant was trumpeting, and the servants were running about shouting and vociferating in the wildest confusion; and mingled with the other sounds came the screams of some creature in agony, and at intervals accompanying the screams there was a deep, muffled roar.

There was such a turmoil that it was some time before I could ascertain what had happened. Then I learnt that a tiger had entered the patch of coarse grass, had caught a wild hog, and was devouring it. The screams continued for some time, but growing fainter and fainter. Presently they ceased, as did also the muffled roars; at the same time the horses became quiet, and the elephant stopped his trumpeting. We concluded from this that the tiger had finished his meal and had departed.

The next morning the patch of grass was examined. In an open space among the clumps of grass we found a large wild hog lying dead; one hind leg had been completely devoured, and the blood apparently also sucked out of the rest of the body. After this I was careful never to encamp near patches of this tall grass, nor adjacent to a wooded ravine.

The reason that tigers are so rarely seen is that they mostly pass the day in slumber and in the recesses of the forest and grass jungles. Occasionally, however, they do wander abroad, and then they are sometimes met with. A gentleman I knew had once this experience. It was in the Shewalics. He was driving through one of the western passes, on his way to Mussoorie. At a turn in the pass, to his consternation, he beheld a tiger; it was on the other side, some little way in advance, and walking leisurely onwards in the same direction as himself.

After a moment's hesitation he decided to drive on in

the chance of passing it; but his vehicle was an old one, and the wheels rattled loudly. The tiger heard, stopped, and turned round. There were some seconds of extreme anxiety, then relief; for the tiger, either alarmed at the appearance of the vehicle or at the noise of its wheels, turned again, broke into a trot, and disappeared in an adjacent gorge.

The tigers do not confine themselves entirely to the forests and jungles at the base of the Himalaya. They occasionally wander up the valleys, even, it is said, as far as the snowy range.

The Government at that time gave a reward for the killing of the more dangerous wild animals, such as tigers, leopards, and bears. Before the reward could be claimed the skin of the animal had to be shown me. In the course of my residence in the Doon, in this way a great number of tiger skins were brought before me, and I learnt some things regarding them which perhaps may interest the reader.

The skins of the young tigers are by far the handsomest: the fur is longer, softer, and thicker, and the colours deeper and richer. With advancing age the colours grow paler, and the fur shorter and less close. By the appearance of a skin the age of the tiger can thus be roughly guessed, also the season of the year in which it was killed, for under the intense sunlight of the hot weather the colours, especially the yellow, more or less become lighter and less brilliant. The skins of the old male tigers are generally much marked with scars, the results of the wounds received in their many combats.

Most of the tigers whose skins were brought in had been shot from platforms built on the branches of trees, or from behind a barricade of some kind or other; but in some instances they had been shot in the most sportsmanlike manner by a hunter on foot, and with no other protection than his own firearm. One such case I especially remember. An elderly man, a hunter, or, to use the native term, "a shikaree," by profession, came to me with two skins; one skin was that of a tiger, the other that of a bear. He stated that he had shot them the day before in the forest, and he brought them to show and so claim the reward. In reply to my inquiries, he described to me the whole adventure.

He had heard of a tiger, and gone out in search of it; he found it, and shot it dead. He had just reloaded, when he heard a crashing among the trees behind; he turned and saw a bear coming towards him. The situation was alarming, but the man kept his presence of mind; he waited till the bear was quite near, and then fired and shot it, as he had the tiger also, dead.

Now, considering that the man was old, and that he had no better weapon than a matchlock, the feat was certainly a remarkable one. From the inquiries I made, I satisfied myself that the man's story was true, and the two skins also bore testimony to its correctness, for they showed that each animal had been killed by a single bullet.

The bear of the Doon is certainly small, but still for a man it is a most deadly antagonist; and, moreover, unlike the tiger, there is no escaping it, for it can not only run, and run fast, but it can also climb trees, and that with perfect facility.

The skin of this tiger, though not large, was the handsomest I ever saw, for the tiger was young, and the skin most beautifully marked; and, moreover, it had been shot in the cold weather. It was so handsome that I had it prepared, and subsequently brought it with me home to England.

The tigers in India, like the wolves formerly in this country, are the wild beasts the most often introduced into legends and fairy tales, and with which the most superstitions are associated. Among others they are supposed occasionally to be animated by sentiments of religion. I have seen pictures where they are represented as standing in attitudes of reverence around a fakir performing austerities, and there is a belief that occasionally they will sweep with their tails at night the terraces on which devotees of especial sanctity sit and meditate during the day.

Such influence over tigers is mostly attributed to the devotees of past ages; but I remember hearing of a devotee in quite recent times who thought he possessed it, and, with disastrous results to himself, attempted to exercise it. The affair occurred in a station where I once held office, but it occurred some years previously. One of the English officials, in the course of a shooting expedition, captured a quite young tiger—a mere cub. He brought it home and kept it. It was playful at first; then, as it grew larger, it became dangerous, and had to be placed in a cage. It was nearly full grown when the devotee, in the course of his wanderings, arrived at the station, or rather at the city near which the station was situated. He was practising an austerity, and was pledged to maintain absolute silence for a certain number of years. He heard of the tiger, and made it understood that he would proceed to its cage, put in his arm, and stroke it with impunity.

A great crowd accompanied him. The devotee, very confident, advanced to the cage and thrust in his arm between the bars, and then uttered a piercing yell; for, as might have been expected, the tiger, when he saw the arm, immediately seized it. Somehow or other the devotee was rescued, but with his arm terribly lacerated, and also with his reputation for sanctity entirely ruined. Moreover, he had lost all the benefit of his long austerity, for by his screams and other exclamations his vow of silence had been violated.

Tigers, chained or in cages, used formerly to be often kept by wealthy natives and at the native courts, and in a manner that we should consider very insecure. I remember even now my astonishment on coming on a tiger thus kept in one of the streets of Lucknow; it was on the occasion of my first visit, some years before the annexation. The gentleman with whom I was staying drove me through the city one afternoon. In the course of the drive we turned suddenly from a rather narrow lane into the principal thoroughfare; there was a crowd, and we had to wait till it had passed. While thus waiting I happened to look round, and there close beside me, lying on a low wooden platform, I saw an enormous tiger; he lay half asleep, with his head resting on his paws. He was secured only by an iron chain attached to the wall behind, and fastened to an iron collar round his neck.

All along the edge of the platform men were seated, chatting, smoking, or resting, and apparently perfectly indifferent to the huge creature so near them. I suppose they were safe; but it seemed to me as if by a sudden bound and stretch of his forearm the tiger might either break his chain or reach some of the men who were nearest him. A little further on in the street we passed another tiger similarly chained on a platform, and with a whole row of men similarly sitting along the edge. Possibly there may have been more tigers on other platforms elsewhere.

But I suppose that in no court in India were so many tigers maintained, or allowed so much liberty, as in the court of the Emperor Jehangire, the cotemporary of our James I. According to native tradition, the Emperor possessed supernatural influence over wild animals, which rendered them incapable of harming him. The King of Persia, so the story goes, heard a report of this and sent an ambassador to ascertain if it was correct; the ambassador when presented found the Emperor seated on his throne stroking and petting two great tigers, and the tigers as gentle to him and submissive as if they had been puppies or kittens. Astonished at the sight, he informed his master that the report he had heard was more than true. "This Emperor of Hindostan," he wrote, "exercises not sovereignty, but godship."

The native tradition, at least so far as the presence

of the tigers at the Emperor's court is concerned, is confirmed by the accounts of the English travellers of the period. Hawkins, who was two years at Agra in attendance at the court, speaks of fifteen young lions which used to roam about the palace "and hurt no one." But he adds that the Emperor, whom he describes as horribly cruel, used occasionally to make some of his soldiers wrestle with them, and then the case was different. The soldier who wrestled with the lion was of course torn in pieces.

Terry, who afterwards visited the court when at Ajmere as chaplain to Sir Thomas Roe, the ambassador sent by King James, speaks also of the wild animals at the palace, especially of a "very great lion" that used to walk among the crowds "as gentle as a dog, harming no one." Terry states, however, that he was always accompanied by a number of keepers.

I should explain here that these early travellers applied the term "lion" indifferently both to the real Indian lion and also to that much more powerful animal the tiger. We may conclude, therefore, according to native traditio that the animals they speak of as lions were really tigers.

All who have seen tigers, even in menageries, must have been struck with their activity and grace of movement; but it is only when observed free in the forests and jungles that one becomes aware of their enormous strength. A tiger, so I have often been assured, will crush in the head of a bullock with a single blow of his forearm, and will carry at full speed up the side of a mountain in his jaws the body of any cattle he may have seized and killed.

The tiger being an animal so fierce, active, and powerful, it may be supposed that of all sports tiger-shooting must be one of the most exciting and dangerous. As ordinarily it used to be practised in large parties, and on elephants, it was really one of the tamest and safest, so safe that accidents were of the rarest occurrence. I remember, however, one very sad one. As it happened in the Doon, and as its incidents were very singular, I will relate them.

A young officer at Dehra heard of a tiger in one of the neighbouring forests. He went out on an elephant in search of it; he took with him only his soldier-servant, a Goorkha. The elephant was not trained for shooting, and it carried no howdah, but only a pad. The tiger was found; the officer fired and hit it. The tiger, mortally wounded, crawled under a tree and there fell. The elephant was urged towards it; being untrained, on coming near the tiger it took fright and became unmanageable. To save themselves, the officer and his servant seized hold of a branch of the tree that stretched above them as the elephant rushed off into the forest.

The Goorkha servant, light, active, and loosely clad, swung himself up and sat astride on the branch. The officer, heavier and encumbered by his tighter-fitting dress, was unable to do so, notwithstanding all the efforts of his servant to assist him. He had to remain suspended, holding on by his hands alone. The situation must have been terrible, for the tiger lay below him still alive, and he felt his own strength failing. Presently the grip of his hands relaxed, and he fell. He felt too much shaken to move, and had his leg within reach of the tiger's jaws. The tiger had just sufficient life remaining to enable him to seize the leg and crunch it. The officer was rescued, and eventually recovered, but it was with the loss of his limb. What made the case sadder was that he was remarkably handsome and a soldier of much promise. The event occurred long before I had charge of the Doon, but at a time when I happened to be at Mussoorie on leave. I tell the story as I then heard it.

I will conclude my account of the tigers by the correction of a very prevalent error in regard to some of them. It is commonly supposed, especially in this country, that the tigers termed "man-eaters" are tigers of unusual ferocity. It is quite otherwise. They are tigers whose strength and activity have become diminished by age. Unable to catch the deer and wild animals, as before, they approach the villages and prey on the sheep and cattle or, if they happen to meet with any, on the human inhabitants; and this they continue to do when opportunity offers, not from any special partiality for the flesh of man, but because it happens to be easily obtainable.

Having said so much on the tigers, I ought not to leave unmentioned their near but less imposing relations, the leopards. Although smaller and weaker, the leopards are far more numerous than are the tigers, and they are also more frequently met with. When travelling through the forests I have many times seen them crossing the road before me, occasionally alone, more often two together. They much infest the lower ranges of the Himalaya. They do not, like the tigers, confine themselves to the valleys; they wander up the mountains as high as the forests extend. Though far inferior in size and strength to the tiger, the leopard excels the tiger in agility and grace of movement. Of the agility of the leopard I once saw a striking instance. It was at Mussoorie. I was walking one afternoon along a road that led round a thickly wooded hill. Suddenly a deer leaped out of the wood, crossed the road, and descended the hill on the other side. I was a little surprised, as deer were rarely seen so near the station. Almost immediately after I heard a noise in the trees above. The sound came from behind me. I turned, and saw a leopard spring out of the wood. It gave one leap on to the road, then bounded over the railing, and went headlong down the mountain-side, and at racing speed.

Now the mountain there was extremely steep, as steep, indeed, as it could be for trees to grow on it. A man could not have safely descended it save on hands and knees, and clinging to the grass and underwood; and yet the leopard, far heavier, tore down at full gallop. Nothing but the most extreme agility could have prevented him from rolling over and over to the bottom, or being dashed against the trees.

Leopards when young can be tamed; but as they grow older they are apt to become dangerous. I have heard of them being kept as pets. One was so kept at the Lucknow Residency some years before the annexation. My brother happened at the time to be there on a visit. He told me that the leopard used to wander at will all over the house; it was as tame as a dog, and would let anyone stroke it, though not everyone cared to do so. It was, however, a great terror to strangers who came on it unexpectedly.

There was a story about this leopard, or some other that succeeded it, that it eventually became savage and was killed. I tell the story as I have heard it, without, however, vouching for its correctness. Indeed, of that I entertain some doubt. The story, certainly sufficiently exciting, is as follows:—

A gentleman, a visitor at the Residency, was lying asleep in the morning. His right arm hung slightly over the bedside. He awoke with a feeling of pain, and, to his horror, saw the leopard beside him and licking the back of his hand. The leopard's rough tongue had scraped the skin and drawn blood. The gentleman attempted to pull away his hand; the leopard growled. The gentleman repeated the attempt; there was another growl, and louder and fiercer. It was early morning; there was no one near to give assistance, and yet if no assistance came the position of the gentleman seemed desperate, for, with the taste of blood, the animal would soon get maddened and tear him to pieces. But the gentleman remembered that he had a loaded pistol beneath his pillow. He cautiously drew it out with his left hand, placed the mouth of the barrel to the leopard's skull, and fired. The leopard fell dead, and he was saved.

I will follow this story by another, which in contrast

will, I fear, appear exceedingly tame, but of the truth of which I can vouch. A young officer at a station where I once was had a pet leopard. It was very gentle still; when it got big it was thought more prudent to have it kept chained. The chain was a strong one, but, nevertheless, in a few days the leopard broke it, wandered about, killed a few fowls, and was then recovered and brought home and secured by a chain still stronger. This too he presently broke, and, if I remember right, a third one also. How he did so was a mystery. It was at length solved. It was not the result of any desire of the leopard to escape, but merely the consequence of his incessant activity. Except when eating or sleeping, he was for ever pacing round and round and backwards and forwards. The chain by these movements got at length knotted and twisted into the rigidity of a bar, and at some moment snapped with the leverage of the leopard's strength and weight pressing against its further end.

The tigers and leopards are the natural inhabitants of the Doon and its forests; the bears may be regarded rather as visitors or immigrants, for their proper home is the Himalaya. They are small, that is, for bears. In size they do not very much exceed a well-grown English sheep, and their fur, though very long, is not particularly thick. It is black in colour, with generally a patch of white on the chest.

Notwithstanding, however, their small size, the bears in the Himalaya are far more dreaded than even the tigers. I once asked a villager the reason. He thus explained it. The tiger, he said, if he attacks a man, kills him; but these bears—and here he applied to them a most insulting epithet—if they meet a man, will mutilate and leave him. Of the truth of this statement I soon after had a sad illustration. I met a villager being led by another. He seemed ill, and one side of his face was concealed by a cloth. I inquired what was the matter. In reply he lifted the cloth, and displayed a terrible spectacle. The entire face, eye, cheek, and skin, was gone. Nothing remained but one great half-healed scar.

He had gone to cut wood in the forest above his village. There a bear attacked him. These bears of the Himalaya, I should mention, do not hug, as the bears of Europe are said to do; they bite, or they rise on their hind legs and strike with their forepaw. This bear did so. He rose, and with his front paw struck the man on the head. The claws tore away the face. How the man escaped I forget; I suppose that either the bear left him, or that he had companions that drove it off.

During the hot season the bears mostly reside in the valleys and on the lower slopes of the mountains. As the cold weather approaches they ascend to the summits, and there for the winter they remain. They come up to feed on certain fruits and berries that they then find in the higher forests. The bears that come near Mussoorie occasionally enter the station; at least, in my time they did. They not only entered the station, but, when the fancy took them, they would visit the houses. Their visits were usually paid at night, and mostly to houses that were empty—of which at that season there was always plenty, for during the winter Mussoorie was nearly deserted.

The bears would, however, also prowl round houses in which there were residents; and of this I once had experience. It was in the month of February. I was at Mussoorie on leave; I occupied a house near the extreme end of the station, very lonely, and with woods all around. It must have been near midnight; I was in bed and asleep. I was awakened by a noise in the verandah, a heavy, shuffling sound accompanied by a grunting snuffle. Not a little to my dismay, I recognized the grunt as that of a bear; and then, still more to my dismay, I became aware that there was not only one bear, but two, and further that one of the two was pushing against the door.

I now became really alarmed. I had no gun by me, and the servants were all on the other side of the house; and, moreover, if the bears wanted to enter, I was very sure that the door would not prevent them. I was considering what to do, when, much to my relief, the bears moved off. But it was only as far as the other door. There in a minute or two I again heard their grunting and shuffling; but it soon ceased, and as it did not recommence, I presumed that the bears had finally departed, and I fell again asleep.

In the morning I discovered that as to the final departure of the bears I had been mistaken. On leaving my door they had continued their prowl round the house till they discovered the larder. The door of this they smashed open; that done, they entered, and devoured a cheese.

These Himalayan bears, if caught young, are easily tamed, but afterwards, like the leopards, they are not to be trusted. I once had two given me. One of them was still half a cub, the other nearly full grown. They were very tame and very amusing. I used often to have them brought into the house and let them play about the garden. They were especially fond of climbing the trees, and once up, it was a great business to get them down again. They were perfectly quiet, and never attempted to bite, not even the dogs who sometimes used to run after them; they were never, however, allowed to go altogether loose. When brought into the house or let play in the garden, the man who looked after them always accompanied them. The largest of the two he also generally led, except, of course, when it was permitted to climb a tree. I had these two bears for nearly a year, then I was transferred to a distant station, and as I could not very well take the bears with me, I presented them to a native landowner, who had often expressed his desire to possess them.

After discussing these grander creatures, the bear and the tiger, it may seem superfluous to speak of the wolves. I do so, however, on account of a curious superstition, or rather belief, which prevails in India regarding them. I shall presently mention it. There are wolves in the Doon and in the neighbouring wastes and forests; but in comparison with the other larger and fiercer wild animals they attract but little attention. In the plains it is different. The wolves there are nearly the only beasts of prey, and in the parts where they are numerous they are regarded with great terror.

They seldom attack adults, either women or men, but they frequently carry off children.

Early in my service I was subordinate magistrate at Etawah, a district not far from Agra. In parts of that district, along the banks of the river Chumbul, there are very extensive ravines. They form a perfect labyrinth over many miles of country. In these ravines the wolves abounded. They were not much seen in the day, but at night they roamed abroad, prowled about the villages, and if they found a door open would enter and bear off a child. It is so long ago that I may exaggerate, but I think that hardly a week passed without some such case being reported.

Now it was the belief of the natives that in some rare instances the child thus seized was not devoured, but was brought up by some she-wolf with her own offspring. The belief was not confined to that district, but was universal; it was entertained even by some Europeans: that is, they accepted as reliable the statements that from time to time appeared of the discovery of children that wolves had thus brought up.

Some years after, when I was magistrate of Muttra, the discovery of such a child was reported; it was a boy. He had been found wandering, if I remember aright, near some ravines. When found, he was perfectly unclothed, and though apparently at least twelve years old, he was unable to utter any articulate sound. The villagers who had discovered the boy had taken him to the nearest police-station, describing him as a "wolf-child," and the police as such forwarded him on to me.

His arrival caused the greatest excitement; whole crowds from the city flocked out to behold him; the excitement penetrated even to the zenanas. At the special request of the wealthiest resident in the city, the boy was conducted to his house, in order that his wives and the other females of his family might see him.

Now, through the police, I made the fullest investigation into the matter; nevertheless as to who the boy was, where he came from, or who had brought him, I could discover nothing. But for the statement that he had been brought up among the wolves there was not the smallest foundation; it arose merely from the love of the marvellous, the inability of the boy to speak, his very animal expression of countenance, and the mystery of his sudden appearance. The simple facts were that the boy was an idiot, that most probably he belonged to some party of vagrants, and for some reason or other had been deserted by them when passing through the district. I have little doubt that the other tales of "wolf-children," if we could investigate them, would be found equally unreliable.

Although at various times I have been much in the neighbourhood of wolves, I never but once beheld one—I mean free in the jungle. The occasion was this: I was marching; my tent was pitched by a river. In the afternoon I took a stroll along it; on the opposite side was a wood, and between the wood and the bank of the river there stretched a narrow tract of open ground. Presently I saw walking slowly along this tract what at first sight I took to be a very large dog; then on looking more attentively I recognized him as a wolf, very tall, gaunt, and shaggy. He was a little in advance, proceeding in the same direction as myself, and consequently he did not see me. I stood still and watched him; he went on very leisurely, and, like all wild animals, with extreme caution, constantly turning his head and looking from side to side. Every now and again he stopped, stood still for a minute, and seemed to listen. At length I suppose something alarmed him, or he saw something to pursue, for he broke into a trot, made for the wood, entered it, and disappeared.

I am not quite sure, but I do not think that the wolves in India associate in packs like the wolves of Europe, and with this remark I will leave them.

I commenced my discussion on the animals with the tiger; I will conclude it with some anecdotes and observations on the tiger's great antagonist, his rival monarch of the forests, the stately elephant. But the elephant demands a chapter to himself.

CHAPTER XVII.

ELEPHANTS

THE elephants live mostly in herds; the herds wander through these forests. They are not often seen, but when seen, especially in some open space, they present a most imposing appearance. I once heard it described. An English officer was out shooting in the Shewalics; he had pitched his tent for the night up the side of a mountain in a valley that opens into one of the passes that lead into the Doon. The next morning at daybreak he was sitting outside his tent drinking his tea before starting. The valley below and the pass beyond were filled, as is often the case in the cold season, with a thick white mist.

Presently he noticed towards the mouth of the valley some large, dark forms. They seemed moving, and next he perceived that they were advancing up the valley in his direction; they drew nearer, they became more distinct, and then a whole herd of elephants came into view. As one by one they emerged from the mist the spectacle was most grand, but it was one also that caused a little anxiety. The elephants might notice the tent and advance to inspect it, and if so the result might be unpleasant. It was a satisfaction when the herd turned up another gorge and passed out of sight.

It is not very safe to meet a herd of elephants, but it is still more dangerous to meet the elephants that wander alone or even in pairs. On one occasion I had this last experience. It was long ago, when these forests were broader than they are at present, the roads through them less frequented, and the elephants more numerous. I was travelling by night in a palanquin on my way to Mussoorie. We were about half-way through the forest when suddenly the bearers stopped. I heard a sound of someone shouting in advance; the bearers shouted in reply. Then they put down the palanquin in the road and informed me that we must remain where we were for a time, as the road in front was occupied by two elephants. They had learnt this from the man who had shouted, and who, they said, was the dâk-runner, that is the man on the post-office establishment who carries the mails. On learning this I got out of the palanquin to look around. The night was intensely dark; the trees on either side seemed to form a wall. In front, at no great distance, I saw a moving circle of sparks, something resembling a Catherine wheel. These sparks, the bearers told me, proceeded from the burnt end of stick which the dâk-runner was waving round to check the advance of the elephants; for elephants, like most other wild animals, have an extreme dread of lights or fires when seen in the dark. We remained thus some ten minutes or more, the dâk-runner continuously waving his stick, and at intervals shouting information as to the proceedings of the elephants. The position was a little anxious, as if the elephants advanced we should have to take refuge in the trees, and the palanquin would almost certainly be destroyed.

It was a relief, therefore, when the dâk-runner at length announced that the elephants were moving off, and a crashing among the trees confirmed his statement. The crashing, however, seemed to be coming in our direction; and I also thought that I dimly beheld two great dark forms approaching. This, however, I consider, must have been fancy. If the elephants were really advancing towards us they soon changed their minds, for the crashing grew fainter and fainter, and before long it ceased to be heard altogether; then we felt satisfied that the elephants were well away in the forest. I re-entered my palanquin, the bearers raised it, and we continued our journey.

Such incidents did not always terminate so satisfactorily. I remember hearing of an officer who had to climb a tree, and from thence witness the proceedings of the elephant with his palanquin. The elephant first examined the palanquin carefully, both within and without; then, his curiosity satisfied, he raised his trunk and beat it to pieces. I remember also the case of a lady whose palanquin was similarly destroyed, and who had herself a most narrow escape; but the particulars of it I forget.

It was not uncommon in those days for some solitary elephant to take up his position on one of the less frequented of the forest roads, and entirely stop the traffic, the mails included, for two or three days together. Then he would wander away, return after an interval, and proceed as before. In the end a reward would be offered by the Government for his destruction. Sportsmen would proceed in search of him, and he would be either frightened away or shot.

With regard to one of these elephants I will relate a story. It is a story which, if at all dramatically told, I have found always intensely interests children. The incidents occurred in a part of the forest further to the east, and, as they were told me by the magistrate in whose district that part of the forest lay, I think they may be accepted as correct. About half-way along the road that led through the forest there stood a hut; it was built for the accommodation of the dâk-runners who carried the mails and the police who patrolled the road; and, as a security against the wild beasts, it stood, not on the ground, but on a platform among the trees. The platform, I may mention, rested on four strong horizontal poles, fastened at some height above the ground to the trunks of four trees that happened to grow near together.

It was night; the four men not on duty were in the hut. They had cooked their dinner, and, seated on the floor, were about to eat it. The dinner, as is usual among men of their class, consisted chiefly of "chapatties," that is large, round, flat cakes of unleavened bread. The "chapatties," freshly baked, were piled before them; a large earthen jar of water stood in a corner. Suddenly there fell on their ears a distant sound of crashing among the trees. A solitary elephant had of late been haunting the forest; apprehension seized them that the crashing might be he approaching. Their fears soon became certainties. The crashing drew nearer and nearer; then there was a pause; next the whole hut shook and trembled. The elephant had arrived; he had wound his trunk round one of the trees, and was trying to uproot it. But the tree proved too strong; the elephant was unable to tear it up, or even to break it. He tried another of the trees, with the same result, and then in succession the other two. But though the trees shook, and the poles creaked, and the hut quivered, yet the trees stood firm. The terror of the four men meanwhile may be imagined.

For a minute or so there was quiet. The men were in hopes that the elephant was about to depart, when, to their horror, they perceived coming through the doorway something resembling a huge black snake. It was the trunk of the elephant. He was evidently aware of their presence, and was thus endeavouring to seize them. The men fled precipitately, and forced themselves into the two furthest corners; and these, to their inexpressible relief, the elephant could not reach. He felt in the two nearer corners; in one he found nothing, in the other was the jar of water: this he broke. Then with his trunk he swept the floor, and discovered the pile of "chapatties"; he lifted them two or three at a time, conveyed them to his mouth, ate them, and departed.

These solitary elephants are chiefly those who have been expelled their herd. Each herd of elephants is led and commanded by the strongest male elephant, the one who has vanquished his rivals. But as years pass, and the younger elephants grow up, by one or other of them the supremacy of the leader is disputed. A combat ensues. The vanquished elephant, whichever he may be, is then expelled the herd. Condemned to solitude, he becomes vicious, and is dangerous to men as well as to his own species. This is the accepted explanation; how far it is founded on actual observation I cannot say.

But among the solitary elephants there are some who have not been expelled from a herd. These are tame elephants that have escaped and taken to the forest, and these, it is said, are among the most dangerous of all. Their viciousness is attributed to much the same cause. The wild elephants will not associate with them, and so, like the expelled elephants, they are condemned to solitude. The native explanation for this is, that, having been in captivity and in association with man, they have from their changed food and mode of life acquired an order which the wild elephants dislike, or which marks them as of a different species. It is more probable, I think, that the wild elephants recognize them as not belonging to their own herd.

The elephants in these forests are not considered to be so large and fine as the elephants of the forests far away to the east towards Assam, nor are they nearly so numerous. On these accounts they are but rarely captured, and then only in pits, or, as they are termed, "ogees." The "ogee" in shape much resembles a saw-pit, only it is very much longer and broader, and also slightly deeper. It is dug in the course of some track along which the herd of elephants is accustomed to proceed; it is then covered over with branches of trees, and above them with leaves, grass, and twigs. The elephant, mistaking this covering for the real surface of the ground, steps on it, the branches give way under his weight, and he falls into the pit below. Although the fall is not great—not more than eight feet or so —it is very apt to seriously injure the elephant, and on this account this mode of capture is but seldom resorted to.

Elephants are so extremely cautious in testing the strength and stability of any bridges or embankments before they venture on them that it certainly seems surprising that they should be so easily deceived by these "ogees." I suppose that in the forest, suspecting no evil, they are less cautious. I once saw an "ogee"; it was in the forest just below the Shewalics. A female elephant and her infant had lately been captured in it. The mother, I think, had been hurt by her fall; the infant was none the worse for it. I subsequently made his acquaintance; he was a most amusing little creature; he was about the height of a small donkey, but so broad, and with such thick legs and massive body, that he seemed almost like a solid block, and so strong that he would almost have pulled against an English cart-horse.

The elephants in these forests, as I have said, are but seldom caught. I am glad to be able to add that neither are they ever shot, that is, except those solitary ones that are dangerous. That barbarous destruction of the elephant for the sake of his tusks that prevails in

Africa, or for mere amusement, as in Ceylon, is here unknown.

Like some other things and institutions, the position of the elephant has declined under our rule. He no longer, gorgeously caparisoned, adds to the splendour of the court ceremonials, or carries kings and chiefs in battle, or himself forms an effective portion of the armies. He is certainly still used in warfare, but it is in little more than in the capacity of a drudge: he mostly only draws the heavy cannon and carries on his back the tents and baggage.

Under the early Mahomedan emperors, indeed till up to the end of our fourteenth century, the elephants were regarded as the most important and formidable part of the Indian armies, and that not only by the emperors themselves, but also by their foreign invaders. Timour entered India in the year 1398 of our era. He swept through the Punjaub without meeting hardly any serious opposition; his Mogul troops excited such terror that the Indians fled at their approach. But on reaching Delhi the conditions were changed. The Moguls would here have to encounter not merely the army of the Emperor, but also his elephants. The army of the Emperor they despised, but the thought of encountering these gigantic creatures filled them with apprehension. Their apprehensions were so great that the literary men who accompanied Timour and all the other non-combatants were placed in the rear among the women. Entrenchments were thrown up, and other preparations made, and then with much anxiety they awaited the Emperor's attack.

The morning dawned. Timour drew up his troops, and then, as was his custom, prostrated himself on the bare ground, and, with arms extended, prayed and meditated, till, filled with religious ecstasy, he arose and mounted his horse, assuring his troops of victory. His troops accepted his assurances; nevertheless, as the army of the Emperor approached with the long line of elephants in front, they felt again apprehensions. The elephants drew near, the Moguls let fly their arrows, and their apprehensions vanished. Some of the mahowts were struck, and fell. Their elephants, left unguided, turned and fled; the rest became unmanageable, and followed: wild with terror, they tore through their own army behind, throwing it into utter confusion. Then as Timour, with his Moguls, advanced, the whole Indian army, with the Emperor at its head, fled precipitately, and such as escaped massacre took refuge within the walls of Delhi.

Perhaps it was this disaster that shook the confidence hitherto placed in the elephants, for in the later wars, though the elephants still continued to carry into battle the chiefs and generals, we do not hear of their being used as actual combatants, always excepting, if the historian is to be relied on, at the capture of Cheitore, in Rajpootana, by the Emperor Akbar.

When a breach had been made in the walls by mining, the Emperor, so the historian relates, advanced to the attack mounted on his elephant Asmân-Shakoh (the grandeur of the heavens), and accompanied by his other four war elephants: Budaghur, Jungeah, Gaderah, and Sabadleah. These five elephants not only carried and accompanied the Emperor, but fought themselves most valiantly on his behalf, "each of them," the historian asserts, "doing such things as surpassed all imagination." For courage and endurance Jungeah appears to have surpassed them all, for after his trunk had been cut off by the sword of a Rajpoot chieftain he still continued to fight, and having already slain thirty of the enemy, he now, though trunkless, killed sixteen more.

Although, as I have said, in the later wars elephants ceased to be used as actual combatants, yet the kings, chiefs, and generals continued to enter battle and to fight on them till very shortly before the commencement of our rule. Mounted on their elephants, they not unfrequently sought out, like our knights of old, an antagonist of similar rank in the opposing army. In the combat which ensued the elephants, guided by their mahowts, were sometimes able to afford the chief or general who rode them valuable assistance.

It was not, however, in war so much as in court ceremonial that the elephants made their most magnificent appearance. The procession of the state elephants on the Emperor's birthday and other especial occasions must indeed have been a spectacle most imposing. It impressed extremely the early European travellers. Sir Thomas Roe, the ambassador sent by our James I. to the Emperor Jehangire, thus describes it :—

"After the Emperor had been weighed against gold, silver, jewels, and other articles of value, the state elephants were paraded. They passed in procession before the Emperor, seated on his throne ; they were divided into twelve companies, each company consisting of eight or ten elephants; they were preceded by flags and banners, 'and clothed in gold, silk, and silver.'"

The "first elephant," I presume the one that headed the procession, is described by Sir Thomas as "a beast of wonderful size and beauty." His head was covered with "plates" (of gold, I imagine), "all set with rubies and emeralds."

The procession, when the Emperor commenced his journey to Mando, must have been even still more imposing. A guard of elephants, three hundred in number, each carrying a small cannon, lined the road on either side; and six hundred state elephants went before the Emperor and behind, and all caparisoned in velvet or cloth of gold.

The elephant of "wonderful size and beauty," which Sir Thomas mentions above, was probably the Emperor's favourite elephant, "Indraguj" (the elephant of Indra, in Hindoo mythology the god of the skies). The Emperor in his memoirs gives an elaborate description of this elephant. It had originally belonged to the Emperor's younger brother, Prince Daniel. After the death of that prince it came into the Emperor's possession. It was considered to be the largest and in appearance the most magnificent elephant ever seen in India.

It was so tall, the Emperor states, that a ladder of fourteen steps was required to mount it, so fleet that not even the fastest horse could keep pace with it, so strong and brave that it would not hesitate to attack a hundred of its own species, and yet so gentle that even when "in its most furious excitement," if an infant happened to be in its way, it would stop, raise the infant gently in its trunk, and place it carefully on one side in a place of safety.

This elephant, the Emperor further states, always went attended by a band of music, and preceded by forty horsemen. In another passage the Emperor mentions its allowance of food. It may perhaps interest the reader to hear it. It was as follows:—

Liquor . . .	80 bls.
Boiled rice . . .	320 ,,
Beef or mutton . .	160 ,,
Clarified butter . .	80 ,,

With regard to the beef and mutton, I conclude there must be some mistake.

Hawkins, who was also accredited to the Emperor's court at an earlier period, describes the Emperor's favourite elephant, which I presume must be the same. He speaks of its enormous size and extreme gentleness. Of its gentleness he mentions an instance. He saw it lift up in succession several young children, raise them with its trunk aloft in the air, and then place them with the utmost care again on the ground. Among the children thus lifted was the Emperor's youngest son, a boy of not more than seven years old.

A very full account of the imperial elephants is given in the *Ayeen Akbari*. Among other matters, it is mentioned that a certain number of elephants were kept for fighting, and that each of them had his own special antagonist. Other elephants were kept for amusement, and were taught to dance, to play on musical instruments, to shoot arrows from a bow, and to perform other tricks. It is further mentioned that a special class of men, famed for their skill in teaching these tricks to elephants, were maintained at the court for the purpose.

I suppose that these performances by elephants went out of fashion. They are not mentioned, so far as I know, by any of the early European travellers. I have never heard of their prevailing at any of the modern native courts, nor have I heard any tradition regarding them at the courts of the subsequent emperors. The elephant-fights, on the contrary, remained an institution to the last. They are especially noticed by the early European travellers, and always with condemnation on account of their extreme cruelty. The cruelty was not, however, to the elephants, but to the mahowts who rode them. Each elephant endeavoured to unseat the mahowt of his antagonist, and if he succeeded, then, if he could, he trampled him to death.

Bernier, in describing these elephant-fights, says that they hardly ever took place without one or more of the mahowts being killed. So dangerous, indeed, were they regarded, that the mahowts who were to take part in them, before mounting their elephants, bade farewell to their wives and children, like soldiers proceeding to battle. According to Hawkins, the Emperor Jehangire added a further cruelty to these exhibitions. If a mahowt, when unseated and flung on the ground, was not killed, but merely maimed or injured, the Emperor had him immediately thrown into the river, and there left to drown. "He will be sure to hate me," the Emperor would remark, "as the cause of his suffering. It is better, therefore, that he should be sent to a world where his hate can cause me no evil."

These elephant-fights did not cease with the fall of the Mogul empire. They were continued at the courts of all the greater sovereigns among whom that empire became divided, more especially at Lucknow. They used to be there exhibited till within a few years previous to the annexation. I have heard them described by those who had seen them as the most uninteresting of spectacles. The fight consisted of the two elephants butting each other. This they continued to do till one of the combatants had had enough. Then he turned and fled, his adversary following and butting him behind. Like as in a ram-fight, the elephant that had once turned made no further resistance. So long as the fight continued, each elephant endeavoured to unseat the mahowt of his adversary; but I never heard of the mahowts being killed or seriously injured.

The elephants used for fighting were always the largest and strongest that could be procured. On my first visit to Lucknow, not very long after my arrival in India, I accidentally saw one—I say accidentally, for I came on it unawares. I was being shown over the palace by the gentleman—one of the assistants to the Resident—with whom I was staying. We had gone through the palace itself, and were being conducted to the stables. On the way we passed a detached building. It was a sort of shed, with thick walls and tiled roof, and very lofty; it was partly open in front, and the opening was fitted with a pair of folding gates formed of very massive upright wooden bars. It was near sunset, and the building, facing north or east, seemed dark within. As we passed, out of curiosity I stepped aside to the gates, and looked through the bars to see what lay behind them. I confess that as I did so I started, and moved back; for behind the bars, only a few paces off, stood the very largest elephant I ever beheld, and in the half-light of the shed he looked even more gigantic than perhaps he really was. His tusks, too, were in proportion to his stature: they seemed at least six or seven feet long. As I placed my face to the bars the elephant made a movement forward, and it was then I retreated, for I felt by no means certain that if he stretched out his trunk he might not reach me. I subsequently learnt that he was the champion of the fighting elephants, and was considered to be the largest and most powerful elephant then in all India.

I will conclude this account of the elephant-fights by mentioning that in the days of the emperors they were held at Agra and Delhi on some place on the sands, between the palace and the river. The space required for the contests was very large, and was enclosed by a lofty palisade formed of the strongest timbers. The exact part of the sands selected I could never clearly determine from the descriptions of the early travellers.

Under the native rule, and especially under the Mahomedan emperors, the elephants were frequently used as executioners. No particular elephants were reserved for the purpose. The condemned were made over to any of the elephants that happened to be in attendance. The severity of the punishment was adapted to the offence. If merely death was adjudged, the criminal was laid on the ground and the elephant with his forefoot crushed in his head or his chest, according as the Emperor directed. Death must have been instantaneous, but the sight must have been very sickening. If to death torture was to be added, then the elephant, guided by his mahowt, broke only the bones of the limbs of the condemned man in succession, and now, incapable of movement, he was left, while life continued, to linger in agony. These executions were frequently performed in the palace and before the Emperor himself, his nobles and courtiers, and the crowds of spectators.

Terry mentions a case where the ordinary mode of execution was varied. A man had been convicted of killing his own mother. For such a crime the Emperor considered that a punishment more terrible than usual should be inflicted. The man, by the Emperor's direction, was fastened by a long chain to the hind leg of the elephant, and so dragged along the road, as the Emperor set out on his march to Mando. Terry describes seeing the body in the course of the third march. There was then, he says, little left of it but the skeleton; almost all the flesh had been torn off as the body had been dragged along over the rough surface of the road.

The male elephants occasionally become savage, or as it is termed, "must." When in this state they are more or less dangerous. They are also given to wandering. To prevent their doing so, a chain is attached to one of their hind legs and secured at the other end to a post; but notwithstanding this precaution they still sometimes manage to get loose, and then they are to be avoided. I once saw a "must" elephant which had thus broke loose. It was at Dehra. The Commander-in-Chief was marching through the valley, and was encamped for a day or two just outside the town. He had come, as was the custom of those days, with a great retinue and many elephants.

I was in my tent; I heard a clamour, and was told that one of the elephants in the camp had become "must," had broken loose, and was approaching in our direction. I ran out to see; the sight was disappointing. I had expected to see a furious elephant rushing along with uplifted trunk in a frenzy of rage and occasionally trumpeting. Instead of this I beheld an elephant approaching, walking slowly and deliberately, and in the calmest and most stately manner. He was dragging his chain behind him, and followed by a number of mahowts and their assistants, and after them came a crowd of men and boys. It was from this crowd, who appeared to be highly enjoying the sight, that the noise and shouting proceeded.

The elephant came on, and passed by. A little beyond, and near beside the road, there stood an empty cottage. The elephant here stopped; he turned, looked at the cottage for a minute or so, and then left the road and advanced towards it; and having reached the cottage, he proceeded in the most deliberate manner to demolish it. He first tore off the thatch and scattered the fragments in the air and all around; next he wrenched out the timbers of the roof and broke them to pieces. This done, he commenced to batter down the mud walls. I imagine that he found this business troublesome, for he presently abandoned it, returned to the road, and continued his progress along it in the same calm, stately manner as before. I learnt that he was soon after captured and brought back to the camp, but not before he had in a similar manner destroyed some other cottages.

An iron chain such as this elephant was dragging after him forms part of the equipment of every elephant. In the *Ayeen Akbari* the chain is termed the "dehrneh." Its modern appellation I do not remember. Those in use in the Emperor's stables are described as consisting each chain of sixty links, and each link as weighing three seers, or six pounds. The chains, the description adds, were ordinarily made of iron, but occasionally of silver and even of gold. Assuming the then value of gold to have been twenty times that of silver, the value of one of these golden chains would have amounted to over half a million of our money.

And yet, according to the accounts of the early European travellers, such chains were not unfrequent at the imperial court. Sir Thomes Roe describes the arrival of an elephant at Ajmere, sent as a present to the then Emperor Jehangire by some tributary sovereign. Among its other equipments, it carried a chain of gold, but perhaps this chain was of a lighter construction.

The elephant, as all are aware, is long-lived. Its age exceeds a century, but by how much is a matter on which statements vary. The Emperor Akbar assigns a hundred and twenty years as the duration of the life of an elephant. Popular belief in India credits him with thirty more years in addition. The elephant is considered to reach maturity at the age of fifty, and to continue to live afterwards for twice that period. In most cases, however, the length of an elephant's life must be a matter of uncertainty, for when captured his age can only be conjectured, and after capture he outlives so many owners and attendants that at the end the period when he was acquired must be much a matter of tradition.

The great age to which elephants do live is more striking when particular instances are given than when merely generally stated. The two following cases always much impressed me. The state elephant that carried Warren Hastings was said to be alive, and still on occasions to bear the howdah of the Governor-General, up to a short period before my arrival in India; and the elephant of Sooruj Mull, the celebrated Raja of Bhurtpore, was said to have been still ridden on state occasions by his far-away successors after our capture of Bhurtpore had reduced them from independent sovereigns to the position of little more than large landed proprietors. Sooruj Mull was killed in his march to Delhi in 1763, and between his death and the capture of Bhurtpore a period of nearly seventy years had gone by; and in the interval so many and great had been the changes that politically another world had arisen, and between the two worlds this elephant seemed the connecting link.

As elephants grow old, like as with other animals, their strength declines. In the matter of food, this alone would not much affect them, for they subsist chiefly on leaves and the small branches of trees, and of these in the forests there is always abundance; but as their strength declines, so also do their teeth decay. Indeed, the decay of their teeth commences while their strength is still almost unimpaired, and without teeth or with fewer, though they may pluck the branches, they are unable to properly masticate them. The twigs and branches they devour pass through them but little digested. This loss of teeth occurs equally in the wild and in the domesticated elephant. By the droppings left by a herd, the number of elephants that have passed the period of their prime can always be identified. I do not know if the teeth gradually decay or loosen and fall out whole.

In the early days of our rule elephants were a good deal used by Europeans for riding. In the hot season the evening airing was frequently taken on an elephant instead of, as now, in a carriage; and in the cold season, when travelling in tents, it was similarly on an elephant that marches were made. In my time this custom had been long discontinued. Very few Europeans kept elephants at all; and those who did kept them only for the purpose of tiger-shooting.

For traversing the forests and grass jungles the elephant is indispensable; and for passing through the streets of a native city it is, of all modes of conveyance, the most convenient and agreeable. Raised high aloft, the view of the rider is never interrupted, and he escapes all the closeness and pressure of the crowds below. Moreover, the elephant makes his way through the crowds with an ease and rapidity possible to neither horse nor carriage, and he does so with almost absolute safety to the crowds themselves. Fatal as would be his push or tread, yet he manages to pass along and to clear his passage without hurt to man or animal.

Except, however, for these two purposes, the traversing the cities and the forests or jungles, the elephant as a substitute for a horse or vehicle is not to be recommended, and least of all for the performance of a journey. The pace of the elephant is a series of jolts. Towards the end of the journey, as he becomes tired, the jolts grow rougher; also his speed slackens. He appears every instant as if about to stop, and has to be constantly urged on by his mahowt. What with the jolting and the urging, by the end of the journey the rider is almost as fatigued as the elephant himself.

An elephant cannot be well described as a beautiful animal, hardly even as a handsome animal; yet his vast size and enormous tusks give to him an aspect of much grandeur. But, to appreciate his full majesty of appearance, he should be seen fully caparisoned in gorgeous trappings, and bearing one of the beautiful Indian howdahs, all overlaid with gold.

The height of an elephant is said to equal twice the circumference of his fore foot. I have never, however, tested the accuracy of the statement by measurement, nor do I know whether the height referred to is that of the elephant at his shoulder or at the centre of his back, where it is greater.

The intelligence of the elephant is proverbial, though certainly many of the current stories brought forward to illustrate it are sufficiently fictitious. If the histories are to be accepted, the elephant is also capable of corresponding sentiments of affection. It is related that when the Emperor Kuttub-ood-Deen (pole star of the faith) was slain in a night attack on his camp, his favourite elephant was so affected at his master's death, that he pined away and died also himself of grief. This elephant is also stated by the historian to have been the only white elephant seen in India.

CHAPTER XVIII.

DISAPPEARANCE OF THE WILD ANIMALS

THROUGHOUT India generally the larger wild animals are now less numerous than they formerly were. Over certain large tracts some of these animals have even entirely disappeared. This diminution and disappearance is ordinarily attributed partly to the greater numbers killed by sportsmen since our acquisition of the country, but in a greater degree to the increase of cultivation that has taken place under our rule, for this increase of cultivation has reduced the extent of the forests and waste lands in which alone these larger wild animals are able to exist.

No doubt this explanation, to a certain extent, is correct; still it is not altogether satisfactory, for it leaves some important facts altogether unexplained. The disappearance of the larger animals has in several cases occurred previous to our rule, and it has also occurred where the conditions of the country have apparently remained unchanged. The subject is one which I do not possess sufficient knowledge to properly discuss. I will, however, mention such facts as I happen to be aware of. They relate to three of the largest and most powerful of the wild animals—the rhinoceros, the elephant, and the lion. And first as to the rhinoceros.

The Emperor Babur, the founder of the Mogul dynasty, entered India in the year 1525 of our era. He halted with his army for some time at Peshawar, and there amused himself, as he relates in his memoirs, with hunting the rhinoceros. Now I cannot speak with certainty, for I have never visited that part of the Punjaub, but I do not believe that the rhinoceros is now found either in the neighbourhood of Peshawar or anywhere in the adjacent regions, nor that it was there found at the time of our acquisition of the country.

If in this belief I am correct, then it appears that in the course of little more than three centuries the rhinoceros had entirely disappeared from extensive tracts of country where previously it was abundant; and it is to be noted that the country during the whole of this period had continued under native rule: its conditions, therefore, are not likely to have much changed. We may presume that the forests and wastes which sheltered the rhinoceros in the days of Babur had but slightly, if at all, diminished in extent at the period when the territory in which they are situated passed under the British rule.

But further, in the year 1803 we acquired all that part of the upper provinces which lies at the base of the Himalaya and Shewalic ranges. I have always understood that the rhinoceros was then found throughout the entire length of forest which extends below these mountains; but at the time when I had charge of the Doon the rhinoceros was never met with, nor had been for many years, in any part of the forest to the westward of the Ganges; and to the east of the Ganges it was rarely found except in the district of Philibect, which is situated close adjacent to the frontiers of Nepaul. In the course, therefore, of about half a century the rhinoceros had retired eastwards for a distance of over two hundred miles.

During this period the forests, owing to the increase of cultivation, had certainly very much diminished in breadth; also the wild animals within them had been shot and hunted to a far greater extent than in previous times. But these changes had not caused the disappearance of the other animals. The tigers, the deer, and the herds of wild elephants roamed the forests as before, though in rather diminished numbers. Why then should the rhinoceros have vanished?

Next as to the elephant. There are two great forests in India; they are known among the natives, if I remember the names correctly, as the Chunglee Bun (forest) and the Pâtree Bun. The one is the forest which stretches along the base of the Himalaya; the other forms a belt across the continent of India. It extends, running in a south-westerly direction, from the river Ganges to near Bombay. It covers those ranges of hills and low mountains that separate Hindostan proper from the peninsula below it.

Three centuries ago both these forests abounded in elephants; the forest below the Himalaya does so still. From the other forest the elephants have entirely or almost entirely disappeared. Of their former abundance we have historical proof.

The Emperor Babur, when proceeding on his expedition against Bengal, passed near the town of Calpee. Describing it in his memoirs, he mentions that the forests around were full of elephants. He remarks further, the elephants were so numerous that the greater part of the domesticated elephants in India were obtained from among them. These forests form the eastern portion of the great forest belt. I was once for a short time stationed in their neighbourhood, and my recollection is that no elephants at all then existed within them; certainly none were captured.

The *Ayeen Akbari* was composed more than half a century later. In its account of the "soobah," or province, of Agra, it is stated that elephants were very plentiful in that province, and were there captured for use. The forests in which the elephants were found and captured must have been also a part of the great belt, but one more to the westward. No elephants are now captured in those forests, nor, so far as I am aware, do any exist.

But, further; the historian Firishtah, in his narrative of the events of the reign of the Emperor Akbar, mentions that on one occasion the Emperor, when returning from Mando to Agra, came on a herd of wild elephants in the forests of Sipree. These forests are in the neighbourhood of Indore, and form a still more westerly portion of the belt. Colonel Briggs, in his English translation of Firishtah, comments on this passage. He observes that then, at the time he wrote, there were no elephants in those forests. Colonel Briggs' translation was published about seventy years ago, and must have been composed, we may presume, a little earlier. It would appear, therefore, that the elephants had disappeared within a period not much exceeding two centuries and a half.

But the forests still exist; at least, in my time they did, for I have passed through them: and they have always remained, as indeed have most of the other parts of the great forest belt, under the native rule.

I will now speak of the lion. As compared with the tigers, the leopards, and some other of the larger beasts of prey, the lions have at no time been very abundant in India. The area of their range has also been more restricted. They have never, for example, been found, I believe, to the eastward of the Jumna. In the tracts of country that border that river on the west the lions were, however, in former times tolerably numerous; they were sufficiently numerous to render the hunting them one of the ordinary sports. There are several descriptions of lion hunts and allusions to the sport in the *Ayeen Akbari* and also in the memoirs of the Emperor Jehangire. Some of them I will quote; they may perhaps be found entertaining.

The *Ayeen Akbari* describes one mode of hunting the lion which it states was occasionally practised, and which must certainly have been most hazardous. It was as follows. A man mounted on a buffalo rode up to the lion, and then urged on the buffalo to attack it. A fierce combat of course ensued. In the end the buffalo was victorious: he gored the lion with his horns and tossed him, and finally killed him.

The Emperor Akbar was very partial to lion-hunting, and frequently indulged in the sport. On two occasions, however, when pursuing it, he had narrow escapes; they are thus related: On the first occasion the Emperor, armed with bow and arrows, came on a lion; the lion advanced; the Emperor drew his bow and let fly an arrow; the arrow struck the lion; he fell mortally wounded. But as he fell a second lion suddenly appeared, and with rage and fury bounded towards the Emperor. It came near, then it paused, turned, and fled, its instinct inspiring it with terror at the aspect of the Emperor, "Heaven's favourite."

On the second occasion the Emperor's escape was due to human intervention. The Emperor, as before, was lion-hunting. Unexpectedly three lions rushed forward to attack him. A young Uzbec noble was standing at a little distance; beside him was the Emperor's favourite horse "Kohpârâ" (mountain-sized); it was a horse that feared neither lion nor elephant. Perceiving the Emperor's danger, the young noble sprang at once on Kohpârâ, and galloped forward to his assistance. One lion he seized by the mane, and drove his dagger through its throat. The lion fell dead. Then the young noble caught hold of the other two lions by their necks, each with one hand, and thus holding them, he dashed their heads together, and with such violence that their skulls were shattered, and they also fell dead beside their companion lion.

This young noble afterwards gave an exhibition of

almost equal strength and courage before the Emperor Jehangire, the Emperor Akbar's son and successor. The Emperor was hunting lions in the Punjaub. A lion had been wounded, but was still alive; the noble advanced to it, drew his sword, and with one blow severed the lion's head from his body. As a reward for his courage, the Emperor, as he records in his memoirs, bestowed on the noble high promotion.

The Emperor Jehangire died in 1627 of our era. We may conclude, I think, that at that time the lion existed and was fairly numerous both in the Punjaub and in the other tracts of country I have mentioned. At the time of my arrival in India, which was some years previous to the Mutiny, the lion was, I believe, unknown in the Punjaub, and in the upper provinces it was found only in the district of Banda, which is situated in the extreme south-west.

I will conclude these remarks on the disappearance of the lion with a few words regarding the lion itself, that is to say, the lion as found in India. I should mention that I have never myself seen one, but I have always heard it described as an animal very inferior to the lion of Africa, both in size, strength, and also in majesty of appearance. In Terry's account of his residence in India an engraving is given of the standard of the Emperor Jehangire. The engraving is stated to have been copied from an Indian painting. The device on the standard is a lion couchant, with a representation of the sun either rising or setting immediately behind it. The lion as depicted is a true lion, with shaggy mane and tufted tail.

The disappearance of species of the wild animals suggests thoughts as to the ultimate fate of the wild animals individually. It is a subject on which when in the forests I have often reflected. Many of the animals, no doubt, fall victims to accident or are devoured by the others that are beasts of prey; but the greater number, I imagine, escape both accident and enemies, and live to grow old, and then I think that their end must be sad. Those that wander alone when they feel that their vital powers are failing may seek and find a shelter where they may lie concealed and die undisturbed.

But those that move in herds will remain with the rest so long as their strength enables them. Then they will fall behind and be left, for among animals there is but little compassion to weakness, to sickness, or to age. Thus left, they will suffer: they will feel the solitude, also the abandonment. Besides, they will be haunted by fears. Enemies abound, and they must be conscious that if discovered they now no longer possess the power to resist or to escape.

For a longer or shorter period they will thus remain; then they will lie down and not rise again. Perhaps they pass calmly away; perhaps the wolves, the jackals, or the birds of prey find them and approach, and then in their last hours they are tormented.

The animal dead, its body rapidly disappears. This is not surprising, for in these forests there are multitudes of creatures—birds, beasts, and even insects—ready to devour it. But what is curious is that not only the flesh, but also the bones, appear to vanish. The bones of the smaller animals are doubtless eaten or split into fragments and dispersed, but the bones of the larger animals cannot thus be disposed of; and yet they are rarely, if ever, seen. Perhaps when still fresh they are dragged away and concealed, or perhaps they become hidden by the grass and the falling leaves.

When first I made acquaintance with the forests I was struck by the profusion of animal life, its freedom, and its joyousness. Afterwards these feelings were modified: I was the more impressed by the cruelty, the selfishness, everywhere apparent, the strong among the animals so merciless, the weak so helpless. But after a still longer experience I returned very much to my earlier sentiment. The forests are not, indeed, for the animals an ideal world; there is death, terror, and much suffering and privation. But then in the free life and otherwise there are compensations. On the whole, as compared with the animals that live subject to man, the lot of these inhabitants of the wilds is one to be envied.

CHAPTER XIX.

THE TOUR CONTINUED

AFTER this description of the Doon, I will resume the narrative of my tour. I remained at Dehra about a week, and then I set off on my return. I marched along the valley in the direction of the Jumna, and re-entered the plains through one of the western passes. The first march was a long one, but very pretty—all fields of rising crops, interspersed with groves of mango trees and neat little grass-hutted villages. Now and then the road was bordered by hedges of aloes or wild rose and white raspberry, and always along the horizon on one side was the great wall of the Himalaya, on the other the green, forest-covered slope of the Shewalic. As we went on the slope grew lower, and the peaks behind it came into view; they were so many, so small, and so sharp, and so close together, that they somewhat suggested the idea of a gigantic saw. Soon after this we reached our encamping-ground.

Close beside the encamping-ground was a grove of mango trees, and a little below it was a river. It was the same small river I have already mentioned which flows into the Jumna through the length of the Western Doon, and whose waters may be said, with a little exaggeration, to roll over sands of gold. To pass away the time while the tents were being pitched, I strolled down to the river and sauntered beside it. During the rainy season the river contains a considerable amount of water. It was now nearly dry; only a small, shallow stream wandered through a wide bed of sand and boulders.

Scattered over the bed there were numerous pools of water. The water which had come down from the mountains was clear as crystal. In nearly all the pools there were shoals of the minutest of fishes; they were so small that each alone was hardly visible. I presume that they had been but just recently hatched. It was most interesting to watch them: they rose, they sank, they darted from side to side; occasionally they stopped suddenly in the shade and seemed to disappear; in a minute or so they were swimming about as before.

As I watched the little creatures, I began to speculate as to their future. In the hot season most of the pools would dry up, and then what would become of the fishes? Would they die, or would they burrow in the sand and lie torpid, like the frogs, till the water came again in the rains and revived them? The largest and deepest pools might, however, remain. But then, as the fishes grew, how would the water contain them or supply them with food? Would the fishes remain small as they were till the next rains came, or devour each other, or what?

As I thus speculated the sun began to approach the horizon. Seen in its mellow beams, the river-bed presented a reddish glow that reminded me of the gold that was in it. There is really gold in the sand, and that everywhere, though not much. When work in the fields is slack, some few of the villagers employ themselves in collecting it. They obtain just about sufficient to supply themselves with the means of subsistence. When formerly I was in charge of the Doon, I happened once to be encamped near this river, though higher up the stream. The thought occurred to me to procure some of its gold as a memento. I sent for two labourers who understood the process, and set them to work to wash the sand. They washed all day, and by the evening they had collected about a teaspoonful of grains of gold. I had them melted down, and they formed a ball the size of a large pea. I kept the ball as a curiosity till the Mutiny, when it was either lost or plundered.

The tents were now pitched, and I returned to the camping-ground, and there I found some visitors awaiting me. There was a village near. The proprietors had known me in former days; they had heard of my arrival, and were come to pay their respects. While dinner was getting ready we sat and chatted. We talked of old times and recent events, and among these I learnt that a herd of elephants had just lately come through the Shewalic and eaten up a good part of their sugarcane crop. Very possibly this might have been the same herd whose tracks I had seen behind the dâk bungalow as I entered the Doon. The proprietors took their loss cheerfully, as they knew that they would get compensation for most of it from the Government.

Next morning after breakfast the tents were struck, and we continued our journey. We crossed the little river, and proceeded up the road that led to the mountains. The march was very pleasant; the road was good, the ascent was easy, and the forest on either side most picturesque. The trees were tall and shady, they grew near together, and there were but few patches of coarse grass or brushwood. As we entered the mountains the conditions a little changed; the road was rough and broken, and the ascent extremely steep, but though steep, it was not long. In less than an hour we reached the summit, and here we were to halt for the night.

Our encamping-ground was a small level space a little above the road. There were a good many stones lying about it, and these, before the tents were pitched, it was necessary to remove, for the place swarms with scorpions, and it is under the stones and boulders that they chiefly conceal themselves. The scorpions are not only numerous here, but are also unusually large; some that I saw were the largest, blackest, most bloated, venomous-looking creatures of their kind that I ever beheld. But unless touched or trod on, they did not appear at all aggressive. When exposed by turning over a stone, their first impulse was always to escape and conceal themselves, and it was wonderful into what narrow cracks and fissures they were able to force their way and hide. It was also a matter of wonder to me why they should so frequent this spot, and still more what in it they could find to subsist on, for the whole space about was nothing but stones, rock, sand, or boulders.

Our encamping-ground, though in the midst of the wildest of mountains, was not so solitary as might have been expected. There was a police-station close by, and also one or two sheds occupied by dealers in provisions; for the pass is much frequented, and most of the travellers who go through it halt here for the night. From a point not far off the Doon can be seen, and as there was still some daylight remaining, I strolled along the footpath that led to the point to take a farewell look. The head policeman accompanied me. From the point only the further slopes of the Doon were visible, and over these the shadows were stealing. The view, all forest and mountain, when seen thus was rather dreary. A few white peaks of the far-away snowy range a little relieved it. These could be seen through that vast gap in the lower ranges along the bottom of which the river Jumna flows.

By the time I returned to the camping-ground the tents had been pitched, and many travellers had arrived with carts, cattle, and ponies. The little halting-place had quite a cheerful aspect. Among the other travellers was a fakir. He presently came up to where I was standing, made his salaam, and addressed me; he was a young man, and for a fakir he looked clean and respectable. Moreover, as soon as he spoke I perceived that he was educated. Before long he told me his story.

He had been a clerk in a Government office. There had been some family quarrel, he thought himself aggrieved, and so, half in anger, half in devotion, he had assumed the yellow dress and become a fakir—one of that class of fakirs who for ever wander from shrine to shrine, "whose home," as the Persian saying poetically expresses it, "is where the evening finds them."

As he told me his history, I soon perceived that he heartily repented the step he had taken; indeed, he presently plainly told me so. He said he was weary to death of his endless wanderings, and would gladly return to secular life. I expressed my sympathy, and then he asked me if, to enable him to do so, I would bestow upon him some small appointment. There was something in the man's manner and story that touched me. Had it been possible, I would have granted his request; but, alas! he had taken that step which there is no retracing. The Hindoo who assumes the yellow dress abandons for ever home, caste, and family; cuts himself at once adrift from all his former life.

He presently took his leave, and went back to the halting-place, where were the other travellers. He approached a party who were commencing their evening meal; there he seated himself at a short distance, and contemplated them much in the manner of a dog awaiting scraps from his master's table. No doubt, when their own hunger was satisfied, the travellers would give him any food that remained.

The head policeman had gone off on some business. He now returned. I pointed out to him the fakir, and expressed some of the compassion his story had excited. In this feeling the head policeman did not share. He entertained for the man and his class the utmost contempt. He described them one and all as an idle, worthless, drug-eating set of vagabonds; and his opinion was only what I have heard other natives frequently express.

The fakirs of India have always been regarded as one of the great curiosities of the country. Some brief account of them may perhaps be not uninteresting to the English reader.

The ordinary fakir, the one most commonly met with, wears a yellow dress, and has long yellow hair. The hair is plaited and coiled round his head, and when thus coiled has much the appearance of a turban. The yellow colour is, of course, the result of a dye, though Ibn Batutu, the early Mahomedan traveller, supposed that it was natural and was caused by excessive fasting. The yellow is of an ugly brick-dust tint, and the hair itself has a dead, withered appearance. The extraordinary length of the hair of some of the fakirs used to excite my astonishment till I learnt that the greater part of it was artificial. Some is picked up at the bathing-places, where the pilgrims shave their heads; some is their own hair, which has fallen or been combed out and twisted in again; while the very long strands have been procured from the tails of horses.

The faces of these fakirs are always more or less painted, and their eyes have that dull, glassy look which arises from the excessive use of narcotics. The appearance of the ordinary fakir is certainly not attractive; but it is almost beauty compared with that of many of the special varieties. Some of these go nearly entirely unclothed. Their faces are thickly daubed with paint; their naked bodies are smeared with wood ashes. Thus decorated, with glassy eyes and lean, emaciated figures, they have an aspect inexpressibly repulsive. Occasionally it is such as almost to realize the mediæval representations of ghosts and evil spirits.

There are numerous varieties of fakirs. Some are solitary, and live independently; others associate in communities, and own obedience to a superior. At the head of these varieties in point of respectability are the Goshines, at the bottom the Jogees. The Goshines have settled habitations, often engage in trade, and not unfrequently acquire considerable wealth. Except in some peculiarities of dress, they differ but little from the ordinary secular population.

To the Goshines the Jogees are an extreme contrast. They live always in the wastes and jungles, and mostly in small communities; but they do not, I think, own obedience to any superior. They have no fixed abodes, but wander as their fancy inclines. Their appearance is to the last degree wild and squalid. Their long hair hangs loose; their dress consists of a strip of sackcloth wrapped round their loins, and perhaps another broader strip thrown over their shoulders. The Jogees are now rarely seen, and as a sect they have sunk into insignificance. Formerly they were the best known and most celebrated of all the Indian fakirs. They were credited, as, indeed, they still are, with the possession of magical powers. In the most ancient of the Hindoo fairy tales the Jogees as necromancers always occupy a conspicuous place. In later times they were chiefly celebrated as jugglers and acrobats, and as such they are frequently mentioned in the memoirs and histories as performing before the emperors.

Their performances struck all beholders with amazement, and so wonderful did they appear, that they were attributed to supernatural agency; and, indeed, if the accounts of them are correct, by hardly any other means could they have been accomplished. Ibn Batutu, the traveller, relates that he saw one Jogee turn himself into a cube, and in that form ascend to the skies; and the Emperor Jehangire in his memoirs describes exhibitions even more wonderful. The Jogees are even now believed to possess the secret of the transmutation of metals, and to them is attributed the production of all the silver at present to be found in the world; for, there being no mines of silver in India, none are supposed to exist elsewhere.

In former days some of the fakirs were warlike. They went armed and in large bands. Their contests were, however, chiefly among themselves. It is mentioned in the histories that the Emperor Akbar once came on two such bands of rival orders preparing for combat. He endeavoured to dissuade them, but without avail. Then he let them fight it out; but, with his usual humanity, when one side was defeated and commenced to fly, he sent out his cavalry, and prevented the other side from pursuing and slaughtering them.

The most singular of these warlike fakirs were the "Nagas," or "unclothed." They carried arms, but, as their name implies, they wore no garments. They did not, like the other fighting sects, confine their hostilities to rival devotees: they engaged also in purely secular contests. In the troublesome times that followed the breaking up of the Mogul empire, the Nagas took an active part in the numerous wars then prevailing among the various native princes. They were at one period, about the end of the last century, oddly enough, partially commanded by an English sailor, George Thomas, a man of some celebrity in India at the time, and who afterwards succeeded in establishing himself as the independent sovereign of a small territory towards the confines of the Punjaub.

The "Nâgas" existed in the native states of Rajpootana till quite recently; they may do so still. At the commencement of the Mutiny they attached themselves to one of the English officials, and did good service on behalf of our Government.

I believe that many among the fakirs have become such from very pure and sincere motives. I have conversed with some who impressed me as being, according to their lights, truly pious; but these were those who affected no extravagances of dress or behaviour, and who passed their lives quietly in religious contemplation. As to the fakirs in general, I do not think, from all I have seen and heard, that the opinion of them expressed by the head policeman was much exaggerated. The filthiness of the habits and the horrible impurity of the practices that prevail among them are hardly to be conceived. Of this filthiness I once had experience; it was at Hurdwar.

Struck by the beauty of one of the houses there that line the river bank, I entered it to view the interior. The owner, a raja in the west, occupied the house only on the rare occasions when he attended at the great fair; meanwhile he permitted it to be used by fakirs of all sorts as a kind of caravanserai. I found it full of them. Words would fail to describe its condition. The floors were covered with ordure and other impurities. The fakirs with painted faces, glassy, bloodshot eyes, and bodies smeared with wood ashes, seemed hardly human. All were more or less under the influence of narcotics; some were entirely stupefied. They sat motionless, leaning against the walls, as if in a trance or dream. The place resembled less a habitation of men than a den of the impurest of animals. The filth, the odours, the aspect of the inmates, excited in me a feeling of horror.

In former days the lower class of fakirs were in the habit of inflicting on themselves torments, often permanent injuries. These practices, steadily discountenanced by our Government, are now almost entirely discontinued; by the educated natives they were never approved of. These self-tortures frequently consisted of merely temporary sufferings, and being performed at fairs, they partook a good deal of the nature of acrobatic exhibitions. A common one, and which has often been described, was the swinging the performer from a revolving beam by an iron hook run through the muscles of the back. The more serious self-tortures consisted of mutilations, distortions, and the infliction of other permanent injuries, as, for example, the keeping the hand clenched till the finger-nails grew through the back or the fastening, a limb motionless till it withered and stiffened. I once saw a fakir who had thus treated his left arm. The effect was horrible. The arm stood up from the shoulder stiff and shrunk, like the dead branch of a tree; the fingers, pointing in different directions, resembled the withered twigs.

The milder austerities, those not involving permanent injuries, were, oddly enough, occasionally performed for profit and for the benefit of another person. Runjeet Sing, the celebrated sovereign of the Punjaub, whose own habits were anything but ascetic, used, it was said, to keep in his pay devotees of established sanctity thus to perform penances on his behalf.

Among these minor austerities the sitting within a circle of fire was one, according to tradition, formerly much practised. In the Hindoo fairy tales the Jogee is always represented as thus seated when performing his incantations. The circle of fire was a large ring of smouldering logs. The devotee sat in the centre; the heat and the smoke rendered the position one of much discomfort, even of considerable pain. I have a shadowy recollection that I once, soon after my arrival in India, beheld the performance of this penance. It was on the bank of the Kâlâ Nuddee, a small stream that flows past the ruins of the ancient city of Canauje. The circle was about twelve feet in diameter, and the logs were very small and nearly burnt out.

A painless but almost intolerably tedious form of

austerity is the performance of a pilgrimage and measuring the distance by successive prostrations of the pilgrim's body. This when I left India was still occasionally practised. I once beheld it in process of performance. The pilgrim laid himself flat on the ground, face downwards and with arms extended; then he rose, advanced to the spot where his head had rested, and there again lay down, extended his arms, and again rose and advanced; and this he continued to do till I grew tired of watching him. This devotee, I was told, had commenced his journey from some far-away place in the Punjaub. He was proceeding to Juggernath. I forget in how many years after his setting out he was expected to arrive there.

Towards the end of the last century a fakir at Benares attained great celebrity on account of a novel form of austerity he had devised. He slept always on a bed of iron spikes. The singularity of the penance caused it to excite much interest even among Europeans. The fakir and his bed became one of the sights of Benares. An account of both drawn up by Mr. Jonathan Duncan, the English Resident at Benares, is to be found in one of the early numbers of the *Journal of the Asiatic Society of Bengal.* The account is accompanied by a sketch of the bed and of the fakir reposing on it. The bed as there represented has much the appearance of an inverted harrow. This fakir in his youth, so the account states, had been a great traveller, and had even penetrated far into European Russia. How in such remote northerly regions he managed to exist, and still more to endure the cold, is certainly a marvel.

The practices of the Indian fakirs excite in Europeans only sentiments of ridicule and disgust, and yet on reflection it must be admitted that they are but the outcome of the same ideas that animated the Christian ascetics in early and in mediæval times, the same belief that the natural impulses are impure, and that the highest virtue consists in repressing them. Simon Stylites on his column, or Thomas à Becket, his person swarming with vermin, were but the analogies of the Indian pilgrim who measures with his body the road to Juggernath or the devotee who thinks it meritorious to mutilate or distort his limbs. Only in the Indian fakirs the principle is carried out further, and the results are more apparent. Desiring to be higher than man, they end in sinking below the level of the brutes.

I must remind the reader in conclusion that the fakirs I have been describing are the Hindoo devotees only, to whom, strictly speaking, the term fakir ought not to be applied. The Mahomedan religious mendicants, the true fakirs, rarely, if ever, indulge in these extravagances.

I may add that it was on seeing these Hindoo devotees that I first properly comprehended the meaning of the scriptural phrase "sitting in sackcloth and ashes." I then understood that the ashes referred to were not, as I had imagined, the cinders of coal, but the almost impalpable powder of burnt wood. This powder, of a bluish white, when rubbed over the body, gives it an appearance supposed to indicate the abandonment of all worldly enjoyments. The appearance is certainly most ghastly.

The reason for the habit of drug-eating, in which the Hindoo devotees so indulge, may be that perhaps without some such stimulant their life would be unendurable. I believe, too, that the drowsiness which these narcotic drugs induce is regarded as favourable to religious contemplation.

When I came out of my tent next morning I found that all the travellers had departed, and with them also the fakir. The travellers had gone on to their homes or to where their business called them, the fakir to continue while life endured his purposeless, endless wanderings. I wonder if he is still pursuing them. Most likely he has long ere this found rest, for his appearance showed that he had already adopted the habit of indulging in narcotics, and this habit, once adopted, is never relinquished, and has but one termination.

In my above account of the fakirs I have alluded to the marvellous juggling performances of the Jogees before the Emperor Jehangire. A brief description of them may, I think, interest the reader. The tricks exhibited were twenty-eight in number, and the Jogees who performed them amounted to seven. Most of the tricks call for no special notice, for, allowing for a little exaggeration, they do not very much differ from those exhibited at the present day; but with regard to the rest we may endorse the opinion of the Emperor that they will be accepted as true only by those who have seen them. But on this point the readers may judge for themselves. Out of several I select the following:—

The tricks, we may conclude, were exhibited in one of the courts of the palace where, according to custom, there would be in the centre a large stone basin or reservoir of water. Over the face of the reservoir the Jogees drew a sheet. Presently they removed it and displayed the surface of the water frozen, and that so hard and so deep that the ice bore the weight of an elephant which was made to walk across it.

In another performance the Jogees produced a chain; it was fifty cubits in length. The Jogees raised one end and threw it in the air. The chain went up and up till the lower end just touched the ground, and it thus continued to hang suspended from nothing. Next the Jogees drew forward a sack; the mouth of the sack was fastened: the Jogees opened it. Immediately from out of the sack a dog appeared; he walked to the chain and commenced to ascend it. A wild boar followed, and did the same, and after them, all likewise issuing from the sack, came a panther, a lion, and then a tiger. These three also, like the dog and the wild boar, went to the chain and proceeded to climb it; and each of the five animals—the dog, the wild boar, the panther, the lion, and the tiger—so soon as they reached the summit of the chain vanished in succession in the air.

Marvellous as these two performances were, perhaps the third I have selected is even more amazing. The Jogees brought forward a man; then they drew their swords and cut him to pieces. This done, they collected the pieces, piled them in a heap, and covered them with a cloth; then, after a minute or so, they raised the cloth, and there was the man beneath alive and well as before.

It was not only these seven Jogees who displayed their skill before the Emperor. A young nobleman exhibited a feat of manual dexterity, if we can believe the Emperor's account of it, almost as surprising. But this was on another occasion. He produced a small glass bottle; it was made of glass so delicate that the slightest blow would break it. On the outer surface of the bottle there was affixed the image of a butterfly made of wax; above the butterfly was fastened a single peppercorn, and above the peppercorn a grain of rice: a staff was then driven into the ground, and the glass bottle with the wax butterfly, the peppercorn, and the grain of rice placed on its summit.

The young noble now retired to a distance with his bow and three arrows. He shot one arrow; the arrow flew through the air, just touched the butterfly, and carried it away; the next two arrows removed in succession the peppercorn and the grain of rice: and yet the glass bottle, delicate as it was, remained unhurt. To show his admiration for this display of dexterity, the Emperor appointed the young noble to a high command in the army, and also bestowed on him in marriage a niece of the Empress Noor Jehan.

Making allowance for exaggeration and rejecting the descriptions that are manifestly incredible, I do not think that the conjuring performances of the Jogees could have been more surprising than those of the modern Indian jugglers. Some of these are certainly most marvellous. They are by the natives, even by the educated natives, attributed to magic. It is considered that the performers, the acrobats in especial, do not really perform their tricks. They merely create an illusion that causes the spectators to imagine that they behold them.

Very much the same idea was entertained by the early Europeans who visited India, only they attributed the performances not to magic, but to satanic agency. It is mentioned by one of the early travellers that the chaplain to the English mercantile factory at Agra was so convinced that Satan himself assisted these jugglers, that he refused the sacrament to any of his congregation who should witness their exhibitions. In order to properly appreciate the skill of the Indian jugglers, it must be remembered that their tricks are performed without apparatus, generally with bare arms, and in the open air, and in the brilliant Indian sunshine.

Most of the tricks of the Indian jugglers have been described, but the following I have never seen noticed, nor did I ever happen to meet any European who had witnessed it, nor did I myself ever see it performed except on one occasion, and that was soon after my arrival in the country. The trick was this. A hole was dug in the ground about two feet deep, and as much across; it was filled with water to the brim. The performer, a young woman, then advanced to the hole. She wore, as all native women do, a small ring in her nose; she took out the ring and dropped it into the water; then she lay down, her back on the ground, her arms folded across her chest. Her head was over the hole; she lowered it into the water, face and all below the surface. She so remained for nearly a minute. All the while we could see, from the agitation of the water, that her head was moving. Then she raised her head, and there was the ring, or one precisely similar, again in her nose. How the trick was effected I cannot imagine. It was evidently one of very difficult performance, for the girl, when she raised her head from the water, seemed to be much exhausted.

In regard to the tricks performed by the Jogees before the Emperor Jehangire, I may mention a curious circumstance. One of the tricks, so far as I am aware, is now quite unknown in India; but of late years it has, I believe, been exhibited as a novelty in Europe. The trick was this. One of the Jogees produced a book; he turned over the leaves, they were all blank; he turned them over again, and on each appeared a coloured picture.

CHAPTER XX.

THE TOUR CONCLUDED

AFTER breakfast, while the tents were being struck and the baggage laden, I climbed to the summit of one of the adjacent peaks. The peak was not very high, but it was sufficiently so to enable me to get a rather extended view of the small ranges and valleys around. I have spoken already of the wildness of these mountains, but I do not think that till now I had ever fully appreciated it. The scene I looked on resembled nothing so much as a stormy ocean of a sudden turned to stone. It was a very chaos of narrow, winding ridges, deep clefts of valleys between them, and at short intervals tall, sharp, craggy peaks.

I need not describe the pass, except that it was slightly shorter and generally narrower; it did not much differ from the pass by which we had entered the Doon. There were the same perpendicular cliffs, and behind and above them the same miniature peaks and ridges and the same small green slopes and patches of forest. In these peaks and sandy precipices was to be read the history of the mountains and the abyss of time which that history discloses. These ranges must once have formed the bed of some vanished ocean. What countless ages must have passed while that bed accumulated; what æons of centuries must have gone by ere it was raised aloft and moulded by the elements into the forms it now presents!

About midway in the pass there stands a rock which is regarded by the natives as a great natural curiosity. It is termed by them the "Summun Boorj," or "Octagon Tower," the word "summun" being the Hindostanee corruption of the Arabic term "musummin," that is, "eight-sided." It was described to me, before I had seen it, as a nearly exact counterpart of one of the bastions of the Fort of Agra or of the palace of Delhi. The description was, of course, much exaggerated; still, the rock being in shape roughly octagonal, and projecting from the flat surface of a perpendicular cliff, it does really bear a curious resemblance to the bastion of an Indian fortress. It is difficult to understand by what process of weathering the rock could have acquired its present shape.

The march all the way was either level or a slight descent, and the road, though a mere track, as in the other pass, was less broken and more free from stones. We moved in consequence much more rapidly. It was early in the afternoon when we reached our encamping-ground. It was a small open space, just beyond the mouth of the pass. The next morning we proceeded on to the bank of the Jumna. The march was very uninteresting. For the first few miles it lay through a forest, or rather what lately had been one; but most of the larger trees had been felled. The forest now consisted of little more than coarse grass, saplings, and brushwood.

Next we came on land just recently brought under cultivation, and here the prospect was even more melancholy: scanty crops, or fresh ploughed land, alternated with wide tracts of bare waste, and everywhere appeared the blackened stumps of the trees that had been burnt when the forest was cleared away. Here and there as we advanced we came on small villages, but they consisted only of grass huts. We were all glad when the march was accomplished, and we had arrived at the Jumna. Our encamping-ground was that picturesque, half-ruined building known as the "Badshah Mahal," or "Palace of the Emperor." The tents were pitched in the courtyard; the horses were tethered, and the carts and bullocks stationed just outside.

The "Badshah Mahal" is a building little known even in India. Its history is romantic. It may interest the reader if I relate it.

The palace, according to tradition, was erected more than two and a half centuries ago by the Emperor Shah Jeahn, the same emperor who erected that most exquisite of structures, the Taj, at Agra. The Emperor had transferred his capital from Agra to Delhi. There he founded a new city. A canal had in former days conducted the water of the Jumna from the point where it issues from the Shewalic to the Delhi of that earlier period. The canal had long gone to ruin; the Emperor had it restored. When the works at the head of the canal were completed, the Emperor came to inspect them, and this palace was built for his accommodation.

But the presence of the court so near them was not at all desired by inhabitants of the mountains, for in the East the presence of the court means oppression. They could not, of course, compel the Emperor to depart, but they devised a scheme by which he might be induced to do so. In the Himalayas, as in the Alps, goitre is very prevalent. The villagers collected a number of women in whom the complaint was strongly developed, and sent them down to the palace. On some pretext or other the women got admission to the zenana. The ladies of the zenana were horrified at the appearance of their swollen throats; the women, as they had been instructed, informed the ladies that their swollen throats were caused by the water of the region. They also added that if the court remained here the throats of the ladies themselves would before long become the same. Then ensued a scene: the ladies believed the statement, and assailed the Emperor with tears, entreaties, and threats of suicide. In the end the Emperor had to yield, and returned to Delhi.

Such is the tradition. It is current all over the mountains as well as in the neighbouring parts of the plains; I have over and over again heard it related. Nevertheless a well-educated Mahomedan, the manager of a property near, assured me that there was no truth in the story whatever. The palace, he said, was merely erected, as a compliment to the Emperor, by the nobleman to whom the superintendence of the works of the canal had been committed; but the Emperor, he said, never occupied it, never even visited the spot, or if he did it was only in the course of some hunting expedition. Still, however, it is difficult to believe that a tradition so widely spread should have had no foundation.

But, whether the Emperor ever occupied the palace or not, his stay in it could not have been long, nor was the visit, if it really occurred, again repeated. A century passed away, and the Mogul empire was in the throes of dissolution. Then followed a long period of war and confusion. The population diminished; the land around fell gradually out of cultivation; where there had been fields and harvests, the coarse grass, the trees, and brushwood grew up. Ere long the palace became embosomed in forest; and so, silent and deserted, visited only by the wild animals, for near a hundred years it thus remained. Except in the immediate neighbourhood, the very tradition of its existence passed away; then by a sort of accident it was discovered.

One of the ancient emperors had constructed a canal to irrigate the upper portion of the Doab, that is, the tract of country that lies between the Ganges and the Jumna. The water of this canal was drawn from the Jumna at a point a few miles below this palace. The canal had long gone to ruin, and when the Doab came into our possession it was little more than a dry trench, partly filled with pools of water during the rains. Some thirty years after we had acquired the country, the Government decided to restore the canal. For the construction of the dam and other buildings at the canal head bricks were required. The engineer in charge was preparing to have them manufactured, when the owner of a village in the neighbourhood happened to call on him. The engineer consulted him as to the best place for erecting the kilns. The village proprietor informed the engineer in reply that the doing so was quite unnecessary, for a few miles off in the forest there were bricks in any amount lying ready to his hand; and then he related to him the story of the palace.

The engineer, mounted on an elephant and accompanied by a gang of labourers, set out to discover it. They passed through miles of forest, often having to cut a track with their axes; and then they came, not, as might have been expected, on a collection of mere crumbling ruins, but on a real palace, with halls, courtyards, enclosing walls, gateways, and bastions, and all almost as perfect as when, near two centuries before, the Emperor had abandoned it. The scene must have recalled the tale of the sleeping beauty; and, to complete the resemblance, there in the great hall lay a beauty ready to receive them, not, indeed, an enchanted princess, but a magnificent tigress. She lay there surrounded by her cubs, as in ancient days may have reposed the ladies of the zenana.

It is a pity that the palace as it then was was not left to continue. The greater portion, I regret to say, was demolished, and the materials carried away and used in the construction of the dam, the bridges, and the other buildings of the canal. I have been told by those who had seen them that the parts of the palace thus destroyed possessed but little of beauty or architectural interest; that they were mostly merely enclosing walls, offices, or apartments for servants. Still all lovers of the picturesque must regret that they were not allowed to remain, for we should then behold the palace complete as when the Emperor left it; we now see only isolated buildings and fragments of walls.

At the time of my visit the palace was in the possession of a Christian family, who had obtained a grant of a large tract of the freshly cleared land in its vicinity. When visiting their property they were in the habit of residing in what remained habitable of the palace; and this, for the short period of my stay, their agent invited me to occupy. This habitable portion of the palace was very small; it consisted of only two rooms, a very large hall, the same in which the tigress had taken up her abode, and one smaller half-octagonal chamber beyond. This chamber formed the summit of a great tower that rose sheer from the river some forty feet or more below.

The view from the windows was one of the wildest I ever beheld. At the base of the tower the river ran deep and still; further away it was shallower, and flowing over rocks and boulders, was broken into a thousand eddies, often into long sheets of foam. The opposite shore displayed a desolate expanse of sand and stones, interspersed by patches of brushwood and tall, coarse grass; then a long slope of forest led up to a very wilderness of mountains. The prospect was unrelieved by field or village or any habitation of man. As the day declined the loneliness of the scene became oppressive; when night came on it was still more so, for then the forest woke up, and to the melancholy, monotonous murmur of the river below were added the cries of the wild animals in the woods and wastes beyond, among them, and more frequent than I had ever heard it before, the deep, dull roar of the tiger.

Once or twice during my stay at the palace I amused myself in the afternoons by short excursions on the river. There was a rude, clumsy fisherman's boat lying somewhere on the bank; in this I had myself rowed up the stream, and then I floated down again with the current. Seen from the water, the appearance of the palace was very imposing. The bank of the river on which the palace stood was—I speak from memory—at least forty feet or more in elevation, and for the entire distance to which the palace extended, this lofty bank had been scarped perpendicular, and faced with a massive wall. The wall and the great octagon tower which projected from it rose from the stream with an aspect of much grandeur. Once I crossed the river and paid a visit to the head of the canal.

The head of the canal is some few miles above the palace, not far from the spot where the Jumna issues from the Shewalic. The river is formed by the union of two streams, the Jumna and the Tonse, and of the two the Tonse is by far the largest. It is broader, deeper; it bears along many times the greater volume of water. In appearance it is the most imposing, and yet, while the Jumna is known throughout the world, few people, save in its immediate neighbourhood, are aware even of the existence of the Tonse. I suppose this pre-eminence accorded to the Jumna must be in consequence of its more illustrious origin, for, while the Tonse rises only among the lower mountains, the Jumna issues from one of the loftiest peaks of this western portion of the true Himalaya, the ranges of perpetual snow.

The old palace could never have been large, at least for an Indian palace, but the outer walls must have enclosed a considerable area. The principal structures that now remain are the hall and chamber I have described, a gateway much ruined, and a courtyard. This courtyard must formerly have been the garden, and have been adorned with canals of water, basins, and fountains. I was told that when first discovered a large basin or reservoir of white marble stood on the terrace before the hall. I could not ascertain what had become of it.

Judging from the buildings that remain, the palace could not, even when entire, have possessed any special architectural beauty. It displays, however, all that massive solidity of construction combined with that exquisite finish and delicacy of detail which characterises the Mahomedan buildings of the Mogul period. Of this delicacy and finish the raised walks of the courtyard are a beautiful illustration. They are formed of brick, as, indeed, is nearly the whole of the palace; but the bricks which compose the surface of the walks are those extremely small ones that in hardness and smoothness of texture are almost equal to terra cotta. They are arranged so as to form simple but very pretty designs, and so small are the bricks, and so exquisite is the manner in which they are joined, that the designs to some extent have the appearance and beauty of mosaics.

I remained a few days at the palace, and then I returned along the bank of the canal, that canal whose restoration, as I have mentioned, led to the discovery of the palace. The first march was to the head of the canal, the point where it receives its water from the Jumna. The length of the march was not very great, but it had brought about an entire change in the scenery, a change that, I must confess, I found agreeable. Instead of the wilderness of waste and forest, I now looked over a wide, open plain, half enclosed by long blue lines of distant mountains, and here and there above them rose some of the glistening peaks of the snowy range. The plain was still mostly wild, but not far off there were fields with rising crops, groves of mango trees, and some few villages.

Where the plain was uncultivated, it was covered by a low, shrub-like plant, which produces a curious berry. The berry is oval in shape, very small, of the colour of red coral, and of almost equal hardness; on the broader end is a little round patch of black. This berry is termed the "ruttee," and is used all over India by goldsmiths and jewellers as the standard by which small ornaments, pearls, and precious stones are weighed. Though less in weight, it corresponds to the "carat" of the jewellers of Europe. There must be countless millions of these berries in use over India, yet I do not know of any place, except this belt of waste land below the Shewalic, where they are found, and, moreover, from this part of the waste I never heard of their being exported.

I remained for the day at the canal head. The next morning I continued my march, proceding, as before, along the canal bank. Canals, as a rule, are straight and formal; but this canal, laid out in unscientific days, is different. It bends, it winds, it narrows, and widens again with all the variety of a river. The banks are broad, and are bordered with avenues of shady trees. Bridges cross it continually, and at intervals of every few miles there are locks and falls; and at many of the falls the water is utilized to turn small mills for the grinding of corn. Before the first march was completed I had entered the cultivated country; the second march brought me home.

I have mentioned that the late harvest had been deficient in quantity, and that some fears were entertained that it would be followed by a scarcity. Before the cold weather had passed these apprehensions were realized. There was such want of food, so much distress, that the Government thought it necessary to give assistance. The assistance was given quickly and liberally. In all the districts where the scarcity prevailed relief works were established, and those in want of food were provided with employment. The employment was chiefly on the roads, and consisted in repairing or improving them.

As the men thus employed amounted in every district to many thousands, a large number of officials were required to overlook and to pay them; and these officials had to be selected and appointed in extreme haste. Under such circumstances, there was opportunity for much peculation which the European authorities were quite powerless to prevent, and, according to rumour, these opportunities were very generally taken advantage of. More relief money, it was said, was given by the Government than was distributed, and pay was drawn for many more minor officials than were ever really employed. Of the correctness of this last rumour I once had an amusing illustration.

In the course of my morning walk I came on one of these relief parties; they were engaged in repairing the road. The overseer in charge was standing by, and with him were several children. All were quite small; the youngest he carried in his arms. The sight struck me as odd. I asked my attendants what was its meaning, whose the children were, and why they were there. My attendants smiled, and informed me that the children were the overseer's and also his assistants, and were now engaged, they supposed, in overlooking the labourers.

The overseer, when I inquired of him, admitted the correctness of my attendants' statement. The children were, he said, his assistants, and he added that they performed their duties as such most efficiently, even the child in his arms never for an instant permitting the labourers to loiter or idle. To confirm this assertion, he called the child's attention to some labourers close by. They had paused in their work to listen to our conversation. The child had a switch in his hand. Under his father's direction, he waved the switch at the men, and made some inarticulate noises, for he was too young to speak plain. The men appreciated the situation, made a pretence of being frightened, and commenced to shovel up earth again with intense assumed activity.

The higher relief officials had, of course, greater opportunities of enriching themselves, and that they occasionally availed themselves of them I had also about this time an example. A man came before me as a witness in some case. I had known him when I had previously held office in these parts. He was then very poor; he had some small appointment and nothing besides. He now, from his dress and manner, appeared to be very well off. When he had retired, I remarked to my office people on the change in the man's circumstances, and inquired how it had occurred. The answer I received was suggestive. He had been entrusted with the distribution of the relief funds on the occasion of the last scarcity.

I will relate another story more serious. I must first explain that the grain in India is not stored in barns or warehouses, as it is here, but in pits beneath the soil. These pits in shape a good deal resemble the "oubliette" dungeons of our mediæval castles. They are round and deep, grow narrow at the top, and have for their entrance only a small circular aperture. The entrance is covered over with earth, and the situation of the pit often is known only to the owner.

About the year 1836—I forget the exact date—there occurred a famine in these upper provinces. I have always heard it spoken of as one of the most terrible ever known. The English Government made every effort to relieve it; nevertheless whole villages were nearly depopulated, and the poor died in thousands. So extreme was the distress, that all the distinctions of caste were disregarded. The Governor-General was then marching up the country. Wherever his camp halted, cooked food in abundance was laid in great trays on the ground. I have been told by those who beheld it that as soon as the trays were laid whole crowds of starving poor, Hindoos and Mahomedans, Brahmins and men of the lowest castes, rushed forward almost like famished animals to devour it.

Many years passed by, the famine had become a memory, when there again arose fears of a scarcity. In the district where I then was, diligent search was made for concealed grain-pits. In one village several such pits, and very large ones, were discovered; they were full of grain, but the grain, alas! was all decayed and putrid. It was then ascertained that the pits had been filled with grain by their then owner just previous to the great famine. When the famine occurred the price of grain rose and rose, but the owner would not sell, waiting till the price should rise still higher. In the end he overreached himself; the crisis of the famine passed, and prices fell, and the owner, disappointed of the profit he had hoped to make, in his anger let the pits remain unopened, as they were.

The discovery of the pits made some sensation among the natives. The decay of the grain was regarded as a judgment, for through the avarice of this one man, the owner, many hundreds of his fellow-men no doubt had perished.

India, from time immemorial, has been always subject to famines. It was formerly thought that the famines were much the result of the native misgovernment, and that under our humaner and more enlightened rule they would cease. Experience has shown that these opinions were erroneous. Good government may alleviate the sufferings of famines, but it is powerless in India to prevent their occurrence, for they arise from a deficiency of the rainfall, and over the rainfall man has no control.